European Debt Restructuring Handbook

Leading Case Studies from the Post-Lehman Cycle

Consulting Editors **Kon Asimacopoulos** and **Justin Bickle**

Consulting editors
Kon Asimacopoulos and Justin Bickle

Publisher
Sian O'Neill

Editors
Carolyn Boyle, Jo Moore, Liz Rutherford-Johnson, Jeremy White

Production
Paul Stoneham

Publishing directors
Guy Davis, Tony Harriss, Mark Lamb

European Debt Restructuring Handbook: Leading Case Studies from the Post-Lehman Cycle
is published by
Globe Law and Business
Globe Business Publishing Ltd
New Hibernia House
Winchester Walk
London SE1 9AG
United Kingdom
Tel +44 20 7234 0606
Fax +44 20 7234 0808
Web www.globelawandbusiness.com

Printed and bound by CPI Group (UK) Ltd, Croydon, CR0 4YY

ISBN 978-1-905783-65-6

European Debt Restructuring Handbook: Leading Case Studies from the Post-Lehman Cycle
© 2013 Globe Business Publishing Ltd

DISCLAIMER
This publication is intended as a general guide only. The information and opinions which it contains are not intended to be a comprehensive study, nor to provide legal advice, and should not be treated as a substitute for legal advice concerning particular situations. Legal advice should always be sought before taking any action based on the information provided. The publishers bear no responsibility for any errors or omissions contained herein.

Table of contents

Introduction

Kon Asimacopoulos
Kirkland & Ellis International LLP
Justin Bickle
Oaktree

The past decade has transformed the restructuring landscape in Europe. The number of companies with complex corporate and financing structures has increased to levels unseen before at any time in history. While efforts have been made by both the European Union and various country jurisdictions to improve their restructuring and insolvency regimes, restructuring practitioners and their clients have had to extend the boundaries of what was supposed to be achievable in order to restructure corporate groups' balance sheets in a manner that reflects value and preserves the going concern.

When we first set out to compile this book, we were both struck by how fortunate we were to advise and/or invest in a market as dynamic and fluid as that which we have seen across Europe in the past several years. No one could have predicted the effects of the collapse of Lehman Brothers on the global financial markets in late 2008, or the impact this would have on debtors and other stakeholders in restructuring corporate debt across multiple European jurisdictions over the following few years. Both of us first developed our restructuring experience during the collapse of the high-yield bond market, which took place at the beginning of this century following over-exuberance in the telecommunications and cable sectors, and the fallout from the deregulation of the European energy market. Nothing we saw or learned during that downturn prepared us for the challenges that faced the entire European restructuring community in early 2009, when a chronic lack of liquidity seized up global credit markets and began to impact on real-economy businesses, each with over-leveraged balance sheets, multiple stakeholders and complex legal documentation, and each facing the potential use of multi-country insolvency regimes, which threatened stakeholder value while being untested and/or wholly uncertain in outcome.

Four years after the start of the global financial crisis, this new publication brings together Europe's leading restructuring lawyers, who were and remain instrumental in shaping the way that European restructurings are conducted and implemented today. We were conscious that no single publication had captured the response of the European restructuring legal community to the crisis and no single record existed of the key balance-sheet restructurings which have advanced and shaped the market. We hope, therefore, that this practical handbook represents a single record of the era by those involved and leads the reader through each restructuring in detail, explaining what happened, the difficulties, issues and challenges involved and providing examples of the key legal techniques used to preserve corporate value.

Each chapter is a detailed case study by key lawyers centrally involved in the leading consensual workouts. Compiling such lists is always subjective, but in each instance we wanted to include those restructurings that demonstrated innovation, positively impacted on the market and proved influential far beyond their own stakeholders.

Given our view that Europe is likely to continue to see such restructuring activity in the coming years, we have also included in the concluding chapter some thoughts on the lessons learned to date, as well as some suggestions as to how the European restructuring landscape may continue to develop in the coming years as over-leveraging continues to haunt the eurozone.

We are very grateful to all of the legal practitioners who took the time and trouble to contribute to this publication, and are proud of the way that our profession has worked together to cope with sometimes impossible expectations and workloads to achieve great legal innovation while preserving economic value for debtors, creditors and other stakeholders during these unprecedented times.

Preparation of the next edition is already underway, covering restructurings completed following finalisation of this publication.

Publishers' note
The case studies included are open to different interpretations and the views/ interpretations expressed are the authors' own. Readers should seek legal advice before taking action based on the information provided.

McCarthy & Stone

Richard Tett
Freshfields Bruckhaus Deringer LLP

1. Synopsis

In 2008, as a result of the sharp downturn in the UK housing market caused by the credit crunch, McCarthy & Stone plc found itself over-leveraged and it became clear that a restructuring was needed. In 2006 (before its restructuring) the company had been valued at approximately £1.1 billion and had approximately £1 billion of debt.

At the heart of the restructuring were two schemes of arrangement of the trading companies which enabled the majority to bind the minority and prevent non-consenting creditors from seeking to extract leverage. This was one of the first times that a scheme was successfully used to restructure bank debt. The two schemes interlinked with two administrations and effectively left behind over £250 million of junior creditors that no longer had an economic interest (see Mann J, *In re Mytravel Group Plc* [2004] EWHC 2741).

Most significantly for the wider restructuring market, it was the first time that schemes of arrangement, which are used to drag a minority within a class, had been combined with pre-packaged administration sales, which are used to leave behind out-of-the-money junior creditors. As such, this represented a creative new restructuring solution; the same structure has since been used to implement other restructurings such as IMO Carwash and Gallery Media.

The schemes of arrangement that were used in the restructuring were transfer schemes which involved the transfer of numerous assets – for example, several thousand properties were transferred out of McCarthy & Stone (Developments) Limited. This is in contrast to the more usual situation where, under the scheme of a holding company, essentially only shares in subsidiaries are transferred. A further complexity of the restructuring was that a bespoke arrangement was needed to address loss-sharing issues with the Facility E revolving credit facility.

2. Background

2.1 The McCarthy & Stone business

Over the past 30 years, the McCarthy & Stone Group has become the leading developer of private retirement accommodation in the United Kingdom. It has been responsible for the construction of approximately 40,000 homes and is well positioned to benefit from demographic trends that will generate a rapidly increasing population of potential customers.

In October 2006 McCarthy & Stone plc was acquired by a consortium of

investors, including Bank of Scotland plc, West Coast Capital and Aldersgate Investments Limited, through a newly incorporated parent company, Mother Topco Limited (subsequently renamed McCarthy & Stone Group Limited). The acquisition took the form of a recommended cash offer under the Takeover Code, pursuant to which Mother Bidco Limited (a subsidiary of Mother Topco Limited) acquired the entire share capital of McCarthy & Stone plc. Pursuant to the acquisition, trading in McCarthy & Stone plc shares on the London Stock Exchange was suspended and its shares were de-listed on December 18 2006.

Under the terms of the acquisition in 2006, shareholders in McCarthy & Stone plc were offered cash consideration (or a loan note as an alternative) for the sale of their shares. The terms of the acquisition valued the entire share capital of McCarthy & Stone plc at approximately £1.1 billion (gross). There was approximately £1 billion of debt in McCarthy & Stone plc at this time.

To finance the acquisition and for working capital purposes, Mother Bidco Limited was provided with £930 million in committed existing senior facilities, £100 million in a mezzanine facility and £83 million of investor loan notes.

3.   Pre-restructuring corporate structure

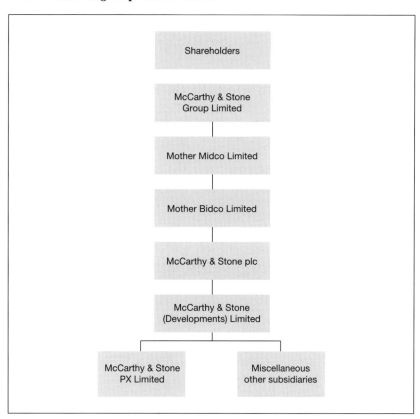

As noted above, in 2006 McCarthy & Stone plc was the subject of a public-to-private transaction which involved the use of new acquisition special purpose vehicles (SPVs). In terms of where the assets were located, McCarthy & Stone plc owned various IP and head office-related assets. McCarthy & Stone (Developments) Limited held the main property assets and McCarthy & Stone PX Limited held the properties from the part exchange programme.

4.   Pre-restructuring capital structure

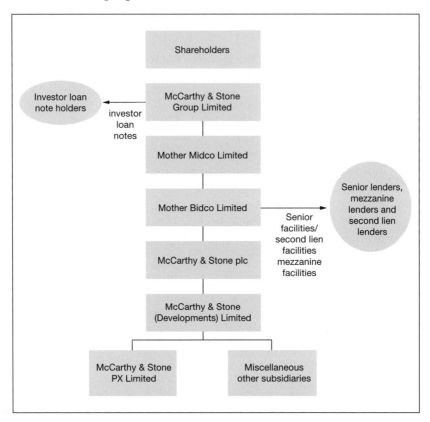

A number of facilities were in place, some with different security packages. Broadly speaking, these can be summarised as follows:
- three senior term loans – the Facility A, Facility B and Facility C term loans;
- a senior Facility D property revolving credit facility;
- a senior Facility E working capital revolving credit facility;
- a second lien Facility F second lien;
- a mezzanine facility; and
- investor loan notes.

At the time that the financing was put in place, the intention was that the senior

Facility D property revolving credit facility would have first ranking security over certain property assets and second ranking security over the other assets. Senior Facilities A, B, C and E would have first ranking security over those other assets and second ranking security over the aforementioned property assets. The Facility E working capital revolving credit facility was undrawn at the time of the restructuring, but there was a *pro rata* loss sharing agreement in place with the Facility A, B and C lenders. All of this debt was borrowed by Mother Bidco Limited and guaranteed by companies across the McCarthy & Stone Group.

The second lien Facility F, the mezzanine facility and the investor loan notes ranked in that order behind the senior Facilities A to E.

5. Financial situation of the group in the lead-up to restructuring, and restructuring triggers

5.1 Effect of the downturn on McCarthy & Stone

During the course of 2008, the McCarthy & Stone Group, like its competitors, began to experience the effects of a sharp downturn in the UK housing market. This led to a significant decline in new home sales and a reduction in house prices generally. Although this downturn affected the McCarthy & Stone Group's performance, the boards of McCarthy & Stone plc and McCarthy & Stone (Developments) Limited expected the market to recover in the medium term. Further, the expectation was that the fall-out of competitors from the market would be likely to offer opportunities for any market participants that could maintain a significant presence in the market through the downturn and rescale their activities following the recovery of the market.

Until March 2008, the McCarthy & Stone Group's operational performance was ahead of expectations. Sales of 2,327 units in its financial year ending August 31 2007 were the highest since 1990. Further, sales of 989 units in the six months to February 28 2008 were the highest ever achieved over the same six-month period.

However, the six months to August 31 2008 saw the beginning of the effects of a serious decline in the wider housing market. The £211.6 million turnover for this period was 26.1% below that of the equivalent six months to August 31 2007.

A primary reason for the continuing decline was the tightening of mortgage financing in the wider market. This meant that the McCarthy & Stone Group's potential customers were having increasing difficulty in finding purchasers for their own properties in order to release the equity required to finance the purchase of a McCarthy & Stone retirement apartment. The reduced ability of the McCarthy & Stone Group's potential customers to sell their own properties was reflected in a reduced level of reservations during the four months ending January 2 2009, which was 49% below the comparative period in the previous year. A large proportion of the McCarthy & Stone Group's customers are needs-based and, historically, around 90% are equity financed from the sale of their previous home. While they do not require mortgage finance, they are dependent on selling their home and that sale often depends on the buyer having access to mortgage finance.

The continued deterioration in the wider housing market led to a fall in house

prices that was more severe than anticipated. The average sale price, net of incentives, stood at £180,800 per unit during the financial year ending August 31 2007 and £190,400 per unit during the six months to February 28 2008. However, the average sale price fell to £176,400 per unit during the six months to August 31 2008 and £165,600 per unit over the four months to January 2 2009, showing an overall decline of 13% from the six months to February 28 2008.

5.2   **Non-payment of interest and breach of financial covenants**
On November 28 2008 the McCarthy & Stone Group failed to make interest payments that were due to the senior lenders, second lien lenders and mezzanine lenders. The group also breached certain of its financial covenants. The McCarthy & Stone Group entered into a forbearance and waiver letter dated December 2 2008 in relation to the non-payment of the interest due to the senior lenders. The group also obtained a temporary waiver from over 90% of the senior lenders in relation to certain other events of default, including the breach of financial covenants.

Following the group's non-payment of interest, Bank of Scotland designated an early termination date under the hedge agreement. Accordingly, Bank of Scotland terminated the interest rate swaps on December 22 2008, crystallising a liability of Mother Bidco Limited of approximately £61 million that both McCarthy & Stone plc and McCarthy & Stone (Developments) Limited had guaranteed, but which remained unpaid.

The temporary waivers and forbearance expired on February 12 2009, but some of the senior lenders agreed to extend those temporary waivers and forbearance until February 27 2009; a new waiver and forbearance letter was thus entered into on February 12 2009. A further letter was entered into in early March 2009 that, among other things, extended the temporary waivers until April 30 2009 and provided for certain additional waivers, including in respect of any events of default that were triggered by the proposed restructuring.

6.   **Composition of lending syndicate and syndicate dynamic**
The McCarthy & Stone Group debt was widely syndicated between a mixture of banks – both UK and continental – as well as a variety of collateralised loan obligation (CLO) funds. Some debt traded during the restructuring, but this was not material and did not particularly affect the process. One reason why distressed debt investors did not purchase the group's debt in the secondary market related to uncertainty over both the priority of payments in the waterfall and security hardening after the privatisation in 2006.

At the McCarthy & Stone Group's request, a coordination committee of the senior lenders was formed in July 2008. The group appointed PricewaterhouseCoopers LLP to advise the coordination committee in September 2008, and agreed to meet the costs of PricewaterhouseCoopers and the coordination committee's legal advisers.

The coordination committee comprised both banks and CLOs and represented the different lender groups. It was made up of Allied Irish Banks plc, Bank of Scotland plc, HSBC plc, Lloyds TSB plc, NIBC Bank NV and Cairn Financial Products Limited.

7.   **Restructuring negotiation process**

Commencing in mid-2008, the McCarthy & Stone Group held discussions with its shareholders, investor loan noteholders, senior lenders, second lien lenders and mezzanine lenders. It also received indications of interest from potential third-party purchasers as a result of a third-party marketing process that was conducted by Rothschild. Discussions among the various stakeholder groups focused on the restructuring of the McCarthy & Stone Group's facilities, although the various stakeholders were unable to reach agreement as to a proposed restructuring solution.

The various proposals that were put forward, together with the indications of interest from the third-party marketing campaign, attributed an enterprise value to the McCarthy & Stone Group below the total debt exposure of the senior lenders and the hedge counterparty. Therefore, the shareholders, investor loan noteholders, mezzanine lenders and second lien lenders did not appear to have an economic interest in the group.

The senior lenders then put forward their own restructuring proposal and it seemed unlikely that there would be a consensual arrangement with the other stakeholders. In these circumstances, the boards of McCarthy & Stone plc and McCarthy & Stone (Developments) Limited considered that the senior lenders' proposal (ie, the restructuring) was in the best interests of their companies and those stakeholders that continued to have an economic interest in the companies. In reaching this view, the boards also considered a number of other options as discussed later in this chapter.

7.1   **Shareholders and investor loan noteholders**

Initially in 2008, the McCarthy & Stone Group entered into discussions with its shareholders and investor loan noteholders to explore a range of potential restructuring solutions, including the possibility of additional (new money) equity investments. The discussions continued until October 2008, and these stakeholders were provided with detailed financial information about the McCarthy & Stone Group. However, it was impossible to reach an agreement that could be taken forward as a potential consensual restructuring solution to be discussed with other key stakeholders (eg, the senior lenders, second lien lenders and mezzanine lenders). The markets also continued to deteriorate, especially in light of the collapse of Lehman Brothers in September 2008.

7.2   **Mezzanine lenders**

An *ad hoc* committee of certain mezzanine lenders was formed in September 2008. On December 4 2008 the mezzanine lenders, following the non-payment of interest due under the mezzanine facility agreement on November 28 2008, served a request notice on the McCarthy & Stone Group under the intercreditor deed. This triggered a standstill period of 90 days, during which the mezzanine creditors were not entitled to take any enforcement action against the McCarthy & Stone Group. The standstill period expired on March 3 2009.

On December 18 2008 the *ad hoc* committee of the mezzanine lenders submitted a restructuring proposal to the senior lenders. This was rejected and, over the following two months, various proposals were submitted by the *ad hoc* committee and certain mezzanine lenders.

In February 2009 the boards of McCarthy & Stone plc and McCarthy & Stone (Developments) Limited were informed by the coordination committee that it had presented these proposals to the senior lenders together with a comparison of the various proposals and the restructuring proposed by the coordination committee. Following consideration by the coordination committee and the senior lenders, the coordination committee confirmed that these mezzanine proposals would not receive the necessary acceptance by the senior lenders to be pursued in their current form.

7.3   Senior lenders

As adviser to the coordination committee, PricewaterhouseCoopers was given access to detailed financial and legal information about the McCarthy & Stone Group, and had continuous discussions and correspondence with the group's management and Rothschild.

On October 14 2008 the McCarthy & Stone Group met with the senior lenders to present its business plan and possible operating scenarios. The boards of McCarthy & Stone plc and McCarthy & Stone (Developments) Limited drew the senior lenders' attention to various financial challenges that the group faced.

As a result, the senior lenders put forward their own restructuring proposal. In particular, having reviewed in detail the provisions of the intercreditor deed with respect to the different classes of senior lenders, certain important ambiguities and uncertainties in interpretation were identified. The coordination committee determined that to resolve such ambiguities and uncertainties in these provisions would probably require expensive and protracted litigation. Therefore, the coordination committee and the majority of the senior lenders agreed a commercial resolution of these issues and supported the restructuring as implemented using the two schemes of arrangement and two administration pre-pack sales.

Throughout the restructuring process, the McCarthy & Stone Group continued to have an active dialogue and hold regular meetings with the coordination committee to provide updates on trading forecasts and short-term cash flow forecasts, as well as to discuss the key terms of the restructuring.

7.4   Third-party valuations of the business

In parallel with discussions with the coordination committee and other stakeholders of the McCarthy & Stone Group, Rothschild pursued a third-party marketing process on behalf of the McCarthy & Stone Group with a view to securing a buyer for the group (or its business) as a potential option by which the business could be placed on a secure financial footing. Third-party proposals were carefully considered in conjunction with other restructuring options involving the existing stakeholders of the business.

Rothschild directly contacted an initial 14 parties, comprising a variety of potential financial and trade purchasers, which were deemed to be credible participants in the process based on previous activity in the house-building sector. A general market awareness of the McCarthy & Stone Group's financial status and of Rothschild's involvement with the group through press reports and otherwise led to an additional nine potential buyers initiating contact with the McCarthy & Stone Group, bringing the total number of potentially interested parties to 23.

As the marketing process developed, two parties made bids valuing the group on an enterprise value basis at £350 million to £400 million – further, both bids required the senior lenders to continue as lenders to the group (although at a reduced level) under amended facilities. Discussions with the coordination committee led McCarthy & Stone plc and McCarthy & Stone (Developments) Limited to believe that these proposals would be unacceptable to the senior lenders.

Separately, independent chartered surveyors were retained to produce a valuation on a 'managed sales' basis which estimated the value of the portfolio at approximately £517 million. Further, the surveyors were commissioned to produce a second valuation report, estimating the value based on sales in a distressed situation with a restricted marketing period of three to six months. The aggregate value of this 'distressed sales' estimate was reported as £353 million. Although the managed sales estimate was higher than the distressed sales estimate, the boards of McCarthy & Stone plc and McCarthy & Stone (Developments) Limited were also advised that it would take a number of years to realise the value implied by the managed sales estimate, and the proceeds realised would be subject to market uncertainty and expected continuing decline in the housing market.

7.5 Position of the boards

The boards of both McCarthy & Stone plc and McCarthy & Stone (Developments) Limited believed that, in the absence of a successful restructuring, part or all of the McCarthy & Stone Group was likely to enter into an insolvency procedure. If the group entered into administration or any other insolvency procedure (other than in connection with the implementation of the restructuring), then – given its financial position and the outlook for the house-building sector generally – the boards believed that it was likely that the proceeds available to the group's creditors would be considerably less than if the restructuring were implemented. The boards thus considered that continuing to run the business as a going concern offered a greater probability of higher recoveries for the scheme creditors.

There were no proposals from among the McCarthy & Stone Group's existing shareholders, second lien lenders, mezzanine lenders or external third parties that provided new financing to the group in a way that the senior lenders found acceptable for rebalancing the group's capital structure. As a result, the boards concluded that the restructuring proposed by the senior lenders would be in the best interests of McCarthy & Stone plc, McCarthy & Stone (Developments) Limited and their stakeholders, and would create a stronger foundation for the restructured McCarthy & Stone Group's business going forward and allow the continuation of trading without the damaging effects of doing so in an insolvency process.

8. Implementation of restructuring

8.1 Schemes of arrangement

The restructuring was implemented by way of court-approved schemes of arrangement for McCarthy & Stone plc and McCarthy & Stone (Developments) Limited pursuant to Part 26 of the Companies Act 2006.

Both schemes of arrangement were asset-transfer schemes and involved only the senior creditors. McCarthy & Stone relied on the *Re Tea Corporation* case ((1904) 1 Ch 12), with the result that out-of-the-money creditors were not a party to the schemes on the grounds that they had "no economic interest". As the schemes of arrangement could not deal with the out-of-the-money creditors, pre-packaged administrations were used, effectively to leave them behind. The senior lenders and hedge counterparty creditors received new debt and equity under the terms of the schemes of arrangement.

The classes of creditors in the schemes of arrangement were as follows:

- McCarthy & Stone plc hedge counterparties;
- McCarthy & Stone (Developments) Limited hedge counterparties;
- McCarthy & Stone plc senior Facility A, B and C lenders;
- McCarthy & Stone (Developments) Limited senior Facility A, B and C lenders;
- McCarthy & Stone plc senior Facility D lenders; and
- McCarthy & Stone (Developments) Limited senior Facility D lenders.

The Facility E lender of record was not party to the schemes, but was bound by a separate agreement.

8.2 Pre-packaged administrations

The pre-packaged administration sales transferred all of the assets of the two trading companies to newly incorporated companies in consideration for:

- the assumption of the majority of trading liabilities; and
- the discharge of part of the senior debt by way of the issuance of new debt and equity.

All of the guarantees and security in the transferred assets were released to ensure that the creditors could not make a claim against the newly constituted group. The administrations were planned well in advance of the sanction hearing in relation to the schemes of arrangement and were fully disclosed to the court. The appointment of the administrators took place only after the schemes of arrangement had been sanctioned by the court. Given the nature of the business, the court agreed that the administration orders could take effect out of business hours.

In this instance, the court also agreed that the newly incorporated companies could use the same company names, thereby allowing the directors that were continuing with the restructured group to comply with the rules on phoenix companies.

8.3 Implementation steps

Mother Bidco Limited, McCarthy & Stone plc and McCarthy & Stone (Developments) Limited entered into a lock-up agreement with certain scheme creditors and the senior Facility E lender of record which, among other things, each agreed to take the steps necessary to support and implement the restructuring before April 30 2009 (or such later date agreed with the coordination committee, provided that it was before June 1 2009).

Of the classes of scheme creditors, 100% of the hedge counterparties, 77.1% of

the senior Facility A, B and C lenders, 81.3% of the senior Facility D lenders and the senior Facility E lender of record (albeit not a scheme creditor) entered into the lock-up agreement on March 18 2009 (these percentages being calculated against the total value of claims of that class against the McCarthy & Stone Group).

The restructuring was effected through the following steps:

- The McCarthy & Stone business was restructured as Hackremco (No 2579) Limited (Holdco), Hackremco (No 2580) Limited (Newco 1), Hackremco (No 2581) Limited (Newco 2) and Hackremco (No 2582) Limited (the SPV), in accordance with the structure diagram on page 18.
- The facility agent (on instructions from the requisite majority of scheme creditors) accelerated all of the scheme creditors' existing debt under the existing senior facilities agreement, while the hedge counterparty creditors took steps to make the amounts that were owed under the hedge agreement due and payable, and called in the guarantees that were given by the group under the existing senior facilities agreement and the hedge agreement in respect of the debt owed by Mother Bidco Limited.
- Immediately after the McCarthy & Stone plc scheme became effective, the senior Facility E lender paid the E loss share amount to the senior Facility A, B and C lenders in respect of the senior Facility E lender's obligations under the intercreditor deed. In consideration for such payment, the senior Facility A, B and C lenders assigned approximately 7.5% of their participations under existing Facility A, existing Facility B and existing Facility C to the senior Facility E lender, in accordance with the terms and conditions of the Facility E agreement, and released the senior Facility E lender from any further obligations that it might otherwise have had under the intercreditor deed.
- Immediately after the completion of the assignments envisaged by the Facility E agreement, McCarthy & Stone plc's assets were transferred to Newco 1 pursuant to the McCarthy & Stone plc business sale agreement, in consideration for:
    - Newco 1's assumption of the assumed plc liabilities; and
    - the discharge of £87.1 million of McCarthy & Stone plc's liabilities to its scheme creditors under the guarantees that it provided under the existing facilities agreement. This was effected by Newco 1 borrowing (pursuant to the debt discharge agreement) £16.6 million from the scheme creditors and by the issuance of both Holdco shares to the unlisted scheme creditors and SPV shares to the listed scheme creditors.
- After the McCarthy & Stone plc scheme became effective and the McCarthy & Stone plc business sale agreement was completed, McCarthy & Stone (Developments) Limited's assets were transferred to Newco 2 pursuant to the McCarthy & Stone (Developments) Limited business sale agreement in consideration for:
    - Newco 2's assumption of the assumed McCarthy & Stone (Developments) Limited liabilities;
    - Newco 2's issuance of five million Newco 2 preference shares to McCarthy & Stone (Developments) Limited; and

- the discharge of £487.9 million of McCarthy & Stone (Developments) Limited's liabilities to its scheme creditors under the guarantees that it provided under the existing senior facilities agreement. This was effected by Newco 2 borrowing (pursuant to the debt discharge agreement) £487.9 million from the scheme creditors.
- As a result of these steps, the restructured McCarthy & Stone Group became indebted to the scheme creditors in an aggregate amount of £504.5 million.
- The debt was transferred between the scheme creditors and Newco 1 in respect of a portion of Newco 2's debt under the new facilities agreement, in consideration for which Newco 1 agreed to become indebted to the scheme creditors in the same amount and on the same terms of the new facilities agreement. In satisfaction of Newco 2's debt to Newco 1 as a result of the debt transfer under the debt transfer agreement, Newco 2 issued 41.4 million Newco 2 shares to Newco 1 at a premium of £0.80 per share. Following completion of this step, the aggregate amount of the restructured McCarthy & Stone Group's indebtedness to the scheme creditors remained at £504.5 million.

Before the schemes became effective, McCarthy & Stone plc and McCarthy & Stone (Developments) Limited were placed into administration. The purpose of this was to achieve a better result for each company's creditors as a whole than would be likely if the company were wound up (without first being in administration).

After completion of the restructuring:

- the scheme creditors owned (directly or indirectly through the SPV) 100% of the issued ordinary share capital of Holdco and indirectly owned 100% of the issued ordinary share capital of Newco 1 and Newco 2;
- McCarthy & Stone (Developments) Limited held five million Newco 2 preference shares of £1 per share;
- the restructured McCarthy & Stone Group was indebted to the scheme creditors in an aggregate amount of £504.5 million;
- Newco 1 and Newco 2 respectively owned the McCarthy & Stone plc transferred assets and the McCarthy & Stone (Developments) Limited transferred assets, and were liable for the assumed McCarthy & Stone plc liabilities and the assumed McCarthy & Stone (Developments) Limited liabilities, respectively; and
- the senior Facility E lender held approximately 7.5% of the participations under existing Facility A, existing Facility B and existing Facility C.

9. Final closing structure

The final closing structure is illustrated on the following page.

10. Comments on importance of this restructuring, other concluding remarks

The McCarthy & Stone restructuring was highly complex and one of the first restructurings of the post-Lehman downturn to scheme bank debt successfully. It required the development of various new solutions to unlock the complex financial

Final closing structure

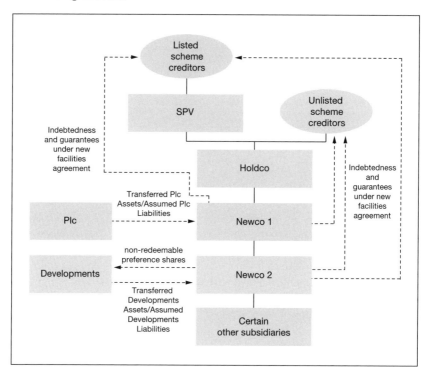

structures that had been created in 2006. It took nearly a year to negotiate and implement, and was ultimately highly successful.

As one of the first and most complex leveraged buy-out restructurings in this downturn, the market has used McCarthy & Stone as a precedent. The particularly new and creative feature was the use of the schemes of arrangement to restructure the senior debt, thereby addressing any hold-outs in the senior debt, combined with the pre-packaged administrations, thereby leaving behind the out-of-the-money junior creditors.

The author would like to thank Catherine Balmond and Stacey Quaye from Freshfields Bruckhaus Deringer LLP for their help in preparing this chapter.

IMO Car Wash

Adam Al-Attar
South Square

1.   Synopsis

In recent years, schemes of arrangement have enjoyed a resurgence as the implementation tool of choice in large restructurings. In many cases the subordinated creditors or equity holders have been crammed down by the terms of a scheme or, in the case of a scheme in contemplation of an asset transfer, left out altogether on the basis that they are 'out of the money'. Therefore, a critical question for all parties in such restructurings is how to determine who is 'in the money' and who is not.

Uncertainty remains over the appropriate basis of valuation that should be employed by a company in proposing a scheme of arrangement and used by the court in deciding whether it has the power to approve a scheme and whether it should do so. Thus, valuation informs both the question of jurisdiction to approve a scheme and the separate question of whether it is fair to do so. The latter question is also tied up with the scope and content of the duties of the scheme company's directors. A court will not approve a scheme if it is proposed in breach of duty or if its implementation would amount to a breach of duty. Insofar as valuation resolves the question of whose interest the company's directors must consider in discharging their duties to the company, valuation is not merely relevant as a fact for the court to consider at any convening hearing or approval hearing. Rather, it should – and does – shape the restructuring from the outset.

The principles, if any, that apply to the valuation of a company have not been debated in the English courts in the same way as in the US courts. The focus of this case study is to assess the extent to which the IMO schemes of arrangement in 2009 have advanced the development of such principles in the English courts. Justice Mann's judgment is reported at *Re Bluebrook Ltd* [2010] 1 BCLC 338. The conclusion of this chapter is that the IMO schemes of arrangement have left wide open the challenge of articulating in legal terms a concept of intrinsic value that differs from the value that a company has in the market now. No less crucially, it remains to articulate the principles, if any, on which the court should decide to use the 'intrinsic value' concept, rather than the value of the company if liquidated as at the scheme date, in assessing the class or classes to which the scheme has been put and the fairness of its terms.

2.   Intrinsic value and market value

The terms 'intrinsic value' and 'market value' are used below to differentiate, very broadly, two ways of looking at the value of a company. Market value is the price that

would be agreed between a willing buyer and a willing seller at arm's length for the company – whether for its shares or its business and assets, and whether as a going concern or on a break-up basis. 'Intrinsic value' does not necessarily coincide with market value. It assumes a going concern and recognises that the price which would be agreed between a willing buyer and a willing seller at arm's length depends on the circumstances at the time that the question is asked; moreover, some of these circumstances may be considered exceptional, reflecting a distortion relative to the value that would be agreed in a perfect market.

The concept of 'intrinsic value', as the term is used here, has been explained in other words by reference to the optimal use of the assets comprised within a company's business.[1] The combination of assets within a given business might represent the most efficient use of such assets relative to any other potential use, and the market value might nonetheless fail to reflect that intrinsic value because of an inadequate perception of the company's future performance or a lack of funding generally, such that the market price is driven down relative to the price that would be agreed in normal conditions.

The 'intrinsic value' concept tends to favour a restructuring between those with an existing interest in the company. If such interests are measured by reference to intrinsic value, a solution such as the rescheduling of the company's debt may produce a better outcome than a sale of its business and assets, as a rescheduling of debt does not expose such interests to the vagaries of the market, which at a time of distress may be sharp and severe. A simplified example is the market for certain financial products in September 2008. There was no market for certain products, such as collateralised debt obligations in respect of US sub-prime mortgage bonds, because of the perception of the quality of such assets. Many of these products may well have been worthless, but all were regarded as such because of the prevailing perception among buyers at the time. As a consequence, assets which had a value – in the sense of being capable of producing an income stream – had no price in the market.

This raises two questions: would a court be receptive to the use of the 'intrinsic value' concept, and would English law permit it? The risk inherent in such a concept is that it may require the court to make judgements on market conditions and perceptions that it is not equipped to make.

As to the former question, it should be apparent that the concept is underpinned by economic theory, engaged to justify a value that differs from the market value. The courts tend to regard a market valuation (as of a given date) as the best evidence of value, taking into account and reflecting expected future value, which may or may not be realised and is necessarily speculative. In *BNY Corporate Trustee Services Ltd v Eurosail-UK 2007-3BL plc*,[2] in considering the correct test for balance-sheet insolvency and the value of contingent liabilities, Lord Neuberger explained that "one has to value a future or contingent liability in a foreign currency at the present exchange

---

1   Crystal and Mokal, "The Valuation of Distressed Companies – A Conceptual Framework", (2006) 3 *International Corporate Rescue*, Issues 2 and 3.

2   [2011] 2 BCLC 1.

rate. By definition, that is the present sterling market value of the liability. The present exchange rate between two currencies can be analysed as the market's assessment of the future, in the sense that it is the rate at which each currency is seen to be equally likely to appreciate or depreciate as against the other. As events in Autumn 2008 graphically illustrated, the market is not always right, but it almost always represents the best one can do when it comes to valuation in the financial and legal worlds."[3]

In light of the above, a court might be reluctant to substitute a value derived from a concept of intrinsic value in place of an assessment of market value. To continue the simplified example above, it would require the court to be sufficiently confident in its judgement on value to prefer that value to the market price. Such a decision might be justifiable in the simplified scenario in which income continues to be received, but in more complex cases the court is likely to be reluctant to disregard the market price. In contrast, the US courts are equipped to distinguish between situations of financial and economic distress – broadly speaking, the former refers to financial difficulty attributable to excessive debt and the burden of servicing it, whereas the latter reflects a more fundamental economic deficiency in the company's business.

On the issue of permissibility under English law, even if the court were receptive to the use of a value other than market value, it might be unable to give effect to such use in most cases because of the scheme of rights agreed between creditors and members and between creditors themselves. For example, if the senior lenders should have rights of enforcement against the debtor, to which right the junior lenders' rights are also subject, then giving effect to a concept of intrinsic value – so as to require a rescheduling of the senior debt (including for the benefit of the junior lenders), as opposed to a sale in the market (and solely for the benefit of the senior lenders) – would require the court to override the terms of the senior lenders' right, which is to enforce and thereby to expose the company and its assets to the market.

Mann's decision provides an insight into these two questions. The judge gave full effect to the intercreditor agreement and favoured the market valuations of the scheme companies to the valuation of the mezzanine lenders because the companies' valuations showed an exercise of judgement as to what the company was worth in the circumstances in which the restructuring was proposed. However, the judge was required to choose not between a concept of market value and a concept of intrinsic value, but rather between rival market valuations. Therefore, the judgment does not close the door on the development, in English law, of principles similar to those applied in proceedings under Chapter 11 of the US Bankruptcy Code.

3.   Background to existing group operations

At the time of the restructuring, IMO Car Wash was the world's largest carwash company, washing over 30 million cars a year across 14 countries. The group was founded in Germany in 1965 and was subject to a number of institutional buy-outs, with Bridgepoint Capital taking ownership in 1988 and JP Morgan Partners acquiring

---

3   at 68.

the business in 2004. In 2006 US private equity firm The Carlyle Group purchased the existing group through a £450 million leveraged buy-out.

The existing group's biggest markets were the United Kingdom and Germany, but it also had operations in Australia, Austria, Belgium, the Czech Republic, France, Hungary, Luxembourg, the Netherlands, Poland, Portugal, Spain and Switzerland. It principally operated conveyor wash services. The existing group's business revolved around commission-based agreements with individual sites. The site operators were largely self-employed and responsible for their own staffing, which kept the group's employee headcount to a minimum. Nonetheless, it employed over 200 staff, many in administrative roles.

4.   Corporate structure before restructuring

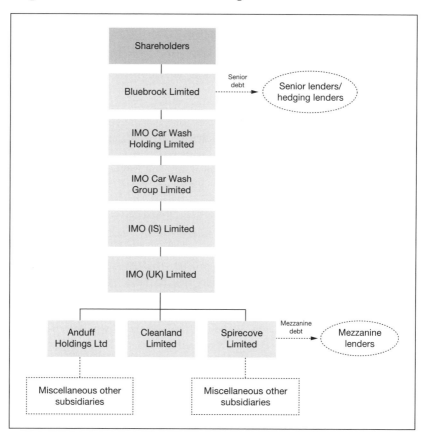

Bluebrook Limited was the holding company of the existing group, with IMO (UK) Limited and Spirecove Limited being its indirect wholly owned subsidiaries. The operating companies sat below IMO and Spirecove in the corporate structure. Bluebrook was beneficially owned by The Carlyle Group, which retained a majority stake together with certain minority shareholders.

5. Pre-restructuring capital structure

The existing group was funded pursuant to two principal facility agreements:

- a senior facilities agreement, originally dated February 8 2006, which was provided to Bluebrook; and
- a mezzanine facility agreement, originally of the same date, which was provided to Bluebrook and subsequently novated to Spirecove.

The senior facilities agreement and the mezzanine facility agreement were secured by way of first-priority security over all of the scheme companies' assets.

As of May 31 2009 a total of £314.2 million was outstanding under the senior facilities agreement and £119.3 million was outstanding under the mezzanine facility agreement. Between that date and the date of the approval hearing, the outstanding amounts increased through the further accrual of interest by approximately £1.2 million a month and £1 million a month, respectively. The existing group also had £980,000 outstanding under hedging agreements.

The position between the senior lenders, the mezzanine lenders, the hedging lenders and other finance creditors was regulated by an intercreditor deed, originally dated February 8 2006, whereby the senior lenders had priority for all purposes and at all times. The security agent was required to act in accordance with the instructions of the majority senior creditors until after the senior debt discharge date. Before that date, enforcement by other creditors was prohibited without the consent of the facility agent acting on the instruction of the majority senior creditors (except in permitted circumstances that were irrelevant to the schemes). The intercreditor deed included terms to the following effect:

- Ranking of debt – for all purposes, Clause 2 of the deed ranked senior debt first and mezzanine debt second, followed by other levels of debt.
- Subordination – Clause 6 of the deed prevented the mezzanine lenders from receiving any payment other than those permitted under the clause until the senior debt had been discharged. This clause also included a 'turnover' provision, whereby mezzanine lenders had to pass to the senior lenders any payments that they received in respect of their debt which were not permitted under the clause.
- Release – Clause 11.4 of the deed allowed the security agent to release security and liabilities on an enforcement, provided that the proceeds realised from the enforcement were applied in accordance with the ranking of debt under Clause 2 and the waterfall under Clause 14.
- Mezzanine purchase option – Clause 12 of the deed provided the mezzanine lenders with the option to purchase the senior lenders' debt at par if the mezzanine lenders were not content with the enforcement actions taken by the senior lenders;
- Subordination on insolvency – Clause 13 of the deed stipulated that on the occurrence of an insolvency event, the mezzanine debt would be subordinated to the claims of the senior debt.
- Waterfall – Clause 14 set out a waterfall provision for the application of the proceeds of an enforcement. The clause provided that after the payment of

certain fees, costs and expenses, proceeds were to be applied in the discharge of the senior debt and only subsequently against the discharge of the mezzanine debt.

6. Financial situation of the existing group in the lead-up to restructuring, and restructuring triggers

The existing group had materially underperformed relative to the business plan agreed in 2006. The business plan had contemplated that the existing group would achieve earnings of £57.2 million before interest, taxes, depreciation and amortisation in 2008 with just over 1,000 sites; however, the figures for 2008 were approximately £37.6 million from 925 sites. Bluebrook had outperformed the business plan in the first five months of 2009, but such performance did not generate enough cash to prevent a breach of the terms of the senior facilities agreement and the mezzanine facility agreement.

By certificates dated February 14 2009, the existing group had confirmed breaches of the senior facilities agreement and the mezzanine facility agreement, specifically:

- a breach of the existing group's leverage ratio, being 11.13x against required covenant levels of less than 8.28x under the senior facilities agreement and 9.11x under the mezzanine facility agreement; and
- a breach of the existing group's interest cover ratio, being 1.21x against required covenant levels of more than 1.47x under the senior facilities agreement and 1.32x under the mezzanine facility agreement.

The breaches were irreparable because the ultimate beneficial owners of the existing group, CEP Participations Sarl SICAR and CEP II Co-Investment Sarl SICAR, and their affiliates were unable to provide the required funds to exercise equity cure rights. The existing group had also defaulted on interest payments. These defaults were due to trading performance and consequent projected cash flows. Therefore, the existing group had insufficient cash resources to continue as a going concern without the support of the senior lenders. Moreover, the existing group had made a loss of £356 million for the year to date and had excess liabilities over assets of £342,458,000 following a write-down of purchase goodwill (in line with applicable accounting standards), because of its failure to maintain the covenants mentioned above. Accordingly, the existing group had an unsustainable capital structure. It was able to continue trading only with the forbearance of the senior lenders and thanks to the standstill imposed on the mezzanine lenders by reason of the terms of the intercreditor deed.

Without a form of restructuring that would be satisfactory to the senior lenders, it was highly likely that they would enforce. In any event, it was very likely that the board of directors or a creditor would place the existing group into a form of insolvency proceeding. The senior lenders were not required to act unanimously in relation to enforcement – a majority greater than two-thirds was sufficient to direct the security agent to enforce.

Against this backdrop, the scheme companies sought to initiate a consensus restructuring involving the senior lenders and the mezzanine lenders.

7. Senior lenders and mezzanine lenders

The syndicate of senior lenders included some Icelandic banks which had entered insolvency proceedings in Iceland in 2008. A steering committee was formed, which comprised banks and hedge funds. Likewise, the mezzanine lenders formed a creditors' committee to represent them in the negotiations.

8. Restructuring negotiation process

No sooner had the existing group breached its covenants than a standstill agreement was put in place whereby the senior and mezzanine lenders, among other things, agreed to waive interest payments.

The Carlyle Group took the initiative on or around February 17 2009 and presented a plan. This attributed a value of £202 million to the existing group and would have seen a cash injection by the sponsor of £25 million, a write-off of 30% of the senior debt in exchange for 33% of the equity and a write-down of 100% of the mezzanine debt in exchange for 3% of the equity. The proposal was rejected by all lenders.

This was followed on or around February 19 2009 by a proposal by the mezzanine lenders' committee, which was unacceptable to the steering committee because – as was made clear to the mezzanine lenders' committee on February 23 2009 – it assumed a value for the existing group in excess of the senior debt.

At a meeting on or around March 5 2009, the two committees agreed on certain principles which the steering committee considered necessary in any consensual restructuring:

- the existing security and priority arrangements would be respected; and
- no sums would be payable to the mezzanine lenders until such time as a full recovery had been made on the senior debt.

On the basis of these principles, it was proposed that the mezzanine lenders be issued equity warrants in the restructured group to provide a financial return in future in the event of an exit (ie, a sale, listing or change or control), with an enterprise value in excess of an amount of the existing group's senior debt. The steering committee formalised this proposal as a counter-proposal to the mezzanine lenders' committee on or around April 7 2009.

At a further meeting held between members of the two committees on April 20 2009, the mezzanine lenders' committee raised the possibility of receiving "a little straight equity (ca 2% to 4%) as a sweetener"; however, this idea was rejected and the steering committee's proposal was refined without the incorporation of terms to that effect. The second steering committee proposal would have yielded a return to the mezzanine lenders in circumstances where the enterprise value on an exit exceeded £325 million (ie, approximately the amount of the senior debt, plus accrued but unpaid interest).

On or around May 5 2009 the mezzanine lenders' committee provided a mark-up of the steering committee's proposal which amounted to a counter-proposal. It required that the mezzanine lenders be issued with 5% of the equity in any restructured group notwithstanding the reduction in the senior debt to an amount of approximately £185 million. The steering committee rejected this proposal.

The mezzanine lenders' committee provided a further mark-up of the steering committee's proposal on or around May 19 2009, again requesting 5% of the equity in any restructured group. The steering committee discussed the proposal, but ultimately rejected it on June 17 2009, having previously indicated that agreement was unlikely. To the steering committee, it appeared that the mezzanine lenders' committee was unwilling to respect the security and priority provisions of the existing financing arrangements. These were essential for the steering committee in any consensual restructuring. The steering committee accordingly decided that it needed to progress towards a restructuring solution without the support of the mezzanine lenders' committee. At the approval hearing, the mezzanine lenders' committee had sought to characterise the response of the steering committee as a failure to engage in meaningful or substantive negotiations. However, on the former's own evidence, the steering committee's proposals were unacceptable to the mezzanine lenders' committee "given their view of the value of the existing group".

9. Restructuring proposal

The preferred proposal that was ultimately put forward by the existing group stated that:

- the senior debt was to be accelerated and demand for payment made against Bluebrook, IMO, Spirecove and other existing group companies;
- the existing group's business was to be transferred to a new, restructured group owned by the scheme creditors in proportion to their holding of the existing senior debt;
- approximately £252.1 million of the senior debt was to be novated to the restructured group, of which £67.1 million was to be capitalised and issued to the scheme creditors, leaving the restructured group owing the scheme creditors a reduced amount of senior debt of approximately £185 million;
- the remaining senior debt (subject to a residual £12 million) was to be released as against the scheme companies and their affiliates as guarantors of the senior debt;
- the claims of the mezzanine lenders against any subsidiary of the scheme companies which was to form part of the restructured group were also to be released; and
- the claims of the mezzanine lenders were to be released by the security agent in accordance with the intercreditor deed.

In order to implement the proposal, three identical schemes of arrangement would be prepared in respect of Bluebrook, IMO and Spirecove. The use of a scheme was necessary only as a result of the need for unanimous consent from the lenders to compromise claims – this was unachievable due to the participation in the syndicate of Icelandic banks which were in insolvency proceedings in Iceland and were accordingly unable to obtain the requisite internal consents to vote in favour of the restructuring proposal.

Following the court approval of the schemes, Bluebrook, IMO and Spirecove were to be placed in administration. Unless their administrators took a different view,

these companies – together with other existing group companies acting at the request of the security agent – would enter into transfer agreements to transfer all assets of the existing group to a new restructured group consisting of three companies: Holdco, Midco and Newco. Holdco would be owned by the senior lenders.

10. Implementation

The schemes were approved by the senior lenders, with only two senior lenders (which held no more than 5% of the senior debt) voting against the schemes at the creditors' meetings. However, the mezzanine lenders challenged the schemes at the approval hearing. They contended that the schemes operated unfairly to them by depriving them of potential future value of the company.

The combined effect of the scheme and the anticipated asset transfer in administration was to allow the transfer of assets from the existing group to a new corporate structure. The company and the senior lenders claimed that the value of the existing group and its assets was significantly and demonstrably lower than the senior debt; as such, the mezzanine lenders had no economic interest in the existing group. Accordingly, no assets would be left in the old existing group to pay the mezzanine lenders. This was the basis on which the company had sought to enter into a compromise with the senior lenders and had chosen not to engage further with the mezzanine lenders. Therefore, the mezzanine lenders were not required to approve the scheme, since their claims were not being compromised.

However, the mezzanine lenders did not accept that the value of the assets was lower than the value of their debt. They sought to challenge the scheme, claiming that it would be fair and reasonable to allow them to participate in the restructured group on terms that, after payment of the senior debt and a return on equity, would allow them to obtain some value. It was further suggested that the scheme should not be approved, since it would deprive the mezzanine lenders of any prospect of benefiting from the future value of the assets, whereas there was sufficient prospect of them having an economic value in the assets, which should not be ignored.

The mezzanine lenders sought to put their challenge first as a challenge to the jurisdiction of the court to approve the schemes, and second as a challenge to the application of the scheme companies to the court to exercise its discretion to approve the schemes as approved by the respective meetings of the senior lenders.

The first challenge pointed to a hard-edged question of whether the scheme companies had correctly convened the appropriate classes of creditor for the purpose of considering whether to accept or reject the terms of the proposed scheme. If the class or classes of creditor are incorrectly constituted, such that the members in each class cannot consult together in their common interest, the court has no jurisdiction to approve the scheme, even if all of the members do so.

The latter point reflected a broader challenge to the fairness of the schemes. It dovetailed with the mezzanine lender's secondary case that the scheme companies' directors had acted in breach of their duty in proposing the schemes on the terms approved (ie, on terms which did not grant the mezzanine lenders the right to participate in the restructured group).

It was (and still is) common to both questions that the court should have regard to what has been termed 'the relevant comparator' – that is, the circumstances which would be likely to result but for the approval of the proposed scheme. Justice David Richards had explained in *Re T&N (No 2)* that in determining whether the class or classes are properly constituted for the purpose of considering a scheme, it is essential to identify the relevant comparator.[4] Only by reference to that comparator can the pre-scheme and post-scheme rights of creditors be assessed for the purpose of determining whether the class or classes have been correctly constituted. Similarly, in asking whether a creditors' scheme of arrangement should be approved, the court will have regard to the relevant comparator. In *Re Marconi plc* the judge explained that an intelligent and honest scheme creditor would give special consideration to a comparison between the likely (or even probable) future of the company in the absence of a scheme and, alternatively, its future under the scheme being proposed.[5]

The relevant comparator is a question of fact which turns on the circumstances of the scheme company at hand. For example, it has been held that if the company is solvent, the relevant comparator (should the proposed restructuring fail) is a continuation of business, whether or not this is in a run-off or a solvent winding-up.[6] In contrast, if the company is insolvent and would cease to trade if the proposed restructuring were to fail, the relevant comparator is insolvent liquidation.[7] However, if more would be realised for creditors by an administration than an immediate winding-up, the relevant comparator is administration, which is the proper course having regard to the duties of the company's directors. The further question in such a case is how the administration is likely to be conducted – for example, through an asset transfer by way of sale or some other realisation of value. Therefore, the relevant comparator can involve a more complex counterfactual than a simple solvent or insolvent winding-up.

The dispute in *IMO Car Wash*, between the companies and the senior lenders on the one hand and the mezzanine lenders on the other, can be understood in terms of a dispute about the relevant comparator. However, one of the principal difficulties faced by the mezzanine lenders was to articulate what that comparator was. If they could not do so, the dispute would be reduced to a more straightforward dispute about the quality of the valuation evidence.

For the companies and the senior lenders, the existing group was insolvent on a cash-flow basis, and continued to trade from available cash only as a result of forbearance by the senior lenders as to interest due. It was also insolvent on a balance-sheet basis, having regard to the value break within the senior debt. From this perspective, the relevant comparator was a sale in the market at that point in time, whether by:

- enforcement of the senior lender's security in accordance with the intercreditor deed – which had been inoperative on the facts for a time, only because a minority of senior lenders were themselves in insolvency

---

4   [2007] 1 BCLC 563, at 87.
5   [2003] EWHC 1083 (Ch), at 13 and 14.
6   *Re British Aviation Insurance Co Ltd* [2006] 1 BCLC 665, at 88 to 97.
7   *Re Telewest Communications plc (No 1)* [2005] 1 BCLC 752, at 28 and 29.

proceedings and could not be relied upon to operate the required mechanisms in an acceptable timeframe;

- a sale in administration, which was the more appropriate insolvency proceeding relative to a liquidation, but which would have been terminal to existing group's trading; or
- a voluntary arrangement, which would have been ineffective given the lack of support by the senior lenders and the secured rights in issue.

An informal workout had been attempted, but had failed to produce a consensual compromise. In these circumstances the senior lenders could say that but for the schemes, it was highly likely that the security in respect of the senior debt would be enforced.

By contrast, the mezzanine lenders objected to the characterisation of the relevant comparator as a sale in the market at that point. For the mezzanine lenders, the existing group had an intrinsic value, which was realisable in future; in light of such realisation, value would be returned to the mezzanine lenders and perhaps to other creditors. In order to realise that value, and to prevent its appropriation by the senior lenders, a scheme was required on terms other than those proposed by the senior lenders, and which would allow a wider participation in the restructured group.

In making such an argument, the difficulties for the mezzanine lenders were, first, the failure to articulate what was meant by 'intrinsic value' and, second, the problem of identifying a reason to allow such a basis to override the rights agreed under the intercreditor deed in the circumstances.

The first difficulty reflects the aspect in which UK law is regarded, by some, as deficient in comparison to US law. In *IMO* the respective valuations produced by the companies and the mezzanine lenders were market valuations, and accounted for and reflected the expected future value – a feature most obviously apparent in the income approach or discounted cash-flow analysis. The mezzanine lender's valuation differed in the use of a technique, known as the 'Monte Carlo analysis', which produced a probabilistic range of values, rather than a single value. In this respect, the dispute in *IMO Car Wash* did not engage with the debate about the principles (if any) to be applied in order to determine the appropriate basis for valuation. The court applied the existing law to determine the relevant comparator.

The court was led to its conclusion as to the relevant comparator by the second difficulty encountered by the mezzanine lenders – namely, the rights under the intercreditor deed. The terms of the contractual subordination were, in a sense, deeper than any structural subordination or any subordination imposed by statute (eg, in respect of members as against creditors in a winding-up), because the terms of the intercreditor deed comprised a free agreement between the companies, the senior lenders and the mezzanine lenders, among others. By the terms of the intercreditor deed, the senior lenders were entitled to priority in all respects and were entitled to enforce in their own interest – an enforcement which was said, on the evidence, to be highly likely, and which had only not occurred because of the temporary disability of a minority of the senior lenders that were the subject of foreign

insolvency proceedings. The agreed rights pointed to a sale in the market at that point as the relevant comparator.

Therefore, the question before Justice Mann was whether the court should approve the scheme of arrangement in circumstances in which, if approved, the rights of mezzanine lenders would be rights against a group of companies with no assets and no right of participation in respect of the new group of companies. The question turned on the question of valuation, and not on any wider theoretical question of how to determine the appropriate basis for valuation. The judge was not confronted with the argument that the valuations on which the companies and the senior lenders relied were wrong because of the bases selected. The mezzanine lenders instead produced a rival valuation by use of a different technique, and which did not claim to be correct because of a fundamentally different approach to valuation – that debate remains to be resolved.

For these reasons, the judge devoted considerable time at the hearing to scrutinising the rival valuations, an approach which is reflected in the terms of his judgment.

11.   Scheme companies' valuations

The scheme companies and their legal adviser, Latham & Watkins, had been focused on the determination of valuation from the outset of the restructuring in order to ascertain whether the mezzanine lenders were in the money for the purposes of any scheme. The companies commissioned a desktop valuation, but also tested the market through a third-party sales process which was overseen by the company's financial adviser, Rothschild. Against the background of a senior debt level of approximately £315 million, those exercises indicated the following valuation ranges:

- The market-testing process produced an indicative offer which placed an enterprise value on the existing group of between £150 million and £188 million on a cash, debt-free basis, including a normalised level of working capital. The senior lenders indicated that staple financing might be available to provide acquisition finance to bidders in order to maximise prospective offers.
- The desktop valuation estimated the value of the existing group to be between £235 million and £265 million on a going-concern basis.

The company also undertook a third valuation exercise to 'sense-check' the above analyses. This involved an assessment of the asset value of certain of the existing group's sites on a market-value and restricted-sales basis. An extrapolation exercise was then carried out to produce a valuation of the existing group's entire portfolio, resulting in a valuation range of between £164 million and £208 million.

Perhaps surprisingly, in the context of the scheme and the subsequent transfer of the IMO business which was to survive as a going concern, none of the parties attempted to argue that a liquidation value of the existing group was the appropriate benchmark – in contrast to the arguments raised in *MyTravel* – even though there was evidence from the senior lenders that if the scheme did not go ahead, they would appoint administrators over the entire existing group. All agreed that a going-

concern current valuation was the correct basis for the purposes of the scheme.

In undertaking the desktop valuation exercise, the companies' valuers had taken into account three different approaches in reaching the above value range:

- an income approach based on the cash flows that the business could generate in future. This was essentially a discounted cash-flow analysis, subject to adjustments to reflect the realities of the current market;
- a market approach which was assessed by reference to comparisons with other publicly traded companies and transactions; and
- a leveraged buy-out analysis aimed at assessing how a potential private equity purchaser would look to pay, given its typical expectation of rates of return in the current market.

As previously noted, these approaches produced a valuation peak of £265 million, significantly below the level of the senior debt and, most importantly, significantly above the evidence from the Rothschild sale process, which indicated an enterprise value of between £150 million and £188 million.

The critical point in this case was whether the companies' valuation approach was the correct basis for proposing the restructuring.

12. Mezzanine lenders' valuations

The mezzanine lenders conceded that if the existing group were sold immediately, all proceeds would flow to the senior lenders. However, they argued that this would be unfair, as this valuation took into account the current harsh market conditions. It was further argued that the existing group had an intrinsic value which was greater than this, and that such intrinsic value was properly reflected in a discounted cash-flow analysis that they had commissioned.

The mezzanine lenders had commissioned a valuation from LEK Consulting, which undertook a Monte Carlo simulation to arrive at its valuation. This involved repeated calculations of discounted cash-flow valuations using random sampling of input and assumptions, followed by the aggregation of the results into a range of probabilities of different valuation outcomes.

The LEK report also used comparable transaction valuations and comparable multiple valuations from which data was extracted and applied to the existing group's figures. The valuation produced a range with a median and mean value of between £385 million and £398 million, and accordingly purported to show that the future enterprise value of the existing group would break in the mezzanine debt.

The mezzanine lenders' discounted cash-flow valuation was predicated on the idea that without the constraints of the existing financial covenants, and with the revised debt structure which was envisaged by the scheme of arrangement (or, alternatively, the mezzanine lenders' own proposal), the senior lenders were highly likely to make a full recovery at some time in future, leaving a surplus for the mezzanine lenders. Therefore, the mezzanine lenders argued that they were adversely affected by the scheme of arrangement; (they said) it was unfair that they were excluded from the scheme, as they were economically interested in the future outcome of the company's assets.

Tellingly, the company had not received the mezzanine lenders' valuation report (despite repeated requests) until after it had launched the scheme of arrangement and had participated in the initial directions and class hearing. Accordingly, at the time of entering into a lock-up agreement for the restructuring with the senior creditors and launching the subsequent scheme of arrangement, the valuation evidence available to the directors indicated that the mezzanine lenders had no economic interest in the restructuring, with no evidence from the mezzanine lenders to contradict this.

13.   Scrutiny of rival valuations

The judge was firm in his view that the lack of cross-examination did not mean that he had to accord equal weight to both sets of valuations. He appeared to highlight the difference – and, to some extent, the deficiencies – of the LEK valuation as it had been presented to him, and noted that:

- the LEK report resulted in statistical analysis, conducted by a computer. It did not involve the sort of judgement used in more traditional valuations – although this was not to say that no judgement was involved, as some judgement had been used to select the ranges that the computer would use;
- the use of a Monte Carlo simulation in valuation exercises was not unknown in specialist circumstances. However, it was unacceptable to say that the depressed market conditions constituted a special circumstance which justified an entirely new approach to valuation;
- the process was mechanical and highly technical, without judgement or assessment;
- he had misgivings about the valuation because of the manner in which it and the supporting material had been provided – the mezzanine lenders had delayed requests from the company to produce their valuation materials and were generally perceived by the other stakeholders as having been 'late to the party'. Attention was drawn to the fact that the mezzanine valuation report did not clarify the underlying assumptions on which it was based and was not comprehensive in the sense in which a valuer would wish to comprehend it. Moreover, the report referred to information coming from other sources which were unidentified; and
- as an exercise of assessing what a third party would pay, the judge called the mezzanine valuation "very unconvincing".

14.   Judge's conclusions

Against this background, the judge held as follows:

- The company's advisers had produced expert evidence which was comprehensible and which related to the key question on the facts: how much would a purchaser pay for the existing group now in the current market circumstances?
- In the circumstances of a scheme of arrangement in which the business of the existing group was to continue, a going-concern basis of valuation was the correct basis of valuation.

- Any valuation exercise should use 'real-world' judgements as to the assumptions to be made when valuing the existing group – it should not be a sterile statistical exercise.

Although no single method of valuing a business was automatically favoured over another, the judge did not favour the discounted cash-flow method used by the mezzanine lenders' valuer, which used a Monte Carlo statistical analysis to produce a wide range of potential values that depended on a range of inputs. He described it as producing "not so much a range of values, professionally assessed, but a range of possibilities".

15.   Directors' duties

The mezzanine lenders raised the ancillary argument that since their valuation showed that they were interested in the assets, it was incumbent on the directors to implement a restructuring that would leave the mezzanine lenders with some future interest. They argued that the directors were under a duty to support and promote a deal with the mezzanine lenders – for example, that the interest could be subject to a payment-in-kind instrument, or by promoting a scheme of arrangement involving the mezzanine lenders or some other compromise which would allow the company to continue to pay senior interest while not writing off the mezzanine debt.

The mezzanine lenders ran this argument even though the mezzanine creditors committee, which had been formed in late 2008, had been involved in active (but ultimately fruitless) discussions with both the senior lenders and the company's financial advisers. Moreover, the committee had rejected an offer of warrants as part of the restructuring terms. Nevertheless, it was argued that the company effectively had a duty to negotiate the mezzanine lenders' position for them.

The judge concluded that the mezzanine lenders' case was not a realistic summary of the directors' duties. In particular, he noted that:

- the mezzanine coordination committee was expressly formed for the purpose of protecting the mezzanine lenders' interests;
- the mezzanine lenders had at all material times been 'fighting their own corner' and had never indicated to the directors that they expected them to fight their corner for them – nor did the directors have the authority to do so;
- coupled with the valuation evidence before it, the board was entitled to conclude that if the mezzanine lenders could not have achieved anything in their negotiations with the senior lenders, the company was in no better position to start negotiating something else on their behalf; and
- the company's lock-up to, and promotion of, the scheme was "in substance acknowledging economic and business realities". It could not have an impact on the interests of anyone other than the senior lenders, given the level of debt and the value of the existing group's assets.

The judge also recognised that the directors' options were limited in practice. In discharging their duties to creditors, it was proper for them to take into account the risks of personal liability for wrongful trading if the company continued to trade

without a reasonable prospect of avoiding an insolvent liquidation. He firmly rejected the mezzanine lenders' idea that the board challenge the senior lenders by refusing to implement the scheme until a better deal had been negotiated for the subordinated creditors.

16. **Carry on trading?**

The mezzanine lenders further argued that the IMO business was cash generative, it had not suffered a collapse in earnings before interest, taxes, depreciation and amortisation (unlike most other distressed leveraged buy-outs) and therefore the existing group could survive on its existing cash flows. Accordingly, they argued that the company should have continued to trade within its existing capital structure, even though it was in breach of the finance documents and was not paying senior interest.

The company considered this to be wholly unrealistic. The evidence provided to the court showed that the existing group was balance-sheet insolvent, and that although it was meeting its trading debts, it was unable to pay all of its debts as they fell due, as demonstrated by the failure to pay the interest under the senior and mezzanine debt at the end of March 2009. Moreover, the evidence clearly showed that if the scheme were not approved by the court, the senior lenders would be highly likely to enforce their security, or the company itself might have to apply for an administration order. Thus, the prospect of trading in the existing capital structure seemed remote for the company and was unsatisfactory for the directors from the perspective of personal liability for wrongful trading.

Against this background, the judge held that the existing group was, on any footing, technically insolvent and was suffering from real creditor pressure. Events of default were outstanding under the company's major credit agreements and the valuations showed that the mezzanine creditors were clearly out of the money. It was therefore unrealistic to expect the directors to continue to trade in the face of this, in the vague hope that the mezzanine creditors might be able to return to the negotiating table and reach a new deal with the senior lenders. The company's action in precipitating the restructuring by proposing a scheme of arrangement, with classes drawn up by the company based on the valuation evidence before the directors, had been correct and was in the interests of those to whom the directors owed their duties – namely, the in-the-money creditors, as indicated by that valuation evidence.

17. **Intercreditor agreement and right to purchase senior debt**

One further hurdle that the mezzanine lenders faced was the intercreditor agreement. This contained the usual mezzanine subordination provisions – a fact to which the company and the senior lenders repeatedly alluded in argument. It also contained the right in favour of the mezzanine lenders to purchase the senior debt at par in enforcement circumstances. This has always been viewed as being of benefit to subordinated creditors, but in these circumstances it worked against the mezzanine lenders in practice. The judge drew a negative inference from the fact that they were unwilling to exercise the purchase option (despite having had that suggestion made to them in correspondence), while insisting that they were in the money, and the mezzanine lenders had put forward no reasons for this hesitancy.

Figure 2. Final closing structure

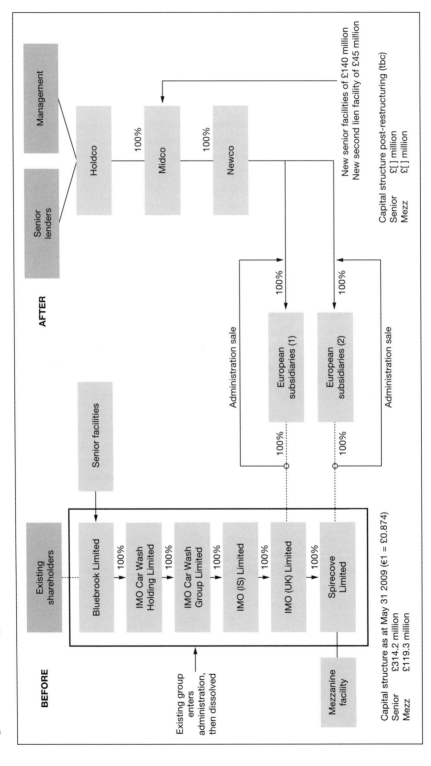

18.   Final closing structure

See Figure 2 on the previous page.

19.   Comment

The *IMO Car Wash* case provides a number of important lessons in the context of the successful implementation of a restructuring:

- Valuation should ordinarily be based on how much a purchaser would pay today for the relevant assets. Whether this is best evidenced by a discounted cash-flow or other desktop valuation, by a sales process or a marketing exercise, or by a combination of these, is likely to be debated on the facts. However, it remains to be seen whether subordinated lenders or equity holders might successfully articulate a concept of intrinsic value which provides a credible legal alternative to a valuation based on a sale in the market at the time of the restructuring.
- Intercreditor agreements are likely to be respected and full effect given to their terms.
- Any buy-out right for the subordinated lenders is likely to be held against them and is likely to be considered redundant going forward. If such lenders had the will and the means to purchase the senior debt, the absence of a right does not prevent an offer from being made.
- The case emphasised both the importance to the parties in a restructuring of careful planning and a thorough execution of the process and, conversely, the imperative for subordinated lenders to make any challenge early and with commitment.

On this last point, the challenge brought by the mezzanine lenders was, in many respects, simply too late, having been made at the approval hearing. By that time, the restructuring had gathered momentum, such that the senior lenders could state clearly that enforcement was highly likely if the schemes were not approved. If the mezzanine lenders had been able to present a fully articulated concept of 'intrinsic value' or a properly funded and convincing rival valuation, the mezzanine lenders would have been better placed to have applied for a declaration as to value in anticipation of the convening hearing. Such a challenge would have posed much more of a threat than a challenge made late in the day, which was susceptible to characterisation as a hold-out, rather than as a serious dispute as to value. For this reason, the debate is not yet over, although it would take a case on the right facts to require any development of more refined legal principles in the area of valuation.

Monier

Melissa Coakley
Mark Hyde
Clifford Chance LLP

1. Introduction

This was the restructuring that everyone said could not be done. This transaction represents the first time that a group of lenders have enforced Luxembourg security to take ownership of a multinational group originally acquired via a major leveraged buy-out, outside of a formal insolvency process and without the cooperation of the sponsor.

In early 2009 Monier Group GmbH found itself with a very short timeframe within which to seek to agree a highly complex €2 billion debt restructuring before a widely anticipated second-quarter covenant breach would tip its main operating company into German insolvency proceedings (the estimated value of the business had dropped to €700 million). Added complications included a large and disparate lender group, an out-of-the-money equity sponsor whose own restructuring proposals were rejected outright by the lenders, an untested Luxembourg enforcement process and a myriad of legal, tax and regulatory considerations.

2. Background to group operations

Formerly part of the LaFarge Group, Monier is a leading international supplier of roof tiles and roofing components, chimneys and ventilation systems. The Monier group has around 9,000 employees, 130 production sites and operations in more than 40 countries, all managed by a Luxembourg-based holding company. Operationally and in terms of headcount, the group is centred in Germany.

3. Pre-restructuring corporate structure

Before the restructuring (illustrated overleaf) the top management of the group who served on the boards at the Luxembourg holding company level predominantly comprised executives, either from the equity sponsor itself or hired by the equity sponsor. As the equity sponsor's tactical approach to the restructuring negotiations was deemed to be so unacceptable by the lender group that it ultimately served to harden the lenders' resolve to take control of the business, management was placed in an unenviable position.

4. Pre-restructuring capital structure

In 2007 Monier was acquired by PAI Partners in a €2.4 billion enterprise value leveraged transaction. The debt structure comprised first-lien debt of €1.7 billion and second-lien debt of €0.3 billion, documented in an English law-governed, multi-

Pre-restructuring corporate structure

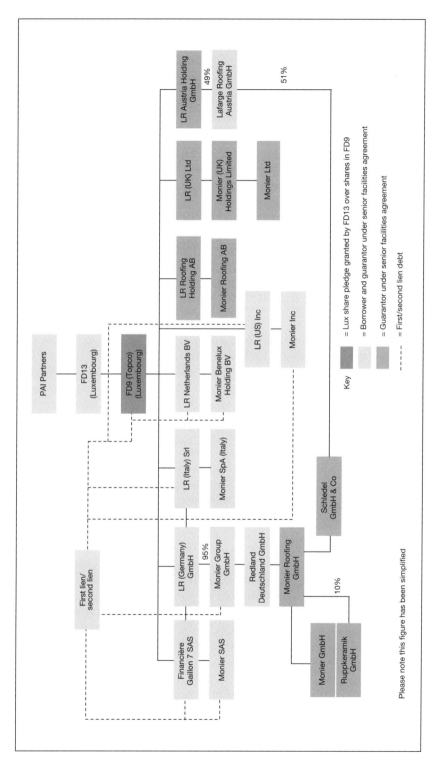

Key

= Lux share pledge granted by FD13 over shares in FD9

= Borrower and guarantor under senior facilities agreement

= Guarantor under senior facilities agreement

= First/second lien debt

Please note this figure has been simplified

tranche credit agreement. The syndication of the debt was heavily oversubscribed, resulting in almost 200 lenders of record, as well as a significant number of sub-participants. As this was a financing which occurred at the top of the private equity market, the security package was relatively light and mostly comprised share security and inter-company loan assignments taken in respect of the Luxembourg holding companies and pledges over shares held in the regional holding companies, rather than security taken at the operating company level. Indeed, the credit agreement itself typified 2007 market conditions in that it was 'covenant light' and contained minimal information reporting rights in favour of the lenders, as well as limited events of default.

5. Financial situation and restructuring triggers

The onset of the global recession meant that companies such as Monier which are reliant on a healthy construction industry were particularly hard hit. Indeed, in the last quarter of 2008 it became clear to the lenders that Monier's enterprise value had plummeted and it was inevitable that it would be in breach of its financial covenants when they next came to be tested. It was apparent to all concerned that on a liquidation analysis, the value of the business would clearly break well within the first-lien debt.

However, the next financial covenant testing date was not until June 30 2009. Equally, no payment of interest was due until this date. The hands of the lenders were effectively tied. They knew that a breach was inevitable, but there were no levers within the credit documentation to enable a default to be called, force Monier to come to the negotiation table or even provide the lenders with any further financial information. The lenders were also painfully aware that as the principal borrower was German, while the heavily over-leveraged position of the group was left unresolved, time was running out before the local directors would be forced to file for potentially value-destructive German insolvency proceedings.

Under German law, it is generally considered mandatory for directors to apply for insolvency proceedings within three weeks of becoming aware that the company is over-indebted on a balance-sheet basis in the absence of a positive continuation forecast.[1] The potential personal liability consequences are stark for non-compliant directors under German insolvency law. Experience from other German restructurings indicated that only a credible restructuring proposal signed by a majority of lenders, coupled with appropriate standstill or non-petition arrangements, would avoid the occurrence of an insolvency filing shortly after June 30. Given its strategic importance to the group, a filing in Germany could also have potentially sparked off a domino effect of insolvency filings throughout the rest of the key Monier operating companies, almost certainly obliterating any potential lender recoveries.

The equity sponsor was well aware of the lenders' contractual position, and

---

1   Legislative changes relating to the 'overindebtedness test' (which came into force after the Monier restructuring) have provided an element of additional breathing space for German directors in certain circumstances.

appeared to use the developing hiatus to its own tactical advantage, presumably hoping that the lack of information or rights of access to Monier would preclude the lenders forming a rival restructuring plan, compelling them to accept the sponsor's own restructuring proposal.

6.   Composition of lending syndicate and syndicate dynamic

However, the information vacuum did not prevent the lenders from mobilising to form steering committees in order to try to start restructuring negotiations with Monier on behalf of the syndicate. Somewhat unusually – and possibly due to the sheer number of lenders – the agent arranged for first-lien lenders to elect the members of their committee via a ballot process. The committee which emerged (the 'co-com') was a representative mix of institutional bank lenders and one collateralised loan obligation covering an appropriate geographical spread. However, due to the fact that each lender within the syndicate held relatively small amounts of debt, together the co-com members represented only around 15% of the first-lien debt.

The second-lien lenders also formed their own committee, although they were significantly less active, presumably as the second-lien debt was so obviously out of the money from a liquidation standpoint.

Once the co-com was up and running, engagement with Monier and the equity sponsor was painfully slow, with the co-com's engagement letter and associated fee arrangements taking more than three months to agree. It was widely speculated that this was part of delaying tactics by the equity sponsor, designed to frustrate the lenders' efforts further. Initially, Monier's advisers tried to impose a 'lock-in' arrangement on the co-com (of the type more commonly used for bondholder committees), which conferred extremely limited information-sharing rights in respect of the rest of the syndicate. Eventually, as the grip of the equity sponsor began to loosen, terms more akin to the Loan Market Association standard for appointment of coordinating committees were agreed and Monier agreed to allow the co-com's financial advisers some access to the business to perform a liquidation analysis for the lenders.

During this process, another interesting development began to unfold. It became clear to the original par lenders serving on the co-com that some first-lien debt was being sold at a discount to secondary market investors. Before long, a consortium of sophisticated 'loan to own' secondary investors, which had bought up around 20% of first-lien debt, approached Monier and then the co-com. The consortium made it known that it had the beginnings of a restructuring strategy for Monier and wanted to join forces with the co-com to build a comprehensive proposal to disenfranchise the equity sponsor and take control of the group.

7.   Restructuring negotiation process

As referred to above, the first restructuring proposal to emerge in the process came from the equity sponsor. It involved the sponsor retaining control of the business in exchange for new money financing to be injected on a priority basis and a significant debt write-down on the part of the lenders. The equity sponsor also sought to

emphasise that in its view, the lender group was too large and disparate to be able to coalesce and take ownership of the group in the limited time available, and it would be impossible to effect a transfer of ownership without cash leakage and significant tax issues.

This proposal was flatly rejected by the co-com, with the backing of the lenders. It was at this stage that the co-com decided to work more closely with the consortium to develop a credible lender-led proposal. The co-com recognised that the consortium was willing to dedicate time and resources to the process, and also saw the negative impact of management potentially having to consider two rival first-lien lender proposals. The consortium and the co-com were perhaps slightly unnatural bedfellows, given the institutional differences (and the stark economic fact that par lenders and secondary investors usually have rather different agendas), which meant that much protracted (and often difficult) negotiation took place behind the scenes in respect of the debt and equity term sheets before the restructuring proposal was finalised and presented to Monier.

In the meantime, the equity sponsor improved its proposal, offering to inject new funds, this time on a junior basis, and to transfer some of the equity to the lenders in exchange for the debt write-down. It is conceivable that without the involvement of the consortium (which was focused on providing a considerable slice of the new money in exchange for running the business), this proposal could have found favour with a majority of lenders. However, the joint co-com and consortium plan had gathered momentum by this stage and they decided to press ahead with a lender-only solution, with no ongoing role for the equity sponsor.

7.1   Lender-led proposal

Broadly, the lender-led restructuring proposal was structured on the assumption that it was highly unlikely that 100% first-lien lender consent would be obtained. Following long-established precedent in this area, however, the co-com appreciated the need to ensure that lenders within a class would receive essentially the same economic treatment under the restructuring, no matter whether they consented.

The co-com and the consortium were also obviously keen to find a way to implement the proposal without the need for formal insolvency proceedings and with minimal structural or organisational disruption to the core operating companies. Therefore, a contractual structure had to be found which would treat lenders equally, extinguish the surplus debt, amend the existing credit agreement and move ownership of the group, all with only majority lender consent.

The lender-led proposal comprised the following:

- equity ownership of the group by first-lien lenders, with out-of-the-money warrants for consenting second-lien lenders;
- division of the existing first-lien indebtedness of the group into 'unsustainable' and 'sustainable' portions. The sustainable debt structure that would continue post-restructuring was made up of:
    - reinstated senior debt of €600 million;
    - reinstated revolving credit facility of €50 million;
    - payment-in-kind (PIK) notes (purchaser loans) of €300 million;

- a new money secured super senior facility (provided by certain existing first-lien lenders) of €150 million; and
- an external new money factoring facility of €50 million;
- elimination of the second-lien debt;
- a mechanism for dealing with non-consenting first-lien lenders without cash leakage (ie, non-cash enforcement proceeds to be paid to all lenders);
- a mechanism for injecting new money on a super priority basis without 100% lender consent;
- a subordination or warehousing structure to deal with the unsustainable first-lien debt to avoid substantial tax charges which could have been triggered by a release of such debt;
- no further role for the current equity sponsor; and
- a contingency plan of an English scheme of arrangement, which could be implemented to cram down up to 25% by value of dissenting first-lien lenders. This would have necessitated a shifting of the centre of main interests in respect of the Luxembourg holding company.

7.2   Structural issues

(a)   *Amendment of existing debt*

Many potential restructurings flounder in the context of a potential use of the enforcement of security. Although it usually requires only 66.67% by value of the relevant lender group to accelerate the facilities, make demand and instruct the agents to take action as appropriate, to the extent that the restructuring involves 'rolling forward' at least part of the existing facilities, often the key terms of the surviving facilities can be amended only with the agreement of all the lenders (ie, it is invariably the case that under the credit agreement, such issues as extension of amortisations and decreases of margin will require the approval of all lenders, or at least all lenders affected by such changes).

In the case of Monier, the co-com and the consortium decided that obtaining control of the group was the primary requirement, such that if the restructuring did not garner the support of a substantial majority of the first-lien lenders, a scheme of arrangement would be implemented through the English courts in order to 'cram down' the dissenters and force all lenders to accept the terms of the new facilities. To this end, the restructuring agreement required 75% of the first-lien lenders to execute the document in order to become effective, since by doing so such lenders declared an irrevocable intention to vote in favour of any scheme of arrangement which may subsequently have been promoted.

Notwithstanding the above, the co-com and the consortium determined from a commercial perspective that if only a very small number of first-lien lenders dissented (representing a small proportion of debt), then although those lenders would be unable to prevent the writing down of their unsustainable first-lien debt (as this could be achieved on majority lender instructions), they would potentially be allowed to continue to participate in the sustainable debt on their existing terms, with the exception of any terms which could be amended by majority consent.

Depending on how many first-lien lenders dissented, the cost of the implementation of a scheme was to be weighed against the cost of allowing some lenders a 'free ride' by continuing to benefit from the old margin.

(b)   *Injection of new super priority debt*
In almost all restructurings, it is likely to be the case that new money providers will be prepared to inject new funds only if these are lent on a super priority basis. In this regard, 'super priority' generally means two things: first of all, priority in terms of repayment obligations but also, and arguably more importantly, priority in the event of any subsequent enforcement of security. While in Monier it was clearly a significant advantage that a super senior new money tranche could be made available via a permitted facility change mechanism contained in the credit agreement, the construct was nevertheless a complicated one involving the need to pass a leverage test at the time the funds were made available. For this reason, it was an important feature of the restructuring agreement (see below for additional details of salient features) that a turnover provision was included which was designed to protect the new money providers if, contrary to expectations, the group subsequently failed and the new money facility was, for whatever reason, set aside.

(c)   *Enforcement process*
As referred to above, although the security package was limited, importantly the lenders did have the benefit of security over the shares in the main Luxembourg holding company ('Topco'). It was clear that the simplest way for the lenders to take control of the group with minimal disruption to the core businesses would be to enforce the Topco share pledge and to sell the group into a new lender-owned holding structure by way of a Luxembourg private sale process.

The co-com was clear from the beginning that no liquidity was available to purchase the shares in Topco or to fund any associated cash leakage to non-consenting lenders. Therefore, a structure had to be developed which allowed for non-cash consideration to be paid if required to non-consenting lenders as the consideration in respect of enforcement of security. Generally speaking, under the terms of most, if not all, English law intercreditor agreements, non-cash consideration is not envisaged. However, the Monier intercreditor agreement conferred unusually wide powers of sale (and indeed debt release) on the security agent and did not preclude the payment of non-cash consideration as enforcement proceeds. Even so, leading counsel's advice was that in most cases, the ultimate determinant of whether non-cash consideration may be utilised is the relevant security document itself. In this case, the parties confirmed that under the terms of the relevant Luxembourg share pledge, which would be enforced in the context of a Luxembourg private sale, non-cash consideration (in the form of a PIK instrument) was permissible, provided that the instrument complied in certain key respects with the Luxembourg law concept of 'deferred consideration'.

An added complication was that no precedent existed for a private sale in such circumstances under the relatively newly implemented Luxembourg Financial Collateral Law. Although, as a matter of law, no third-party valuation was required as

part of such private sale, the security agent must be able to demonstrate that the shares were sold pursuant to 'normal commercial terms'. No guidance as to the likely construction of such term by the Luxembourg courts existed at the time. Therefore, in order to protect against any potential challenge to the sale price by a dissenting lender or the sponsor, the security agent commissioned its own independent valuation in order to prove, if necessary, that the Topco shares had no value beyond that of the indebtedness under the credit facilities.

In circumstances where the security agent was effectively being requested to facilitate the writing-off of non-sustainable first-lien debt with a value up to in excess of €400 million and render worthless second-lien debt of €300 million, while at the same time enforcing security in order to deliver the group into new ownership, for good reason the security agent was not prepared to proceed without enhanced indemnity protection, which was negotiated over a long period with the security agent's independent legal counsel. The final agreement reached with the security agent involved the consenting first-lien lenders giving express increased indemnity protection to the security agent and, separately, the provision of additional indemnity protection from the borrowers in circumstances where the existing indemnity recourse to the group was limited to the principal holding company within the security net. In addition, the security agent was able to negotiate an additional layer of protection, which requires the obligors on any subsequent refinancing to ensure that appropriate substitute credit protection be put in place to protect the security agent in respect of a claim which might still be made pursuant to the indemnities granted by the borrowers.

(d)   Debt to equity conversion and equity composition

In order to implement any lender-led restructuring, all of the participating lenders must agree all relevant issues in relation to the establishment of the new company's structure. These include the relevant place of incorporation and the precise holding structure. It is also critically necessary for lenders to reach agreement on appropriate issues regarding governance, in relation to which there may well be tensions between, on the one hand, the 'loan to own' investors, which collectively may hold a significant portion of the debt, and the par lenders, on the other hand. In this regard, and as noted above, the negotiation of the equity term sheet and the shareholders' agreement between the co-com and the consortium took a considerable period of time.

Any restructuring involving a conversion of German debt to equity (as in the present example), whether in respect of a direct or indirect equity holding, raises real issues in respect of equitable subordination if the German borrower subsequently enters into a formal insolvency process. As a matter of interest, while these issues affect all lenders on an equal footing, almost inevitably experience relates that they tend to be the focus of German banks only within a syndicate. Usually, the only way in which the issue can be addressed to the satisfaction of German banks is through the provision of a restructuring opinion from an independent accounting firm in the prescribed manner under German statute, which was necessarily obtained early on in the Monier transaction. Indeed, the appointment of an independent accounting

firm to perform this function (with an agreed ongoing monitoring role) was a prerequisite for obtaining the consent of a significant number of German bank lenders to the lender-led proposal.

8. Implementation of restructuring

Once the debt and equity term sheets were agreed, the lenders were asked to consent to the restructuring by signing a comprehensive restructuring agreement. First or second-lien lenders which did not sign were not offered equity in the new company's structure.

8.1 Contents of restructuring agreement

By signing the restructuring agreement, each consenting lender irrevocably committed to:

- the implementation of the restructuring on the terms set out in the appended term sheets and implementation plan, subject only to the restructuring agreement terminating in certain limited prescribed circumstances;
- a significant write down of existing unsustainable first-lien debt claims against the group via transfer and warehousing mechanism (detailed further below);
- all of the necessary steps which needed to be taken by consenting lenders in relation to the establishment of the new company's structure;
- turnover and loss-sharing provisions to ensure the primacy of the new money facilities;
- additional indemnity protection afforded to the security agent (as noted above); and
- delegation by the lenders of wide powers to the co-com and the consortium in order to instruct the agent and the security agent to implement the restructuring on the terms set out in the term sheet, removing the need for multiple approaches to be made to the lenders for further consents or instructions.

The restructuring agreement also contained:

- appropriate lock-up provisions, transfer restrictions and a standstill from each lender in favour of the relevant obligors in relation to a series of defined defaults – in particular, a standstill in respect of all payments of interest which would otherwise have been due and payable under the terms of the credit agreement on June 29 2009; and
- various undertakings from the obligors, a large majority of which were designed to ensure proper management and operation during the interim period between the signing of the restructuring agreement and formal implementation of the restructuring.

Despite the seemingly impossible task of designing a structure which satisfied the wide-ranging requirements of all of the different lending institutions, all but one first-lien lender signed the restructuring agreement and associated documentation,

which meant that the restructuring could proceed on a contractual basis, with no need for a scheme of arrangement. An overwhelming number of second-lien lenders also consented to the deal in order to receive warrants comprising a 5% stake in the new holding company.

This success was achieved in two ways. First, the co-com and its advisers spent a considerable amount of time speaking to the syndicate members in order to canvass opinion and discuss suggestions and modifications in respect of the structure and documentation – for example:

- German lender requirements to deal with equitable subordination;
- inclusion of the option of warrants or nominee holdings for banks unable to hold equity; and
- collateralised loan obligation issues with indemnification provisions.

Second, the legal team devoted a huge amount of time to dealing with a tidal wave of information requests and queries submitted by the first-lien lenders in respect of the structure of the transaction. Finally, each co-com member and each of the co-com's financial advisers took a group of lenders with which they were in constant email and telephone contact, pressing for updates on credit approvals and signature of documents. Indeed, managing the signing by 200 lenders of a variety of different documents (the combination of which differed according to whether they held first or second-lien debt or both, whether they were participating as new money lenders and which equity option was selected) was a huge administrative task in itself.

The one remaining non-consenting first-lien lender was largely uncommunicative throughout the restructuring process, despite significant efforts to engage by the co-com. However, in a final twist, this lender decided to object to having its first-lien debt written down without its consent via the issuance of winding-up proceedings against various group companies in the English High Court. The timing was dramatic – the papers were served on the afternoon of the scheduled implementation date, literally moments before the demand was to be made which would trigger the enforcement process to transfer the ownership of the group. Confident that the proceedings were unmeritorious and would be dismissed, and in the knowledge that they had the entire syndicate behind them (and also knowing that a last-minute settlement had been agreed with the outgoing equity sponsor), Monier, the co-com and the consortium pressed ahead with implementation.

In the following days the dissenting lender swiftly withdrew its winding-up petition, perhaps realising somewhat late in the process that by seeking to derail the restructuring and thus the future survival of the group, it was at high risk of facing litigation to recover serious consequential losses which could have been suffered by the other lenders and the group.

From a procedural standpoint, the implementation steps were as follows:

- The participating first-lien lenders capitalised a Luxembourg incorporated and tax-resident entity ('Newco') and its wholly owned subsidiary ('Bidco') (also a Luxembourg incorporated and tax-resident entity) to acquire the group as part of enforcement action at the Topco level.

- Enforcement action was triggered by the service of a notice of acceleration on the various borrower entities in respect of their rateable proportions of unsustainable debt. Immediately afterwards, the security agent was instructed to enforce the share security over the shares in Topco to transfer ownership of the group to Newco.
- Under the terms of the restructuring agreement, Newco issued:
  - PIK notes (purchaser loans);
  - shares (carrying voting rights in Newco, but little economic right) and, for those first-lien lenders that could not hold equity, warrants to subscribe for shares; and
  - in order to achieve maximum tax efficiency, profit-participating loan notes carrying the majority of the economic rights in Newco.
- Part of the PIK notes was used as consideration for the purchase of the shares in Topco from the security agent. PIK notes were distributed to all first-lien lenders pro rata to their outstanding accelerated commitments (not just to consenting lenders), either as proceeds of enforcement in accordance with the waterfall provisions contained in the intercreditor agreement or as part of a consensual transfer. Consenting lenders were also required to sign a deed of renunciation to enable their PIK notes to be distributed outside of the waterfall.
- In conjunction with the sale of the shares of Topco to Newco, the following occurred concurrently:
  - The consenting first-lien lenders' sold the unsustainable part of their first-lien debt to Newco by way of a consensual private sale in consideration for a proportionate amount of the PIK notes. Such unsustainable debt was then subordinated.
  - The security agent sold the second-lien debt to Newco for nominal consideration pursuant to the powers given to the senior agent under the intercreditor agreement.
  - As enforcement action could be taken on instructions of majority first-lien lenders, it was determined that any non-consenting first-lien lenders would be compelled to accept PIK notes as proceeds of enforcement. Additionally, although non-consenting first-lien lenders remained as lenders to the group in the new structure, all the surviving first-lien lender claims were reduced *pro rata* to reflect the resized debt package.
  - The claims in respect of non-sustainable first-lien debt which were owned by Newco following the above steps were transferred down through the group to a warehouse vehicle for nominal consideration. The warehouse vehicle, as part of such transfer, became a party to the intercreditor agreement as an intercompany lender and unilaterally renounced any rights it had as a first lien lender under the intercreditor agreement and unilaterally renounced any rights it might have had to benefit from the transaction security.
  - The existing credit agreement was amended and restated to reflect a reshaped debt package and the existing security remained in place,

subject to any consequential local law amendments required to reflect the new structure and any limitations on extending existing security to new or varied obligations. Any amendments to the credit agreement which required all lender consent were not imposed on the non-consenting lender, whose sustainable debt continued with the existing margin and tenor.

- New money facilities were put in place to rank senior to the existing first-lien debt. This was implemented via a facility change under the credit agreement (which allowed for the intercreditor agreement to be amended). As referred to above, the credit agreement prescribed that the addition of a new money facility was dependent on having a capital structure (after the relevant amendments) which did not exceed a specified leverage ratio.

9. Final closing structure

The final closing structure chart is illustrated opposite.

10. Comment

It is no exaggeration to say that the Monier restructuring had a game-changing effect. It demonstrated the willingness of lenders of all shades and colours to become equity owners of a business through the enforcement of security, with all that this entailed. The role of Clifford Chance in the restructuring was recognised by award of the prestigious FT Innovative Lawyers for Legal Innovation in Financial Services title in 2010.

Final closing structure

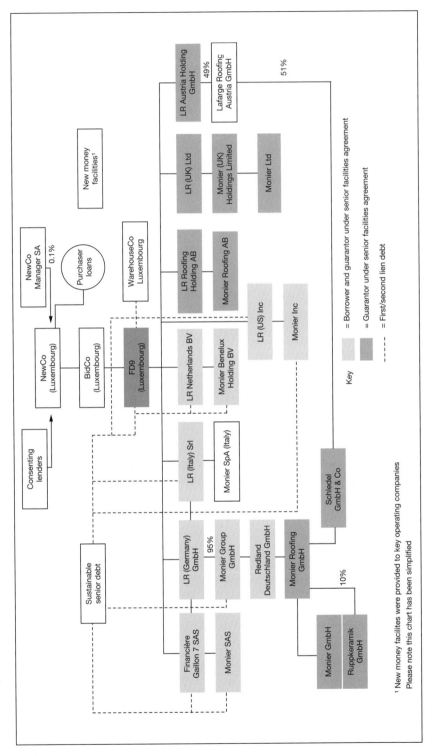

Countrywide

Justin Bickle
Oaktree
Yushan Ng
Cadwalader Wickersham & Taft LLP

The Countrywide restructuring was one of the first examples of a successful loan-to-own transaction in Europe. The restructuring was implemented using schemes of arrangement under Cayman and English law in respect of the primary debtor company, and English law schemes of arrangement in respect of its English guarantor subsidiaries. Recognition of the English law schemes of arrangement under Chapter 15 of the US Bankruptcy Code was sought and obtained in order to give full effect to the compromise contemplated by the schemes of certain New York law-governed debt obligations.

The restructuring reduced the debt of the Countrywide group from £740 million to £175 million and provided significant new money by way of equity investment (£75 million initially, with an additional £37.5 million capital raise for future acquisitions).

1. Background to group operations

Countrywide plc was established in 1986 by Hambros plc. Hambros had acquired two estate agents, Bairstow Eves and Mann & Co, and merged them into a newly created subsidiary, Hambro Countrywide plc. Hambro Countrywide grew rapidly, largely through acquisitions. Acquired estate agencies were left largely intact, operating under their own brand on a highly decentralised basis. A life insurance company was added to the business in 1986. In 1998 Hambro Countrywide plc was demerged from Hambros. Its name was changed to Countrywide Assurance Group plc and the common stock was floated on the London Stock Exchange. In 2004 the life insurance businesses of Countywide were spun off as a separately traded public company.

At the time of the restructuring, Countrywide was the leading residential real estate agent in the United Kingdom, operating under 35 different brands. Its network consisted of 967 owned and 114 franchised real estate offices located in 670 UK towns, and it employed 8,958 people. Countrywide operated five business lines: residential property sales; residential property lettings and property management; the arrangement of mortgages, insurance and related financial products for participants in residential property transactions; survey and valuation services for mortgage lenders and prospective homebuyers; and residential property conveyancing services.

2. Pre-restructuring corporate structure

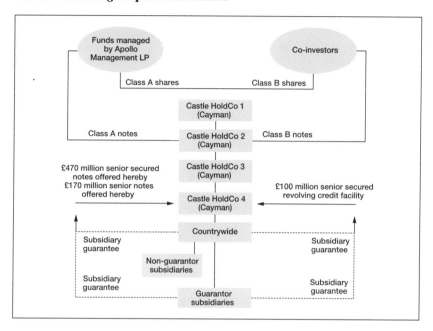

In May 2007 Countrywide was acquired by a group of investors led by global private equity firm Apollo Management LP. The acquisition was made using a Cayman special purpose vehicle, Castle Holdco 4 Limited, and was funded with £640 million in debt and £305.2 million in cash contributed by affiliates of Apollo.

Before implementation of the restructuring, the Castle Holdco board included two non-independent directors, who resigned as part of the restructuring process on March 4 2009. The non-independent directors were excluded from the independent board committee that was formed to consider the scheme proposal (discussed below).

3. Pre-restructuring capital structure

In connection with the 2007 acquisition, Castle Holdco, Countrywide and the group entered into the following debt financing arrangements:

- £370 million in senior secured floating rate notes (the 'cash-pay FRNs') due in 2014, issued by Castle Holdco;
- £100 million in senior secured floating rate payment-in-kind election FRNs (the 'PIK election FRNs') due in 2014, issued by Castle Holdco;
- £170 million in nine 7/8% senior notes due in 2015, issued by Castle Holdco; and
- £100 million in a senior revolving facility (RCF), which ranked in priority to the FRNs and senior notes with respect to proceeds from the enforcement of security.

The documents relating to this indebtedness were governed by New York law.

The RCF and the FRNs were secured by first priority fixed and floating charges over all assets of Castle Holdco, Countrywide and each of the guarantor subsidiaries.[1] The senior notes were secured by second-priority pledges over all of the equity interest of Castle Holdco and Countywide, which ranked behind the security enjoyed by the RCF and FRNs. In addition, the RCF, FRNs and senior notes were guaranteed by the guarantors.

At the time of the restructuring, approximately £90 million of the RCF had been drawn, approximately £488 million was outstanding under the FRNs and approximately £166 million was outstanding under the senior notes. In addition, approximately £3.1 million was outstanding in respect of certain hedging arrangements.

4.   Restructuring triggers

One of the key influences on the performance of the Countrywide business was the number of residential housing transactions conducted in the United Kingdom. The number of houses being bought and sold fell by around 70% as the global recession hit and mortgage availability became constrained after the collapse of Northern Rock Building Society in late 2007. Within a year, Countrywide had gone from a positive earnings before interest, taxes, depreciation and amortisation of around £115 million to a loss of £15 million.

5.   Countrywide's creditor classes

The lenders to Countrywide comprised a number of different institutions. First, the RCF was owned by traditional banks. This remained closely held throughout the process and only a handful of pieces were traded, including one to distressed private equity specialist Oaktree Capital and one to Apollo.

Next, traditional European and US high-yield accounts had purchased the FRNs and the senior notes at par, attracted to the credit by its strong fundamentals, its former public ownership and the fact that the FRNs were the largest bond issuance denominated in sterling ahead of the global credit crunch.

As the recession gathered pace and Castle Holdco earnings reduced dramatically, those high-yield noteholders were forced sellers, and many could not continue to hold those securities as their secondary trading price declined. The price of the FRNs fell from £1 to around £0.80 before a number of secondary holders began to purchase them; and finally to around £0.30, when Oaktree was able to establish more than a one-third blocking position.

The senior notes declined in price even more rapidly. This resulted in Castle Holdco buying them back at a substantial discount. Apollo also began to accumulate a position in them.

---

1   The guarantors were Balanus Limited, Securemove Property Services 2005 Limited, Countrywide Estate Agents (unlimited company), Countrywide Estate Agents FS Limited, Countrywide Surveyors Limited, Countrywide Property Lawyers Limited, Slater Hogg Mortgages Limited, Countrywide Franchising Limited and Countrywide Estate Agents (South) Limited.

The task for Oaktree as the prospective owner of the business was that it could not purchase the FRNs if it was in receipt of 'material non-public information' about Countrywide's business. This meant that all of its diligence into the business and sector had to be done with reference to public sources only, and it was unable to meet the management team or enter into any dialogue with Castle Holdco. Once it had purchased a position in the RCF, Oaktree also made the purchase via an investment bank behind an information barrier and gained no access to any materials which would ordinarily be available to a secured lender in such situations.

By the time the restructuring came to be implemented, Apollo and Oaktree each held significant stakes in the RCF and FRNs and, in the case of Apollo, also the senior notes. As a result of this, and the disparate nature of the FRN and senior noteholder community, no formal or informal coordinating or steering committee was established. As discussed in more detail below, the restructuring was formulated and driven by Oaktree and Apollo in their capacities as significant creditors of the group and prospective new money providers. Oaktree and Apollo agreed to work together (the 'noteholder group') to pursue a consensual restructuring of the group in order to preserve its going concern and best position the business for the future.

6. Restructuring negotiation process

6.1 Scheme proposal

In February 2009 the noteholder group put forward a proposal to Castle Holdco for a restructuring to be implemented by way of schemes of arrangement. The scheme proposal involved a reduction in the indebtedness of Castle Holdco and the injection of £75 million of fresh equity capital from new equity investors.

The scheme proposal was intended to:

- deleverage the group;
- create a sustainable capital structure;
- maximise recoveries for existing creditors (according to rank and priority); and
- allow Countrywide to take advantage of depressed industry conditions through acquisitions of estate agency businesses, particularly in London, and to increase its penetration into the residential lettings market, which is counter-cyclical in nature.

Following receipt of the scheme proposal, an independent board committee of Castle Holdco was formed to consider the proposal. The committee appointed Tri-Artisan Partners as its financial adviser to assist with the analysis of the terms of the proposal.

After a preliminary assessment, on February 17 2009 the independent committee announced that it supported the scheme proposal and that it intended to approve the filing of the schemes.

6.2 Contingency planning

Some initial thought was given to developing a contingency plan in the event that insufficient support from the senior notes was obtained to implement the scheme

proposal. This was likely to have involved a sale of the Countrywide business and assets to a special purpose vehicle controlled by the FRNs through a pre-packaged administration of the issuer and guarantors of the FRNs and senior notes. The consideration for the sale would have been a credit bid of the FRNs achieved through a contemporaneous FRN scheme of arrangement. However, this contingency plan became evidently unnecessary relatively early on in the process, in light of the high levels of support for the scheme proposal received from the senior notes (as discussed below).

6.3 Consensus building

When the scheme proposal was put to Castle Holdco, indications of support from creditors through lock-up agreements and letters of support had been received, representing more than half of the FRNs and the senior notes by value.

Support for the scheme proposal continued to grow during February 2009. On February 23, following further analysis by Castle Holdco and its financial adviser, Castle Holdco confirmed its support for the proposal and indicated that the necessary documentation would be prepared in order for schemes to become effective in the second quarter of 2009.

By the time the schemes were launched, support had grown to 87% of the total outstanding FRNs and approximately 83% of the total outstanding senior notes.

6.4 Regulatory issues

As the Countrywide group included a Financial Services Authority-regulated entity, Countrywide Principal Services Limited, Oaktree and Apollo had to seek and obtain approval to act as controlling shareholders of the group post restructuring. This was a condition to the effectiveness of the schemes.

7. Implementation of the restructuring

7.1 Key features of the restructuring

The restructuring proposal put forward by Castle Holdco and its guarantor subsidiaries was substantially the same as the scheme proposal put forward by the noteholder group. The schemes were part of a broader restructuring which would see all claims under the senior notes released in exchange for equity, and claims under the FRNs released in exchange for equity and new debt instruments.

(a) FRNs – debt-for-equity swap and debt-for-debt swap

Under the terms of the schemes, the holders of the FRNs released most of their claims against Castle Holdco (save for £175 million of outstanding principal) in return for the issue of new shares by Castle Holdco representing 35% of the equity in Castle Holdco (following dilution by the equity subscription described below) and the right to participate in the additional offering (described below).

The FRN holders also entered into a debt-for-debt swap, whereby they released the remaining £175 million of FRN claims in exchange for the issue by Castle Holdco of new debt instruments (£175 million in 10% senior secured notes).

(b) **Senior notes – debt-for-equity swap**

A similar compromise was implemented in respect of claims under the senior notes, save that all senior note claims were released in return for the issue of new shares by Castle Holdco representing 5% of the equity (following dilution by the equity subscription) and the right to participate in the additional offering.

(c) **Additional offering**

Holders of FRNs and senior notes were also given the opportunity to subscribe, at par value, for £37.5 million in aggregate of new shares in Castle Holdco. Oaktree and Apollo acted as standby subscribers in respect of this offering and undertook to backstop the full amount of the additional offering if the other creditors did not wish to subscribe for their full entitlement.

(d) **Equity subscription**

As an additional part of the restructuring, outside of the scope of the schemes but dependent on their approval, certain equity investors led by Oaktree and Apollo agreed to subscribe £75 million in cash for 60% of the new shares in Castle Holdco, giving them equity control.

(e) **Repayment of RCF and hedging**

The proceeds of the equity subscription and additional offering, together with cash on Castle Holdco's balance sheet, were then used to repay in full liabilities under the RCF and the hedging liabilities. This resulted in a full recovery for all RCF lenders, including Oaktree and Apollo, which had purchased their RCF stakes in the secondary market at a discount.

(f) **Cancellation of shares**

Castle Holdco also carried out a reduction in capital, cancelling the shares existing at the date of the restructuring. This effectively wiped out the existing equity in order to implement the debt-for-equity swap described above.

7.2 Schemes

One of the distinctive features of the Countrywide restructuring was the multiple, interconnected schemes of arrangement that were proposed and pursued by the Countrywide group.

The acquisition vehicle used in the 2007 acquisition was an exempted limited liability company incorporated in the Cayman Islands, Castle Holdco. This entity was the main debtor under the FRNs, the senior notes and the RCF.

Parallel schemes of arrangement under Section 895 of the UK Companies Act 2006 and Section 86 of the Cayman Companies Law (2007 revision) were launched in respect of Castle Holdco. The rationale for the dual schemes was twofold:

- Castle Holdco had received advice that, as it was incorporated in the Cayman Islands, an order of the English court binding Castle Holdco would not be enforceable in the Cayman Islands.
- The debt documents were governed by New York law and, in order to ensure

that any compromise would be binding in the event of challenge in the US courts, Castle Holdco intended to seek recognition under Chapter 15 of the US Bankruptcy Code. Due to doubts about whether a Cayman scheme would be recognised by the US bankruptcy court, Castle Holdco felt that it and the guarantors would be best served by proposing schemes in England and Wales.

(a) Jurisdiction of the English court

As Castle Holdco was not incorporated in England and Wales, the English court had to be persuaded that it had jurisdiction to hear the schemes. Under Section 895(2)(b) of the Companies Act 2006, a scheme can be approved in respect of "any company liable to be wound up under the Insolvency Act 1986". Section 221 of the Insolvency Act 1986 allows companies which are not registered in England to be wound up under the Insolvency Act as "unregistered companies". Therefore, for the purposes of a scheme, the term 'company' can include a foreign company, as long as an English court would assume jurisdiction to wind it up.

The Insolvency Act gives no guidance as to the circumstances in which an English court should assume jurisdiction to wind up an unregistered company (eg, where the company has its centre of main interests or an establishment in the United Kingdom), leaving the matter to the discretion of the English courts. In *Re Drax Holdings Ltd* ([2003] EWHC 2743 (Ch)), relying on case law as to the court's jurisdiction to wind up unregistered companies, Justice Lawrence Collins held that the court would not exercise its discretion to sanction a scheme unless a "sufficient connection" with the English jurisdiction was established.

Castle Holdco argued that the English courts had jurisdiction on the basis outlined above, and advanced the following points as evidence of sufficient connection with the jurisdiction:

- The main asset of Castle Holdco was its shares in Countrywide, a company incorporated in England and Wales with substantial assets within the jurisdiction.
- Castle Holdco was tax resident in England and Wales.
- Castle Holdco's centre of main interest was in England.
- Castle Holdco's board meetings were held in the United Kingdom.
- The documents creating security over the assets of the group were governed by English law.
- Castle Holdco was registered as a foreign company at Companies House for England and Wales.

Castle Holdco also argued that certain creditors affected by the schemes were incorporated in England and Wales and were subject to the jurisdiction of the English court, and that were the company to have been wound up in England, there would have been secured assets that could have been realised by such creditors of Castle Holdco.

(b) Scheme classes

One of the key, and often most complicated, issues for a company proposing a

scheme of arrangement is the correct identification of creditor classes. If Castle Holdco had gotten this wrong, the court would not approve the scheme. Historically, this caused major concerns, as until the final approval hearing (after the creditor meetings had taken place), the court would not express a view as to whether the classes had been correctly identified. In *Practice Statement (Companies: Schemes of arrangement)* ([2002] 3 All ER 96), the High Court agreed that it would, at the time of the initial application to convene the court meeting, formulate a *prima facie* view as to whether the class or classes of creditors put forward were appropriate.

Castle Holdco proposed that the scheme creditors be divided into two classes in order to consider and vote on the proposed schemes:

- FRN scheme creditors – persons with a beneficial interest as principal in the FRNs held in global form through the clearing systems at a certain record date; and
- senior note scheme creditors – persons with a beneficial interest as principal in the senior notes held in global form through the clearing systems at the record date.

Castle Holdco did not subdivide the FRN scheme creditors into separate classes, notwithstanding the difference between the PIK election FRNs and the cash-pay FRNs. In justifying its decision, Castle Holdco stressed the similarity of the FRN holders' rights (ie, having a primary claim against Castle Holdco, guarantees from the guarantors and sharing *pari passu* in a distribution of the proceeds of security under the intercreditor agreement after payment of the RCF and certain hedging liabilities). Castle Holdco argued that the existence of the mechanism whereby cash pay interest could be paid by Castle Holdco by issuing PIK notes did not introduce a difference that would make it impossible for the FRN holders to consult together with a view to their common interests. This argument was further strengthened by the fact that all FRN holders were treated equally under the schemes.

No objections were raised by creditors at the convening or approval hearings as to the composition of the creditor classes.

7.3   Chapter 15 recognition

Chapter 15 of Title 11 of the US Bankruptcy Code is the US version of the Model Law on Cross-Border Insolvency, which provides for relief in the US bankruptcy courts to recognise and assist pending insolvency proceedings in other countries.

In light of the fact that New York law governed the FRN and senior note documents, it was felt that recognition of the schemes under Chapter 15 should be sought so as to minimise any risk of challenge being brought by dissenting creditors in the US courts. There was significant doubt as to whether the US bankruptcy courts would recognise the Cayman scheme of Castle Holdco, and therefore recognition was sought only with respect to the English schemes.

In the order sought for leave to convene the scheme meetings, additional wording was included authorising Countrywide independent board director Michael Salvati to act as foreign representative of the scheme companies in connection with the Chapter 15 proceedings. In its Chapter 15 application, Castle Holdco then

sought recognition by the US bankruptcy court of Salvati as the foreign representative of each of the scheme companies, for recognition of the schemes as foreign main proceedings and for preliminary and permanent relief under Chapter 15 recognising the scheme and ultimately recognising and enforcing the final orders approving the schemes.

Castle Holdco argued that recognition under Chapter 15 was appropriate on the basis that Salvati qualified as a foreign representative pursuant to the English court orders, and that each scheme was a foreign main proceeding in that each was pending in England, which was the centre of main interests for each scheme company (as such term is used in the US Bankruptcy Code). Each scheme was a collective judicial proceeding under which the scheme companies' assets and affairs were subject to the supervision of the English court, and therefore each met the definition of a 'foreign proceeding' as defined in Section 101(23) of the US Bankruptcy Code.

On May 7 2009 the US Bankruptcy Court ordered that:

- the English approval order was entitled to recognition and enforcement in the United States;
- within the territorial jurisdiction of the United States, all scheme creditors were permanently enjoined and restrained from commencing or continuing any action or other legal proceeding inconsistent with the English approval order, the schemes or the US enforcement order; and
- within the territorial jurisdiction of the United States, all scheme creditors were permanently enjoined and restrained from commencing or continuing any action or other legal proceeding against the scheme companies or any of their directors, officers, agents, employees, representatives, financial advisers or attorneys in respect of the schemes or the restructuring.

7.4   Challenges

The primary threat of challenge to implementation of the restructuring was posed by certain minority shareholders in Castle Holdco 1 Ltd and loan noteholders of notes issued by Castle Holdco 2 Ltd (the 'minority equityholders'). In correspondence with Castle Holdco, the minority equityholders expressed themselves to be against the proposal and implementation of the schemes, on the basis that economic value in their investments remained. This was despite contrary valuation evidence received by the respective boards of the group.

At the convening hearing on March 23 2009, leading counsel was instructed to appear for the minority equityholders and to seek copies of the scheme documentation. At one stage a winding-up petition was issued by that dissenting group against Castle Holdco 2, although it was later withdrawn along with the minority equityholders' other claims, allowing the schemes to proceed.

7.5   Approval of the schemes

The English and Cayman scheme meetings were held on April 28 2009 and at each meeting the scheme creditors voted to pass the resolutions. The results of the voting are set out on the next page.

Class	Votes for	%	Votes against	%
FRNs	£445,692,883.53	98.86	£5,137,824.55	1.14
Senior notes	£150,527.734	94.74	£8,350.067	5.26

As a result of the multiple parallel processes, the schemes were expressed to be subject to certain conditions, including that the Cayman court also approve the scheme. Accordingly, at the hearing for the English court to approve the English schemes on May 6 2009, the order was expressed to be subject to satisfaction of the remaining conditions. Castle Holdco was given the ability to apply to the court to alter or vary the approval order if the Cayman court required alteration of the scheme to approve it.

Chapter 15 recognition of the English schemes was granted on May 7 2009 and the final step was completed on May 8 2009, when the Cayman court approved the Cayman scheme. The whole process was executed in three countries in less than three months.

8. Final closing structure

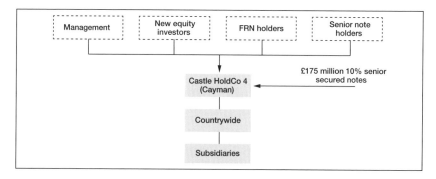

9. Conclusion

The Countrywide restructuring was a textbook example of how a loan-to-own transaction should be conducted in Europe. Its unique restructuring of private debt and public loan securities of a market-leading and highly cyclical business through an expedited consensual process, involving courts in three continents, demonstrated how principals and advisers can work collaboratively to capture and preserve value of a going-concern business at a time of crisis.

The transaction continues to be seen as a landmark in the European restructuring landscape and is the subject of a Harvard Business School case study.[2]

---

2   *In Countrywide plc*, February 11 2011, Reference N9-211-026, published by Professor Stuart C Gilson and Sarah L Abbott of Harvard Business School.

Truvo

Karen McMaster
Yushan Ng
Cadwalader Wickersham & Taft LLP

1. Introduction

This transaction was a market-leading restructuring of a European-based business with no substantive US operations, using the combination of a US Chapter 11 process and English law contractual debt release mechanism under a high yield-style intercreditor agreement.

Truvo Belgium Comm V (together with its related companies, the 'Truvo Group') operates a directories business, based in Belgium but with significant overseas operations. Before the restructuring, the group was significantly over-leveraged (over 12× *pro forma* to the last 12 months earnings before interest, tax, depreciation, and amortisation (EBITDA), with forecasted EBITDA decline). In addition, it anticipated having cash-flow difficulties in the medium term. However, Truvo Group's financing documents were 'covenant light', with no maintenance financial covenants and therefore no immediate trigger event for a creditor-led restructuring. Notwithstanding this, the restructuring was ultimately senior creditor-led and achieved a significant deleveraging of the group's financial obligations.

Leverage of the Truvo Group through the senior debt was in excess of 6×, which led to the view (held at least by management and the senior lenders) that value broke in the senior debt. Accordingly, the key tensions underlying stakeholder negotiations were:

- the requirement to write off subordinated debt in return for consideration that was just a small fraction of face value; and
- the sometimes contradictory drivers for par senior lenders versus secondary investors that acquired the senior debt at a discount (both of which held significant blocking positions within the senior syndicate), in relation to the quantum and structure of the senior debt equitisation.

One of the main achievements of this transaction was securing a relatively quick and clean outcome that reconciled all of the above, thanks in part to creative legal structuring, but no doubt primarily as a result of the commercial rationality and good sense of the key parties involved.

Eventually, following the course of negotiations detailed further below, a US Chapter 11 plan of reorganisation in relation to the holding companies of Truvo Belgium was confirmed with overwhelming creditor support: 100% support of the voting senior lenders (representing 99.28% of the total eligible senior debt claims) and 98.24% (in value) support of the unsecured high-yield bondholders

(representing 86.11% of the total eligible unsecured bondholder claims). The result of the transaction was the write-off of all junior creditor claims against the Truvo Group in return for limited cash payments and minority equity interests in the restructured group, together with partial equitisation and extension of the senior debt. The senior creditors became the new majority shareholders of Truvo Group. Existing shareholders retained no interest.

Implementation of the transaction posed several challenges. While Truvo Belgium was held through US-incorporated holding companies, the group's key operating subsidiaries were all incorporated outside the United States, in jurisdictions which offered significantly less flexible and certain restructuring processes. While a US bankruptcy process was feasible for the holding companies, there was a concern that a bankruptcy filing by the non-US operating subsidiaries might be highly value destructive. The business depended on the confidence of customers and suppliers, which in the key operating jurisdictions would be less familiar with the US bankruptcy process. Accordingly, implementation had to involve the US-UK law combination referred to above and explained in further detail below.

From a more technical perspective, the Truvo restructuring was noteworthy in implementing a number of novel 'market first' structures:

- A number of European restructurings have relied on English law contractual provisions in intercreditor agreements allowing a majority of senior creditors to force the release of junior creditor and minority senior creditor claims in the context of an enforcement sale of the debtor group. The Truvo restructuring faced a further hurdle, in that the intercreditor release mechanism incorporated high yield-style protections in favour of the junior creditors, requiring the group to be sold on a debt-free basis and for cash consideration. The challenge this presented was how to avoid the leakage of the cash consideration to non-consenting senior creditors, which would have made the restructuring far more difficult to finance. A structure was developed for Truvo which achieved this for the first time in the market, and which has subsequently been adopted on other restructurings. In short, the structure involved using a Chapter 11 plan to compel the assignment of both consenting and non-consenting senior lender claims to a newly incorporated special purpose vehicle to prevent leakage, in conjunction with the use of an arm's-length daylight facility to facilitate the cash bid.

- A balance had to be struck between the requirements of par lenders wishing to minimise debt writedowns for internal reasons, versus management and secondary investors seeking a more aggressive deleveraging of the business. This was achieved through a 'split holdco' structure, which allowed individual senior creditors to choose their level of writedown by electing to receive debt instruments in lieu of pure equity in the restructured group, while giving all senior creditors pro rata shareholder voting rights irrespective of their elections.

- The US bankruptcy court granted an injunction preventing creditor action not just against the Truvo (US-incorporated) holding companies that filed for Chapter 11, but also against their European subsidiaries, which did not file

for Chapter 11 for the reason given above. This was unusual in being the first such stay to be granted for the entire duration of the Chapter 11 process, instead of just an interim period.

2. Background to Truvo Group operations

Truvo Group is a multinational provider of local search and advertising services, with a primary focus on publishing printed and online directories. The businesses operated by Truvo Group are leaders in the local search and advertising market, with key local markets in Belgium, Ireland (since disposed of) and Portugal (through a joint venture). Truvo Group also has significant, non-controlling equity interests in leading directory companies operating in South Africa and Puerto Rico. At the time of the restructuring, Truvo Group had more than 1,700 full-time employees.

Truvo Group provides yellow pages and combined yellow and white pages directories to business and residential users. The operating entities also operate more than 20 websites offering local search and advertising information to online audiences. Almost all of Truvo Group's products are provided free to end users, with revenues generated by the sale of advertising.

A decline in revenue, in particular in relation to print operations, resulted in a shift in focus to online directories and products. Revenue declined by approximately 20% from 2008 to 2009 and in the fourth quarter of 2009, as the restructuring gained momentum, the company was forecasting EBITDA to decline to €103.1 million for financial years 2010 to 2012.

3. Pre-restructuring corporate structure

Truvo Group was acquired by funds advised by Apax Partners Worldwide LLP and Cinven Limited in 2004. Cinven and Apax purchased shares in Truvo Luxembourg, which owned the operating group via four Delaware-incorporated holding companies. Truvo Group's main operations are conducted by the company.

The management board of the company was largely independent of the sponsors, with minimal sponsor representation. As at the time of the restructuring, both Cinven and Apax recognised that the equity in Truvo Group was significantly out of the money. To their credit, the sponsors were supportive of the restructuring despite retaining no residual interest in the group, although their actual active role was limited to taking certain minimal steps to facilitate implementation (see page 64).

4. Pre-restructuring capital structure

The senior debt originally utilised to fund the acquisition (the '2004 facilities') was refinanced by a covenant-light senior facility in 2007. Truvo Group's debt at the time of the restructuring comprised:

- €777.6 million ('senior debt') owing under a senior facilities agreement ('senior facilities') the borrowers being the company and Truvo Services & Technology BV. The senior facilities were guaranteed by Truvo USA Inc, Truvo Acquisition Corp, Truvo Belgium, Truvo Services & Technology BV and other subsidiaries; these entities also provided share and asset security. The senior facilities incorporated an undrawn super senior revolving credit facility;

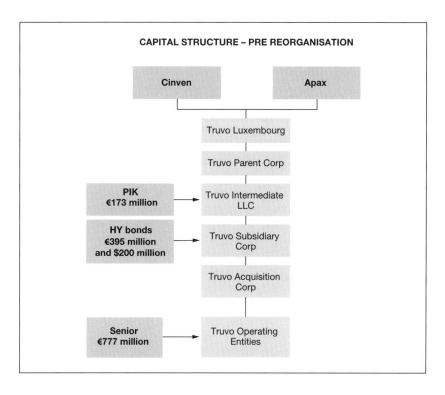

- high-yield bonds comprising €395 million of 8.5% senior notes due in 2014 and $200 million of 8.375% senior notes due in 2014 issued by Truvo Subsidiary Corp. The high-yield bonds were guaranteed by Truvo Belgium, Truvo USA Inc, Truvo Acquisition Corp, Truvo Services & Technology BV and Truvo Corporate CVBA. The guarantees of the high-yield bonds were secured and subordinated to the debt owing under the senior facilities; and
- a €173 million payment-in-kind facility borrowed by Truvo Intermediate LLC. As shown in the diagram above, Truvo Intermediate LLC was a holding company of the high-yield bond issuer. The payment-in-kind facility agreement did not have the benefit of any guarantees from or other direct recourse to Truvo Subsidiary Corp or any of its subsidiaries, so was essentially fully structurally subordinated to the senior facilities and the high-yield bonds.

The priority and ranking of the senior facilities relative to the high-yield bonds was determined by an intercreditor agreement entered into in 2007, which contained customary provisions subordinating the high-yield bond guarantees to the senior facilities. These provisions included a (fairly market standard) mechanism allowing the forced release of high-yield bond guarantees in certain circumstances where the group was being sold in the context of an enforcement. This mechanism is typically designed to allow lenders under the senior facility to recreate a position as if the high-yield bonds had been fully structurally subordinated to the senior facilities. However, the intercreditor agreement also contained customary protections

for the benefit of the high-yield bonds, imposing a number of conditions on the ability of the senior lenders to force a release of high-yield bond guarantees. As discussed further below, satisfying these conditions was one of the significant structural challenges of the restructuring.

5. Restructuring triggers

In mid-2009 the Truvo Group's management approached a small group of lenders with significant exposure under the senior facilities in relation to the use of proceeds of the recent disposal of its Gouden Gids business in the Netherlands. At the time, discussions centred around a proposal to use the Gouden Gids disposal proceeds towards the repurchase of debt at a discount. The Truvo Group agreed to allow this group of senior lenders to engage financial and legal advisers to evaluate the proposal.

The senior lenders objected to the proposal, and the proceeds of the Gouden Gids disposal were ultimately applied in pre-payment of the senior facilities at par. However, these discussions created the impetus to initiate broader restructuring discussions with the Truvo Group, having drawn together those senior lenders into an *ad hoc* committee, the precursor to the formal coordinating committee of senior lenders. For reasons of efficiency, the *ad hoc* committee was comprised of a sub-set of volunteers from the original group of senior lenders approached by the company, with the remaining members of Truvo Group retaining regular communication channels with the *ad hoc* committee.

While there was a clear liquidity wall facing Truvo Group in 2014 when the high-yield notes matured, at the time of the formation of the *ad hoc* committee, Truvo Group had sufficient liquidity to meet debt repayments. Moreover, the senior facility was covenant light, and therefore Truvo Group's deteriorating financial position was not going to trigger a breach of any financial covenants. Accordingly, the initial challenge facing the *ad hoc* committee was to demonstrate to the Truvo Group a need to engage in restructuring negotiations. The senior lenders felt strongly that the payment by the company of the biannual coupon under the high-yield bonds was value leakage in a group in circumstances where it appeared that value was breaking in the senior debt.

Truvo Belgium's management was amenable to engaging with the *ad hoc* committee (and in June 2009 had retained Houlihan Lokey to advise regarding strategic options), but without a clear restructuring trigger its negotiating position was relatively strong and it saw no immediate reason to commence full-blown restructuring negotiations. In particular, the company was unwilling to consider routes that did not pre-suppose junior creditor consent, which it considered to be materially value destructive and high risk. Therefore, the initial challenge for the *ad hoc* committee was to demonstrate otherwise.

6. Lending syndicate

The *ad hoc* committee comprised one bank (AIB) and three collateralised loan obligations (Harbourmaster (now GSO), Alcentra and Avoca Capital), all of which had no holdings elsewhere in the capital structure. The senior lender syndicate

comprised of par lenders as well as institutions that had acquired the debt at a discount to par, with both groups holding significant percentages of the total senior facilities. There were also a number of senior lenders with cross-holdings into the high-yield bonds and payment-in-kind facility.

A significant secondary entrant into the senior lender syndicate was a group of funds related to Elliott Associates LLP and Elliott International LLP, which started the restructuring with a significant high-yield bond position and subsequently also built a large position in the senior facilities (which at one stage became the same size, if not larger, than the aggregate *ad hoc* committee position). No deal could be done without Elliott's consent.

As explained in more detail below, polarisation within the syndicate occurred mainly around the proposed new capital structure and the size of the restructured debt.

The *ad hoc* committee was advised by Linklaters LLP and Rothschild. The company was advised by Houlihan Lokey throughout, and by Weil, Gotshal Manges initially and Cleary Gottlieb Steen Hamilton later on.

An *ad hoc* committee of high-yield noteholders was advised by Bingham McCutchen and Jeffries.

7. Restructuring negotiation process

7.1 Development of Plan B

The company sought, as its primary goal, a consensual restructuring proposal (ie, one that could be accepted by the senior lenders and the high-yield bondholders). It perceived risks associated with senior lender-led security enforcement (discussed further below) and took the position that such risks made it unfeasible to achieve a restructuring without the high-yield bondholders. Therefore, at that stage the company was not prepared to countenance any discussions relating to the potential cramdown of the high-yield bondholders.

In August 2009 the company commissioned an independent business review. The review was completed in October 2009 and supported the view of the senior lenders that the value of Truvo Group was unlikely to break in the high-yield bonds, and was in fact clearly within the senior debt.

In late 2009, something of an impasse had been reached between the *ad hoc* committee and the company, with the *ad hoc* committee cognisant that the wider lender group was unlikely to concede significant value to an out-of-the-money class of creditors, but that the company's insistence on a consensual process without the prospect of a credible non-consensual alternative made that outcome inevitable. The perceived value leakage from the payment of a coupon to the holders of the high-yield bonds in December 2009 exacerbated this position.

In later 2009 and early 2010, a senior lender-led restructuring proposal was developed by the *ad hoc* committee and presented to the Truvo Group. This proposal (outlined further below) aimed to demonstrate that:

- the perceived risks associated with a security enforcement could be overcome;
- without a non-consensual plan or a liquidity trigger, the company was

unlikely to be able to broker a solution which was acceptable to the senior lenders and the high-yield bondholders; and

- the risks and business costs associated with continuing to service debt which was incapable of being repaid or refinanced significantly outweighed any risks associated with the implementation of a non-consensual restructuring plan.

7.2   Chapter 11

The *ad hoc* committee considered various insolvency processes to effect a cramdown of high-yield bond creditors and non-consenting senior lenders. There were cross-holdings within the senior lender syndicate, and therefore a 100% consent senior lender plan did not appear viable.

An insolvency process affecting the company was considered value destructive and to be avoided. The view from Belgium was that there was no local insolvency process at the time which could facilitate the cramdown of an out-of-the-money class of creditor. An English process (potentially an administration sale coupled with a scheme of arrangement of the senior facilities) was considered, but Truvo Group had limited connection to England.

However, the Chapter 11 process had a number of attractive features:

- the company's holding companies were Delaware incorporated, and therefore the jurisdiction of the US court could not be questioned;
- Truvo Group could potentially avail itself of a worldwide stay of execution (discussed further below);
- Chapter 11 could affect a cramdown of a non-consenting class of creditor; and
- the voting thresholds for cramdown within a class were lower than a scheme of arrangement.

Chapter 11 could not affect the release of borrowing or guarantee obligations at the level of non-debtor entities. However, the senior lenders could use the debt release mechanism in the intercreditor agreement that was entered into by all financial creditors at the time of the original financing. The intercreditor release mechanics posed implementation challenges which are described further below.

The Chapter 11 process also had attractive features from the perspective of the directors of the company and its parent entities. The 'business judgement' rule relevant to directors' duties in the United States was sufficiently broad such that an argument could be made to support a Chapter 11 filing, even before the company suffered immediate liquidity concerns. Accordingly, one of the principal concerns of the directors – that they could be criticised for entering into an insolvency process too early, thereby destroying value in the subordinated class of debt (if any) – could be allayed. The fact that Chapter 11 may be a true rehabilitative process, and is seen as such, assisted in this analysis.

During the early part of 2010, the *ad hoc* committee's non-consensual solution was tested and analysed by the company's advisers, and the company's management engaged Cleary Gottlieb to provide US bankruptcy advice. By the end of June 2010 the restructuring proposal was well developed and a plan support agreement had

been agreed between the company, more than 70% of its senior lenders and around 15% of its high-yield bond creditors.

The company did not make a June 1 2010 coupon payment under the high-yield bonds. On July 1 2010, at the expiration of the grace period for the payment of the coupon, Truvo Acquisition Corp, Truvo USA Inc, the high-yield bond issuer and Truvo Intermediary filed for bankruptcy relief in the Southern District of New York bankruptcy court.

7.3   Creditor negotiations

(a)   ***Lock-up agreement***

A lock-up agreement was negotiated between the *ad hoc* committee, the company and Elliott in advance of the Chapter 11 filings. The lock-up agreement contained standard lock-up and support provisions typical of a European restructuring, and also contained provisions relating to voting in the Chapter 11 process. It bound senior lenders in respect of all senior debt held by them, and also in respect of any high-yield bond debt held by them. As a result, due to support from some cross-holders, the debtors filed for Chapter 11 with the support of around 15% of the high-yield bondholders.

(b)   ***Senior versus high-yield bonds***

The debtors filed a joint reorganisation plan which was not supported by the high-yield bondholders as a class, and which provided for a cramdown of the high-yield bond debt. While there had been negotiations with the high-yield bondholders committee leading up to the filing, these negotiations had been unsuccessful.

The plan offered high-yield bondholders 15% warrants in the post-restructured group and €20 million in cash. This was a so-called 'death trap' structure, in that the high-yield bondholder proposal was available to the high-yield bondholders only if it was accepted by the high-yield bondholders as a class. If rejected, the plan provided for the high-yield bondholders to be crammed down as an entire class and receive nothing.

The offer made to the high-yield bondholders was based not on any perceived value within the high-yield bonds, but on the costs associated with a protracted restructuring process. In considering the latter, the *ad hoc* committee was informed by the company's assessment of the costs associated with a contested restructuring proposal, which had been thoroughly calculated and tested.

Soon after the plan was filed, a committee of unsecured creditors was formed (some of whose members were previously members of the high-yield bondholders committee). An objection was filed to the disclosure statement, which was not upheld. The committee also filed several objections to the plan itself, together with extensive discovery requests.

The delay and expense occasioned by the discovery, as well as responding to and hearing the objections, meant that the company was eager to broker a settlement between its creditors. This was achieved on October 5 2010 when a plan settlement agreement was entered into between the *ad hoc* committee, Elliott and the unsecured creditor committee.

The plan settlement agreement revised the offer to the high-yield bondholders to:

- 20% warrants (based on a €150 million strike price);
- a €20 million cash payment; and
- 7.5% of an anticipated tax refund claimed by Truvo Group.

Over 90% (in value) of high-yield bondholders ultimately voted to approve the plan.

The remainder of the equity in the restructured group was allocated to the senior lenders, subject to dilution by the new management incentive plan.

(c)   *Senior versus senior – development of split holdco structure*

Elliott proved influential in the negotiating process. Elliott was not a member of the high-yield bondholders committee, but could engage with them by virtue of its significant high-yield bond position.

The plan contemplated the sale of the company and its subsidiaries to a senior lender-owned special purpose vehicle ('Newco'). The view of the *ad hoc* committee was that in total, Newco could support €600 million of debt on its balance sheet (with the remainder of the senior facilities to be equitised).

The view of non-par senior lenders, including Elliott, was that this structure overlevered the Truvo Group and would make it more difficult for the business to operate and achieve a successful exit. However, it was important to a number of par senior lenders that they retain as much of their debt interest in the group as possible. Some of this gap could be bridged by adjusting the cash pay interest element of the restructured debt, so as to ensure that the group's cash flows were not placed under undue pressure. However, there still remained a gap between the par and non-par constituencies of approximately €150 million.

Eventually, a novel solution was devised, which split the equity holdings of Newco into two new holding companies ('Equityco' and 'PIKco'), which together were to be allocated all of Newco's share capital.

Under the plan, all senior lenders would exchange their existing debt claims against the group for their pro rata share of new debt issued by Newco. In addition, the senior lenders could elect to receive the equity element of their consideration in one of two ways:

- by receiving shares in Equityco, which would remain unlevered and would finance its acquisition of its interest in Newco simply by issuing lenders; or
- by receiving shares as well as payment-in-kind debt in PIKco, which would essentially finance its acquisition of its interest in Newco by issuing both payment-in-kind debt and equity. The payment-in-kind debt would not bear cash pay interest, and there would be dividend restrictions between Newco and PIKco, thereby ensuring that the payment-in-kind debt created no issues for Newco and the operating group.

The shareholdings that Equityco and PIKco received in Newco were reflective of the proportion of lenders that opted for the Equityco option versus the PIKco option.

This structure allowed senior lenders which wished to retain a larger debt claim to elect the PIKco option and receive payment-in-kind debt in PIKco, while at the same time ensuring that Newco and the operating group remained free of these additional debt obligations. The plan also provided that Equityco would always own at least 50.1% of Newco, which meant that the Truvo Group's majority shareholder would not be burdened with the new payment-in-kind debt.

Finally, the shareholder agreements for each of Equityco, PIKco and Newco were such that voting rights were structured on a look-through basis, so that senior lenders would ultimately have the same shareholder rights regarding Newco as they would have had if all senior lenders had received equity directly in Newco.

The final debt structure of the Newco group consisted of:

- a €350 million facility issued by Newco;
- a €100 million second-lien facility issued by Newco;
- a €25 million super senior revolving credit facility issued by Newco; and
- a €52.285 million payment-in-kind facility issued by PIKco, out of the total of €150 million that PIKco was theoretically permitted to issue (reflecting the fact that approximately 35% of the senior lenders chose the PIKco option).

8. Implementation of restructuring

8.1 Impact of credit default swaps

At the commencement of the negotiations, searches of public databases indicated that a significant amount of credit protection had been written on the high-yield bonds.

While creditors did not need to be able to deliver high-yield bonds into an auction (ie, holders of credit protection could cash settle their credit default swaps), there was a concern that locking up high-yield bonds would create a shortage of high-yield bonds for delivery into an auction, creating an artificial spike in the auction price and therefore a lower net cash settlement amount.

Accordingly, in order to incentivise holders of high-yield bonds to support the plan, carve-outs were inserted into the lock-up agreement in order to allow participating holders of high-yield bonds to deliver an amount of high-yield bonds equal to the notional credit default swap protection that had been purchased, into a credit default swap auction. Participating high-yield bondholder support was then calculated on a net of credit default swap basis.

The existence of the credit protection has another implication for the restructuring: while holders of high-yield bonds with credit protection were likely to be supportive of the restructuring plan because it necessitated a credit event, post-auction those high-yield bonds could be transferred to another creditor with entirely different motivations.

The Truvo credit default swap auction took place in August 2010 and the average price for the auction was $0.03 in the dollar. Ultimately, the impact of the credit protection was positive, in that the high-yield bonds delivered into the auction were, on the whole, bought by supportive creditors. Of course, this need not have been the case – there was always the possibility that, particularly in the context of a Chapter

11 restructuring, high-yield bonds could have been acquired in an auction by creditors seeking to gain litigation or hold-out value.

8.2 Restructuring proposal

The restructuring was carried out by the sale of the shares in Truvo USA Inc, the immediate subsidiary of Truvo Acquisition Corp, to Newco, and the issuance of debt and equity by Newco (through Equityco and PIKco) to the senior lenders. These transactions were carried out by the plan.

The plan could not facilitate the sale of Truvo USA Inc free of debt and guarantees given by it and its subsidiaries, or of the company's direct borrowing obligations. Accordingly, it was necessary to incorporate intercreditor debt release mechanics into the restructuring plan.

The debt release provisions in the intercreditor agreement authorised the security agent to release borrowing and guarantee obligations and discharge security in connection with an enforcement sale of a member of the group carried out by it or at the request of an instruction group (ie, 66.6% of the senior lenders). However, the intercreditor agreement also contained high-yield bond protections, which contained restrictions on the security trustee's authority. In particular, in order to release the borrowing and guarantee obligations in connection with a sale:

- the proceeds of the sale or disposal must have been in cash;
- all claims of the senior lenders against the member of the group being sold must have been unconditionally released and discharged, sold or disposed of concurrently with such sale; and
- the disposal must either have taken place via a public auction or have been certified as being for fair value by a recognised investment bank.

The net effect of this was that the senior lenders could not 'credit bid' their debt to fund the purchase of Truvo USA Inc (ie, the purchase price could not take into account any senior debt originally owed by the group or assumed by Newco). Instead, Newco would have to buy Truvo USA Inc valued on a debt-free basis and pay in cash. This gave rise to two issues for the *ad hoc* committee: how to fund the purchase of the shares in the absence of being able to conduct a credit bid, and how to prevent cash leakage to non-consenting senior lenders.

The restructuring proposal dealt with these challenges by:

- providing that Newco would borrow from a third-party financier a daylight facility of an amount equal to the purchase price, in order to fund the cash purchase price of Truvo USA Inc;
- preventing leakage of the cash purchase price to non-consenting senior lenders by using the plan to carry out an assignment of the senior lenders' claims against Truvo Acquisition Corp to Newco, so that Newco became the sole lender under the senior facilities at the time the cash price was paid using the daylight facility proceeds; and
- round-tripping the sale proceeds for Truvo USA Inc to repay Newco as sole lender under the senior facilities (thereby allowing Newco to repay the daylight facility).

The key final steps of the restructuring were as follows:
- Prior to the sale of the Truvo USA Inc shares (and as part of the plan), the security trustee served a demand on the company in respect of the whole of the senior debt, pursuant to the Truvo Acquisition Corp guarantee.
- Under the plan, the senior lenders assigned their claims under the Truvo Acquisition Corp guarantee to Truvo NV in exchange for new debt and equity in Newco, Equityco and PIKco (on the terms described above).
- Newco purchased the Truvo USA Inc shares for market value on condition that the Truvo Acquisition Corp guarantee was assigned to it and that the Truvo USA Inc shares were sold on a debt-free basis.
- In conjunction with the sale of the Truvo USA Inc shares for cash, the security agent released Truvo USA Inc and its subsidiaries from all senior debt and high-yield bond debt, guarantees and securities.

8.3   Worldwide stay

The Truvo Group's legal advisers had identified a risk (though arguable) that the standstill provisions in the intercreditor agreement would be insufficient to prevent high-yield bondholders from taking action to enforce their guarantee against the company when enforcement action was commenced against any member of Truvo Group. This was one of the concerns underpinning the company's initial reluctance to consider a security enforcement cramdown option.

In order to deal with this risk, the Chapter 11 debtors sought an injunction from the New York Bankruptcy Court to prevent financial creditors from taking action against the company and certain other non-debtor subsidiaries. The court granted this injunction, which lasted until the plan was approved. This provided the company with comfort that the business operations could be shielded from claims and was effective in doing so. A similar order had been made in the *Lyondell Bassell* case, but for a limited period. In this case, the New York Bankruptcy Court took an expansive view of the court's jurisdiction and power.

8.4   Daylight facility

A daylight facility was instrumental in addressing the cash sale requirement in the intercreditor agreement. However, it presented various practical problems, and in fact at the outset there were significant doubts as to the feasibility of obtaining a daylight facility sufficiently large to finance the purchase of the group.

After some considerable effort by all parties to identify a willing daylight facility provider, Deutsche Bank agreed to underwrite a daylight facility for Newco. The facility was secured by security over the Truvo USA Inc shares, although it contemplated being repaid immediately upon acquisition of the shares by Newco.

In order for the costs of the daylight facility to be kept at a reasonable level, it was vital that the daylight funding structure insulated the facility provider from any real risk that the moneys would not be repaid at the end of the process. Accordingly, a funding escrow agreement was entered into between Newco, Truvo Acquisition Corp, Deutsche Bank and the security trustee, whereby each party confirmed pre-agreed and irrevocable payment directions, and all of the moneys were moved

through accounts held with Deutsche Bank. In other words, the process was completely hardwired in advance so as to exclude any counterparty risk.

8.5 Negotiations with the security trustee

The security trustee played an important role in the restructuring, and did so in circumstances whereby it had no economic interest in the outcome. Accordingly, the negotiations with the security trustee were relatively prolonged. The security trustee sought (and obtained) an indemnity from senior lenders, which was secured on a super senior basis by the transaction security for the post-restructured debt.

The security trustee was also concerned about the ability of the US bankruptcy court to vary English law claims effectively, and therefore that the assignment of the senior lenders' claims under the plan may be challenged by a non-consenting senior lender. This concern was resolved by providing in the plan for the assignment and delivery by each senior lender of a transfer certificate under the senior facilities agreement, transferring its claim to Newco. All senior lenders voluntarily signed the transfer certificates and the order of the New York Bankruptcy Court did not have to be enforced in this regard.

The security trustee also obtained a fair value opinion in the context of the sale of the Truvo USA Inc shares from a third-party investment bank.

9. Final closing structure

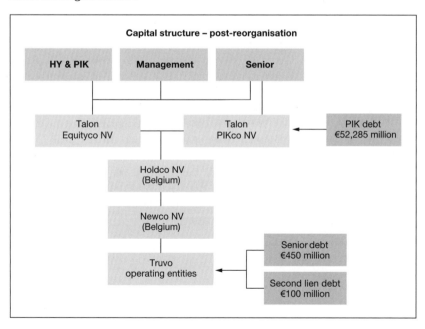

10. Implications of the Truvo restructuring

As has been the case with many recent European restructurings, the two key tensions in this deal were (i) between in-the-money and out-of-the-money creditors on the

one hand and (ii) the differing drivers for senior lenders entering at par versus discount, manifested principally in the extent of senior debt write-off that senior lenders wished to endure, on the other. The fact that, unlike many other concurrent restructurings, a relatively speedy compromise was found between creditor groups which resolved the tensions with a combination of pragmatic commercial compromise and creative legal structuring, is a credit to all parties involved in the deal.

This deal therefore demonstrates how important it is for principals and legal and financial advisers to be highly cognisant of and sensitive to the differing motivations and requirements of both par and non-par lenders, and the need to try to accommodate these differences from the outset.

In terms of process, as far as restructuring transactions go, the Truvo restructuring was remarkably smooth. The non-pre-packaged Chapter 11 plan was confirmed just over four months after being proposed. Overall, a highly complex transaction involving numerous jurisdictions and novel processes was devised, negotiated and implemented within nine months.

While restructurings are inevitably costly exercises for the company subject to them – in terms of both monetary expense and business impact – the potential downsides in this case were significantly mitigated by the efficiency of the process. The impact of the US Chapter 11 process on the group's sales and trading in Europe was in fact minimal.

Finally, the Truvo restructuring was significant in that it demonstrated the ability to use Chapter 11 as a flexible restructuring tool in a European context. It is well known that the reach of the US Chapter 11 courts can, in a jurisdictional sense, be broad. However, this deal demonstrated that the transactional application of a Chapter 11 plan is just as broad – not only is Chapter 11 inherently flexible as a process, but it can be highly adaptable to novel concepts. European-style intercreditor arrangements and English law documents provided the mechanical backbone to the plan. The fact that the US advisers, and indeed the US court, were at the outset unfamiliar with European-style intercreditor arrangements (significantly different in structure from most US-based arrangements) posed no impediment. The speed at which the plan was agreed and confirmed is also testament to the fact that the perceived downsides to a Chapter 11-based restructuring – time and cost – do not always bear out (perhaps indeed, due to the lingering threat of those particular downsides).

Autodistribution

Nicolas Laurent
Samuel Pariente
Bredin Prat

1. **Synopsis**

The Autodistribution group, a European leader of independent distribution of spare parts for cars and lorries, was restructured in April 2009.[1] This was the first restructuring in France to use a structure similar to a US pre-pack for the purposes of reaching an agreement with creditors. The transaction is of particular interest as it showed how the then-applicable French safeguard proceedings could be used to effect a swift debt restructuring without jeopardising a company's operations.

2. **Background and group operations**

First incorporated in 1962, the Autodistribution group is today the French and European leader in the distribution of spare parts for cars and lorries. It is also the main supplier of garage equipment to professionals in the automobile industry. The group currently has approximately 5,500 employees, 117 distributors and 350 suppliers. In addition, the group has 160,000 square metres of storage space and 489 sales outlets.

Pre-restructuring, the Autodistribution group's turnover was €1.1 billion, with earnings before interest, tax, depreciation and amortisation (EBITDA) of €55 million.

3. **Pre-restructuring corporate structure**

Before the restructuring, Autodistribution was owned by Investcorp, a Bahraini private equity fund.

Investcorp had purchased 100% of the shares in a Luxembourg incorporated holding company (Parts Investments) in 2006. This Luxembourg company was the parent company of two financial holding companies, which in turn sat above the leveraged buy-out (LBO) group that owned the operational subsidiaries. The corporate structure of the Autodistribution group before its restructuring is shown in Figure 1 overleaf.

4. **Financial situation in the lead-up to the restructuring**

In 2008 the total LBO debt of the Autodistribution group was €690 million. This was more than 12 times the 2008 EBITDA figure (€55 million). The debt was held by two holding companies, Parts Holdings (France) and Autodis. Parts Holdings (France) had issued €73 million in vendor bonds and Autodis had €394 million of bank debt in

---

1   The information on the restructuring terms set out in this chapter is based on the safeguard plans.

Figure 1

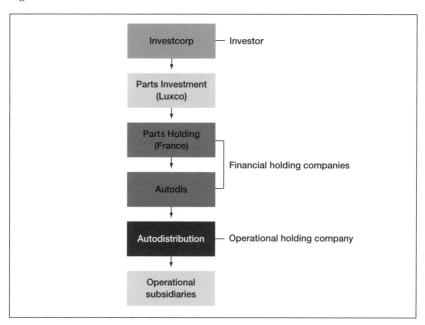

the form of senior and second lien facilities, €93 million of mezzanine bonds and €130 million of intercompany loans. Factoring agreements were also in place with Autodistribution, the operational holding company. This financial situation is summarised in Figure 2 opposite.

In the course of 2008, the group's turnover and EBITDA fell dramatically as a result of the crisis hitting the automobile sector. It became apparent that the financial ratios would not be met in the second half of 2008, and that there would be insufficient cash to service the holding companies' debt.

The change in law on the modernisation of the economy in France made matters worse, as it reduced the time limits for payment of suppliers, thereby increasing the Autodistribution group's working capital requirements by about €70 million in the first half of 2009.

As a result, the survival of the group demanded a major restructuring of its indebtedness at the holding company level and a significant injection of new money at the operational company level.

5.   Composition of lending syndicate and syndicate dynamic

The indebtedness of the financial holding companies was held by vendor bondholders at the level of Parts Holdings (France) and by senior and second lien lenders and mezzanine bondholders at the level of Autodis. Four percent of the vendor bonds were held by 153 private investors (including a number of individuals) and 96% by 17 institutional investors. As is further described below, this unusual allocation of the vendor bonds among very different types of holders led to a tailor-

Figure 2

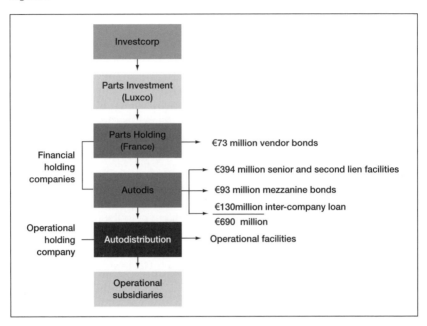

made proposal that resulted in a different treatment offered to holders of the same instrument.

The senior lending syndicate was mostly composed of international banks and funds and the mezzanine holders were mostly collateralised loan obligations (CLOs) and collateralised debt obligations (CDOs). While a large majority of creditors acted as a group and generally followed a common approach throughout the discussions, a handful of dissenting or non-responsive creditors made it impossible to achieve a fully consensual transaction.

6.   **Restructuring negotiation process**

An initial attempt was made to resolve the financial difficulties of the group consensually with the appointment in November 2008 of an *ad hoc* nominee whose role was to "find a consensual solution with the group's creditors and ... seek, as the case may be, a partner likely to buy a stake in the equity and to reinforce the business of the group by injecting cash". As a result of these negotiations, an investment fund, TowerBrook, in a joint proposal with the existing shareholder, Investcorp, agreed to inject €110 million into the business on condition of a restructuring of the existing debt, including an 85% debt write-off and a debt-to-equity swap that would give the lenders as a whole a 20% equity stake (with no voting rights), allocated in different proportions depending on the seniority of the different categories of lender. Under the terms of the finance documents, the amendments necessary to effect such a restructuring on a consensual basis would have required the unanimous approval of the creditors. However, due to the large number of creditors (nearly 200) and their

differing interests, such unanimity could not be obtained, as a minority of lenders refused, for various reasons, to accept the proposal.

At that point in time, it became obvious to all involved that the consensual route had come to a dead end, and that a solution to impose the majority-approved solution on the dissenting lenders while protecting the interest of the equity investors was needed.

Given the failure of negotiations and the difficulties faced by the group, the management could have requested the opening of safeguard proceedings immediately. This is the French equivalent of the US Chapter 11 and is designed to facilitate the reorganisation of a company with a view to allowing the continuation of the business, maintaining employment and repaying the company's liabilities pursuant to a safeguard plan.

The opening of safeguard proceedings triggers a six-month observation period, during which the company is placed under the protection and control of the court. The opening judgment automatically prohibits both the payment of debts incurred before the opening judgment and any legal action against the debtor for the payment of a claim that arose before the opening judgment (ie, an automatic stay). However, creditors (including suppliers) whose claims are subsequent to the opening judgment and are incurred for purposes of the procedure or the observation period, or in consideration for services rendered to the company, must be paid in cash by the company immediately upon delivery of the goods or services (which usually results in a dramatic increase in working capital needs for operating companies subject to safeguard proceedings).

There are two ways to adopt a safeguard plan:

- by submitting the plan to the vote of the creditors' committees and the bondholders' general assembly; or
- by consulting the creditors individually.

Where certain thresholds are met in terms of turnover or number of employees, three bodies must be formed by the administrator to vote on the proposed plan: a committee of credit establishments, a committee of main suppliers and a bondholders' general assembly. Where such thresholds are not met, the administrator can still decide to consult the creditors via the creditors' committee procedure. The safeguard plan submitted to the committees and the bondholders' general assembly may provide for debt write-offs, debt-to-equity swaps and rescheduling of payments, and for different treatments between different categories of creditors within the same committee if justified by differences in their situation. Typically, creditors that have different ranking pursuant to intercreditor arrangements may be treated unequally under a safeguard plan. The safeguard plan must be approved by each committee and the general bondholders' assembly, by a majority of two-thirds of the amount of claims held by the creditors that voted. Once the plan is approved by the committees and bondholders' general assembly, the court will adopt the plan if it is satisfied that the interests of all creditors are sufficiently protected. The plan will then be imposed on all members of the committees and the bondholders, including those that voted against it.

A restructuring plan that imposed debt write-offs or debt-to-equity conversion and approved by the relevant majority of each committee and the bondholders' general assembly could therefore have been imposed on the minority dissenting lenders of the Autodistribution group, whereas a unanimous approval was required pursuant to the contractual mechanisms for any out-of-court negotiations.

However, a traditional safeguard procedure could not provide an adequate solution for the Autodistribution group because of the uncertainty of its outcome. A long process would have had a potentially disastrous impact on the group's turnover, given that a large number of customers were not contractually bound to the Autodistribution group and the suppliers may have been reluctant to supply a company in insolvency proceedings. Moreover, even if a majority of creditors had supported the plan at the time of its conception, there would have been no certainty that the creditors would have voted in its favour at the end of the process.

It was therefore decided that obtaining agreement from the relevant majority of creditors at the same time as the initiation of the safeguard proceedings, in a similar way to a US pre-pack, would avoid the uncertainty inherent in this procedure. This would be achieved by way of a pre-pack agreement entered into by all consenting creditors (representing the required majority for the approval of a safeguard plan), and providing an undertaking by each such creditor to vote in favour of the safeguard plan that would be put forward in the safeguard proceedings, so long as such plan was identical to the plan described in the pre-pack agreement.

Notwithstanding the requirement for creditor agreement to the proposal, this solution was not without risk, particularly to the new investor, TowerBrook. Agreeing to the process meant that TowerBrook had to undertake to provide its investment knowing neither whether the process would be successful nor what the impact would be on the Autodistribution group's results, suppliers and other stakeholders. This was mitigated by including conditions precedent (eg, in respect of regulatory authorisations) in the restructuring agreement to be fulfilled on the date of the vote of the last creditors' committee. The key to the process was therefore the speed with which the restructuring plan could be implemented so as to avoid negative publicity for the company.

7. Implementation of restructuring

The parties agreed to enter into safeguard proceedings and to proceed using the pre-pack mechanism. The pre-pack agreement was signed by the requisite number of lenders on February 26 2009, after almost four months of negotiations. The agreement set out the proposals made to the committees of creditors, the irrevocable voting commitments of the lenders, the conditions precedent to the various steps of the restructuring and the legal documentation that would apply post-restructuring.

The execution of the pre-pack agreement took place a couple of days after the opening of the safeguard proceedings. The initial goal to sign the pre-pack agreement before the opening of the safeguard proceedings (as would be the case for a US pre-pack) was therefore not attained, but the effect ended up being the same as the opening of the safeguard proceedings and the agreement with the relevant majority of creditors was announced at the same time on March 2 2009. As a result, the

negative effect of the safeguard proceedings was immediately mitigated by the positive news that an agreement had been reached with the creditors, and the safeguard could be presented as a purely technical procedure implementing the agreement with the creditors.

Two separate safeguard proceedings were opened simultaneously on February 18 2009 at the Commercial Court of Evry, one for Parts Holdings and one for Autodis. The court-appointed administrator in this process helped to transform the restructuring agreement into a draft safeguard plan to ensure that it was in a form that would comply with the legal requirements for safeguard proceedings. The safeguard plan was then submitted to the creditors on March 5 2009.

This hybrid process needed to accommodate at the same time the complexities of LBO contractual debt arrangements and the mandatory rules applicable to insolvency proceedings, which resulted in a number of technical and legal difficulties.

7.1 Validity of the pre-pack arrangement

As this was the first instance of a pre-pack style restructuring in France, one question was whether the pre-pack would be lawful and binding on the courts. With no provisions in the safeguard law prohibiting such a pre-pack, it remained to be tested whether the French courts would accept this particular use of the safeguard proceeding (given that five different procedures already existed in France), and whether the courts would deem that the creditors had all been treated equally. In particular, there was a concern that the fact that an agreement had already been reached with the creditors before the judicial bodies of the safeguard proceedings were involved could be deemed to constitute an attempt to avoid the safeguard proceedings' mandatory rules. However, care had been taken to ensure that all creditors were given the same amount of information (as ensured by the *ad hoc* nominee) and were able to determine freely whether to agree to the restructuring agreement. Arguably, any commercial court judgment that confirmed the safeguard plan – which itself reflected the restructuring agreement and which was voted upon by the majority of the creditors – was merely an application of the safeguard law and achieved the same aim of allowing the continuation of the business by resolving the company's difficulties.

The Commercial Court of Evry, having ensured that the letter and spirit of the safeguard law had been respected, took a pragmatic approach and supported the process, realising that this was the only opportunity for the recovery of the group.

7.2 Practical enforceability of the pre-pack arrangement

The question then remained of whether the creditors would comply with their undertakings to vote in favour of a safeguard plan that reflected the restructuring agreement. The safeguard plan could not be implemented without the effective positive vote of the creditors, as the mere execution of the pre-pack agreement could not be considered equivalent to the actual vote during the safeguard proceedings. Article 1142 of the Civil Code provides that the violation of an undertaking to do or to refrain from doing something gives rise to monetary damages, as opposed to a

right to specific performance. However, recent case law had confirmed that the benefit of this article could be waived and such a waiver could therefore be included in a pre-pack agreement. Nevertheless, there would always be a risk that a creditor would not comply with its voting undertaking. Such risk could be diminished by combining the waiver of Article 1142 of the Civil Code with other mechanisms, such as:

- an option for the purchase of the debt granted by each creditor for a token €1 in the event of a violation of its voting undertaking;
- an express acknowledgement by the creditors of the serious damage that the company would suffer in the event of a violation of their voting undertaking;
- the designation of an *ad hoc* nominee with the power to act on behalf of a non-complying creditor; and
- the holding of the vote at the commercial court to impress on the creditors the importance of the matter.

In the Autodistribution case, the creditors that were party to the pre-pack agreement all complied with their voting undertaking and the enforceability of these mechanisms was therefore not tested.

7.3 Debt-to-equity swap

The safeguard law specifically provides that a debt-to-equity swap may be imposed on creditors, subject to the relevant majority approving the safeguard plan and provided that a general meeting of shareholders approves the corresponding share capital increase. A peculiarity of the Autodistribution restructuring was that the equity given to the creditors in exchange for the debt write-off was equity in a newly incorporated Dutch holding company (Holdco) and not equity in the debtor company. As a result, the debt-to-equity swap proposed under the Autodistribution safeguard plan could not be based on the mere application of the safeguard law, but required the creditors to take a number of positive steps to effect the swap (eg, subscription to share capital increase, assignments and contributions). The practical question that arose was whether such a debt-to-equity swap, and the required positive steps on the part of the creditors, could be imposed upon dissenting creditors. It appeared that such steps could not be imposed on creditors based on the existing legal mechanisms and the safeguard plan was therefore structured to encourage each creditor to choose individually the proposed debt-to-equity swap. Each creditor was given the option of either a straightforward 85% debt write-off with nothing in exchange for the portion of the debt that was written-off, or the proposed debt-to-equity conversion. All of the creditors opted for the debt-to-equity swap and took the required steps, including the originally dissenting creditors that had not been party to the pre-pack agreement.

7.4 Different treatment of different categories of debt holder

A slightly different treatment was offered to the 153 private investors (including mostly individuals) that held 4% of the bonds in Parts Holdings (France), as it became apparent that a debt waiver and debt-to-equity swap would not be adopted

by these investors. These investors, which had commercial relations with the Autodistribution group as distributors, were offered a cash payment of 30% of their debt. Article L 620-30-2 of the Commercial Code permits differential treatment of creditors in justifiable circumstances (which is usually understood to apply to creditors with different levels of seniority pursuant to intercreditor arrangements), but in this case the proposed plan sought to treat differently bondholders holding the same bond instrument on the assumption that the differential treatment was justified not because the nature or ranking of the debt was different, but because the nature of the bondholders (ie, private versus institutional investors) justified it. While it cannot be certain that this differential treatment would have been upheld by a court had there been a dispute on this matter, the issue did not arise, as the institutional bondholders all accepted the preferential treatment that was awarded to the private bondholders (this acceptance was probably facilitated by the fact that the amount at stake was insignificant).

7.5   Scope of proceedings

The scope of the safeguard proceedings within the Autodistribution group was also a difficult issue to address. On the one hand, the nature of the business excluded the opening of safeguard proceedings at the level of the operating companies, as it would have resulted in a dramatic increase in working capital needs and a potential loss of customers and suppliers. On the other hand, there were immediate liquidity concerns at the level of the operating companies that needed to be addressed urgently. Fortunately, the debt structure of the group was relatively simple, in that most of the LBO indebtedness was at the level of the two financial holding companies, while the operating companies were financed by separate facilities, so that the LBO debt could be treated independently from the operating debt. To address the liquidity needs of the operating companies, a conciliation procedure was opened at the level of Autodistribution in parallel to the safeguard proceedings opened at the level of Parts Holdings (France) and Autodis. The conciliation procedure allowed an emergency injection of new money that benefited from a new money privilege even before the safeguard proceedings of the financial holdings were concluded.

7.6   Timing

The point of a pre-pack is to use the safeguard proceeding as a mere implementation tool for a pre-agreed contractual arrangement, implying that the company should spend as little time as possible in safeguard proceedings.

Arguably, having both safeguard proceedings instituted in the same jurisdiction and in the same commercial court in France significantly reduced the risks and delays inherent to the process. Nevertheless, certain legal timing constraints had to be respected. First, by law all creditor committees had to have at least 15 days to consider the safeguard plan and a further 15 days after the vote during which any creditor could challenge the vote before its confirmation by the court. Second, pursuant to Article L626-32 of the Commercial Code, the bondholders needed to vote in favour of the safeguard plan after the main creditor committees had voted.

In the Autodistribution process, the bondholders' assembly was convened on the same day (in the afternoon) as the creditors' committees and there was therefore no delay between the two votes and a reduced risk of differential voting. The two holding companies were out of safeguard within a month-and-a-half of the opening judgment, comparable to the timing envisaged by the Commercial Code, which provides for a six-month observation period that may be renewed twice (ie, up to a maximum of 18 months).

8. Final closing structure

Below are the key restructuring terms provided by the safeguard plan, a simplified structure chart post-restructuring and a timeline summarising the process:

- Investors – the investors (TowerBrook, Investcorp and management) would hold up to 80% in Holdco.
- Senior lenders – the senior lenders would maintain €107.4 million as rescheduled senior debt and the balance, representing 70% of their claim, would be converted into either 9% of Holdco shares or €9.5 million in equity participation (EP) notes structured as an alternative to straight equity for creditors that could not hold equity instruments. The senior lenders would also be entitled to receive €25.5 million of structured upside participation notes aimed at giving the senior lenders the opportunity to receive an additional return in the event of a significant upside received by the investors.
- Second lien lenders – the second lien lenders would convert 100% of their claims into either 3.6% of the shares in Holdco or €1.8 million in EP notes.
- Mezzanine lenders – the mezzanine lenders would convert 100% of their claims into either 5.4% of the shares in Holdco or €2.7 million in EP notes.
- Vendor bondholders – the vendor bondholders would convert 100% of their claims into either 2% of the shares in Holdco or €1 million in EP notes.
  See Figures 3 and 4 overleaf

9. Conclusion

Autodistribution is without doubt one of the landmark restructuring cases of the past decade in that it maximised the limited flexibility allowed by the rules existing at the time to implement a swift pre-pack style arrangement in a context where no other solution would have allowed the recovery of the business.

This method clearly will not apply in all circumstances, and the structure of the Autodistribution group (ie, two companies holding the majority of the debt, no significant foreign subsidiaries) certainly facilitated the speed of its restructuring. Where debt is held by a number of subsidiary companies in various overseas jurisdictions, this method of restructuring will be much more difficult.

The importance of the Autodistribution restructuring is such that, along with the Thomson restructuring of 2010, it inspired the creation of a new category of safeguard procedure called the accelerated financial safeguard (AFS). The AFS came into force on March 1 2011 and is designed to 'treat quickly' purely financial difficulties of companies. The AFS does not impact suppliers' payables; only the debt

Figure 3

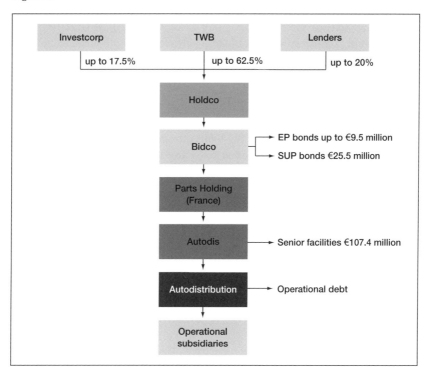

Figure 4

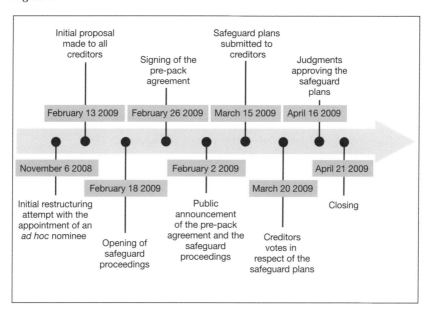

owed to financial institutions is the subject of an automatic stay and is to be dealt with by the safeguard plan. The company can therefore keep trading normally, thus significantly reducing the impact of a safeguard on operational companies. The AFS includes a fast-track feature that is not expressly available in regular safeguard proceedings and which allows for a safeguard plan to be adopted within three weeks to one month. However, a major limitation of the AFS is that the company must satisfy certain thresholds in terms of turnover and number of employees, which will often mean that pure LBO acquisition vehicles (with no turnover and no employees) will be ineligible for the AFS procedure (although it is anticipated that the nature of such thresholds should soon be modified to allow pure LBO holdings to benefit from the AFS).

The technology developed in the Autodistribution restructuring may therefore still prove useful in scenarios where a pre-pack style restructuring is required and where the company is ineligible for the AFS.

The authors express special thanks to Victoria Judd for her contribution to this chapter.

SGD

Eduardo J Fernandez
Willkie Farr & Gallagher LLP
Martin Graham
Oaktree

1.   Synopsis

The restructuring of SGD Group, which was accomplished in a consensual, out-of-court context, provides a vivid illustration of both the beneficial role that a distressed asset investor can play in support of troubled industrial groups and certain particularities of implementing a financial restructuring in France. The restructuring achieved various objectives:

- significantly reducing SGD Group's financial debt burden;
- reinforcing the balance sheets of the group's principal operating companies;
- providing SGD Group with the necessary liquidity to implement a far-reaching capital expenditure programme in a challenging economic climate; and
- preserving SGD Group as an integrated going concern.

2.   Background to group operations

SGD (formerly Saint-Gobain Desjonquères) Group specialises in making, marketing and selling glass bottles used mainly in the pharmacy and fragrance/cosmetic industries, as well as glass bricks, insulators and jars. SGD Group is a world leader in its industry, with a global market share of 19% in the fragrance and cosmetic industry and 28% in the health and pharmaceutical industry, and sales of over €500 million in 2010. SGD Group is headquartered near Paris, France, and has 12 production sites and 10 commercial agencies in France, Germany, Italy, Spain, Brazil, China, Russia and the United States, employing more than 5,000 people (nearly half of whom are based in France).

3.   Pre-restructuring corporate structure

Saint-Gobain Desjonquères was spun out of Saint-Gobain Group in March 2007 via a €671 million leveraged buy-out (LBO) led by French private equity funds FCPR Sagard II A and FCPR Sagard II B (together with their respective fund manager, 'Sagard') and FCPR Cognetas II A and FCPR Cognetas II B (together with their respective fund manager, 'Cognetas'). For the purpose of the LBO, Sagard and Cognetas formed a top holding company, Cougard Holding, in which Sagard and Cognetas each held 50%. Upon completion of the LBO, Cougard Holding held a 78% equity interest in a French *société par actions simplifiée*, then known as 'Cougard Investissement', which had been formed for the purpose of implementing the LBO. The balance of the equity interests in Cougard Investissement was held by affiliates

of the vendor, as to 19.7%, and a special purpose vehicle owned primarily by members of SGD Group's management.

Immediately before the restructuring, Cougard Investissement directly held 100% of the share capital of three entities:

- SGD SA, the principal French company of the group;
- SGD Inc, the holding company for North America organised in Delaware; and
- SGD Germany GmbH, a holding company organised under German law.

SGD SA directly held six subsidiaries:

- four in France – VG Emballage, Verrerie de l'Orne, Verrerie de la Somme and SSV-Saint Remy;
- one in China – SDF Asia Pacific; and
- one in Russia – OAD SG Sitall, which in turn held a majority stake in OAD Sitall.

SGD Inc directly held one subsidiary, SG North America Inc; and SGD Germany GmbH directly held two subsidiaries – SGD Kipfenberg (Germany) and SGD Inversiones Vidrieras Spain, SLU (Spain), which had two subsidiaries of its own (SGD La Granja Vidriera SLU (Spain) and SGD Brasil Vidros Ltda (Brazil)).

The pre-restructuring corporate structure of SGD Group, together with the equity and debt capital described here, is illustrated in Figure 1.

At the time of the LBO, the shareholders of Cougard Investissement entered into a shareholders' agreement setting forth, among other things, certain governance principles for SGD Group. The essence of these arrangements was that the supervisory board of SGD Group was to be controlled by appointees of Sagard and Cognetas, with minority representation for the Saint-Gobain investors and managers. However, in certain circumstances, the Saint-Gobain investors and managers could carry a board vote in the face of opposition from the appointees of the equity sponsors. In hindsight, the governance arrangements introduced for SGD Group at the time of the LBO hindered the company in its attempts to navigate the operational and financial challenges presented by the uncertain economic environment in the months and years that followed.

4. Pre-restructuring capital structure

The LBO was equity funded by Sagard, Cognetas, the Saint Gobain investors and Cougard Management, as well as other investors through their subscription of equity and quasi-equity instruments issued by Cougard Investissement, specifically:

- Sagard, Cognetas, Critical Placements Ltd, Malovat SARL and Jocelyn Lefebvre (collectively and via Cougard Holding) contributed €56,914,286 in exchange for 15,414,286 ordinary shares and 41.5 million preference shares;
- Sagard, Divona A and Divona B (both Cognetas special purpose vehicles), Critical Placements Ltd, Malovat SARL and Lefebvre contributed €109,085,714 in exchange for 109,085,714 convertible bonds;
- the Saint-Gobain investors contributed:

Figure 1. SGD pre-transaction structure

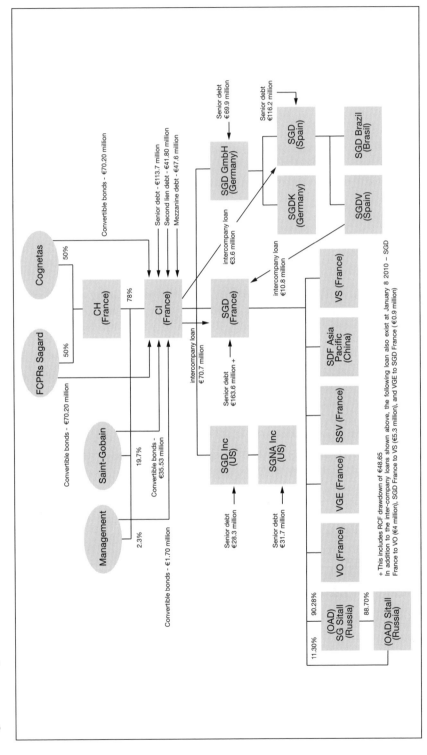

- €14.4 million in exchange for 3.9 million ordinary shares and 10.5 million preference shares; and
- €27.6 million in exchange for 27.6 million convertible bonds; and
- Cougard Management contributed:
  - €1.69 million in exchange for 685,714 ordinary shares and 1 million warrants; and
  - €1,314,286 in exchange for 1,314,286 convertible bonds.

The debt finance for the LBO transaction was provided by a syndicate of European lenders comprising banks and non-traditional lenders (principally collateralised loan obligation-type investment funds). These lenders participated in senior (first and second-lien) acquisition debt facilities and mezzanine bonds, specifically:

- €200.4 million first-lien term B facilities with a maturity date of March 31 2015, priced at Euribor + 237.5 basis points (bps);
- €200.4 million first-lien term C facilities with a maturity date of March 31 2016, priced at Euribor + 287.5 bps;
- an amortisable €50 million acquisition/capex facility with a final repayment date of March 31 2014, priced at Euribor + 200 bps;
- a €60 million revolving facility with a final repayment date of March 31 2014, priced at Euribor + 200 bps;
- a €40 million term loan D facility with a maturity date of September 30 2016, priced at Euribor + 475 bps (together with the first-lien facilities above, the 'senior facilities'); and
- €40 million in mezzanine bonds due March 31 2017, priced at Euribor + 900 bps (375 bps cash and 525 bps payment in kind).

Net leverage for the LBO was 4.2x for the first-lien facilities, 4.7x through the second-lien facilities and 5.1x overall.

Within four months of the LBO and in accordance with the senior facilities and mezzanine bonds, Cougard Investissement, SGD Germany GmbH and SGD SA entered into interest rate hedging agreements with certain first-lien lenders as hedging counterparties.

In connection with the LBO, SGD Group's creditors executed a French law-governed intercreditor agreement providing for their respective ranking and priority. Under the intercreditor agreement, creditors ranked as follows:

- first-lien creditors (first-lien lenders, agent and the hedging lenders);
- second-lien lenders;
- mezzanine creditors (the mezzanine bondholders and agent); and
- other creditors, including funds managed or advised by Cognetas or Sagard, and intercompany creditors.

In case of default on a more senior debt, the senior creditor was entitled to block payment to the subordinated creditors temporarily (or permanently, in case of payment default). Second-lien and mezzanine creditors were entitled to enforce their

security following a standstill period after a payment default, or immediately if the senior creditors accelerated all debt under the first-lien facilities (or all debt under the first or second-lien facilities, with respect to the mezzanine creditors) or enforced at least one security interest. Thus, the second-lien or mezzanine creditors could accelerate and enforce the entire security package if the first-lien creditors enforced a single security interest. Additionally, while the second-lien and mezzanine creditors waived their right to enforce their security interests for the applicable standstill periods, no first or second-lien lenders subordinated their individual enforcement rights under French law. Therefore, any individual senior lender or hedge lender could have enforced the security documents without obtaining consent from the other first-lien creditors.

4.1   Collateral package

The collateral package, in connection with the LBO, secured the first-lien facilities (the first-lien and hedging lenders) with pledges of bank accounts, claims against vendors and shares in the several 'Newcos' and in the French and Spanish target companies. The entities securing the first-lien facilities obligations also acted as guarantors. The pledges made by Cougard Investissement (including a pledge of certain intercompany loans) additionally secured the second-lien facility and the mezzanine bonds. Notably, all guarantees were limited to the obligations of those obligors which were subsidiaries of the French law guarantor in their capacity as borrowers under the senior facilities agreement. Generally, upstream guarantees are prohibited or significantly restricted in France. An upstream guarantee may be valid under French law; however, to the extent that the guarantor has received on-lending proceeds from a borrower, the grant of the guarantee does not violate the guarantor's corporate purpose (as set out in its bylaws) or its corporate interest, and the guaranteed amount is not excessive with regard to the guarantor's assets or financial capacity.

The security pledges and guarantees granted in connection with the LBO are set forth below:

- Cougard Investissement pledged financial instruments accounts relating to shares in SGD SA, bank accounts, certain intercompany loans, claims against vendors, shares in SGD Germany GmbH and shares in SGD Inc. These pledges secured the first-lien facilities, the second-lien facility and the mezzanine bonds.
- SGD SA granted an assignment of intercompany loans and an assignment of trade receivables to secure the first-lien facilities.
- SGD Inversiones Vidrieras Spain SLU pledged claims against vendors, shares in SGD La Granja Vidreiera SLU and its bank accounts to secure the first-lien facilities.
- SGD Germany GmbH pledged bank accounts, shares in SGD Kipfenberg and shares in SGD Inversiones Vidrieras Spain SLU to secure the first-lien facilities.
- Additionally, SGD, Inc, SGD North America, Inc, S SGD Kipfenberg and Verrerie de l'Orne acted as guarantors for the first-lien facilities (under which they were also borrowers).

As the foregoing security interests were granted simultaneously with the drawing of the various facilities, and the various companies granting the security interests were not insolvent at the time, the various security interests granted in connection with the LBO were not voidable under Article L632-1-I-6 of the Commercial Code (which provides that interests granted to secure borrowings after the fact may be declared void if the borrower is insolvent at the time). Additionally, Article L642-12 of the code protects creditors' security interests over assets which they financed (provided that the interests transfer to the new owner of that asset in the context of insolvency proceedings), so that a new owner remains liable for the balance of the acquisition financing even after paying the purchase price for the asset.

Lastly, despite the inclusion of clauses providing for direct enforcement of security upon a default allowing the secured party to take control and ownership of pledged assets, the SGD Group lenders faced certain challenges which would have hindered any enforcement of the security granted by SGD Group with a view to taking control of the group or certain subsidiaries. First, any enforcement action with respect to security granted by a French borrower would be automatically stayed on the commencement of any insolvency proceeding. Moreover, both in Spain and in Germany, enforcement of share pledges would have been required to have been made by way of public auction of such shares (and not transfer of the shares to the secured creditors).

5. Financial situation of group in lead-up to restructuring and restructuring triggers

SGD Group's profitability in 2007 and 2008 (after the LBO) was significantly less than anticipated at the time of the LBO, and the market declined significantly towards the end of 2008 as a result of the worldwide financial crisis. The perfume and cosmetic industries were affected as distributors reacted to contracting consumer demand and producers of perfumery and cosmetic goods (which were the immediate customers of SGD Group) sought to preserve cash by running down inventories rather than ordering new supplies at historic rates. This 'destocking' effect was a global phenomenon which affected many industries worldwide in 2008 and 2009. Heavily leveraged companies such as Cougard Investissement and certain of its subsidiaries were particularly vulnerable to the global destocking effect, since the reduction in sales volumes was not matched by any similar reduction in obligations to pay amounts of principal and interest on their bank debt.

In November 2008, with SGD Group's earnings before interest, taxes, depreciation and amortisation lagging behind budget, one of its works councils (statutorily mandated organisations representing workers in a company with 50 or more employees) initiated an alert procedure. Pursuant to Article L2323-78 of the Labour Code, within the context of an alert procedure, the works council can request information and explanations from the management when it has been made aware of events or facts that could presumably adversely affect the economic situation of the employer company. In light of its highly unionised workforce and the difficult social context within SGD Group, the proactive stance taken by employee representatives was unsurprising. The works council alert procedure did not play a

direct role in the restructuring to follow, but highlighted the need for management/shareholder action.

In December 2008 SGD Group breached certain of its financial covenants under the senior facilities and the mezzanine bonds. Leverage peaked around 6.25x (against a 5.85x covenant), and Cougard Investissement's interest cover stood at 2x (below the 2.2x test). In early 2009 discussions began with senior lenders and mezzanine bondholders to reach a debt restructuring agreement.

In March 2009 Cougard Investissement reached an agreement with lenders in which they agreed to waive the acceleration of the senior facilities and mezzanine bonds until May 15 2009. In exchange, SGD Group agreed to provide lenders with more information about its affairs and presented a business plan. At this time, the group appointed Deloitte to undertake an independent business review of SGD's business plan. Certain lenders, however, notified SGD Group of their intention to terminate or not renew existing short-term facilities and to terminate certain cash-pooling arrangements, foreign exchange transactions and interest rate transactions.

Within SGD Group, performance was uneven across its geographic markets: France and Spain had suffered significant slowdowns in business, which had been further hampered, in the case of France, by product recalls and evidence of declining customer satisfaction. North American operations were flat and basically break-even, while the SGD Kipfenberg and German operations were the group's best performers.

In addition to financial difficulties, SGD Group endured a high degree of management turnover in the period following the LBO. This management instability culminated with the removal of the group's chief executive officer (CEO) and chief financial officer (CFO) during its discussions with SGD Group's lenders. Thierry Dillard, the former CFO who had left the group in September 2008, returned to the group in March 2009 and was appointed CEO. The new management team developed its own business plan in July 2009 with the establishment of a reorganisation project as its primary objective. The plan contemplated a shift towards greater quality-driven production and capital expenditures of €250 million over three to four years.

In early May 2009 SGD Group's statutory auditor (an independent appointee of the shareholders) initiated a second alert procedure and by mid-May the lenders had issued a reservation of rights letter while a *de facto* standstill situation arose.

In July 2009 Cougard Investissement and SGD SA obtained the appointment of *mandataires ad hoc* – essentially, mediators appointed by the relevant commercial court (in the case at hand, the Nanterre *Tribunal de Commerce*) to assist a company's management in analysing difficulties and negotiating with creditors. The *mandat ad hoc* is a confidential and flexible procedure, with no fixed timeframe and no automatic stays of enforcement; the role of the *mandataire ad hoc* is purely to facilitate discussions between a debtor and its creditors. The *mandat ad hoc* proceeding provided the framework to permit SGD Group's new management team to press shareholders and creditors into action on how best to resolve the deepening financial and operational crisis in which the group found itself.

6. Composition of lending syndicate and syndicate dynamic

The senior facilities were syndicated to a large number of international financial

institutions, with RBS remaining as facility agent, term D (second-lien facility) agent and security agent, whereas the mezzanine bonds were syndicated to a limited number of specialised financial institutions. The senior facilities were fairly broadly scattered, with only one or two lenders holding more than €50 million of senior debt. A significant portion of the senior facilities were held by collateralised loan obligations, collaterialised debt obligations and other non-bank institutions.

By early March 2009 the first-lien lenders had formed an informal steering committee led by agent bank RBS. This committee would subsequently evolve into a formal committee approved by the lenders in mid-July 2009 and comprised of RBS, BNP Paribas, Babson, ECM, Highlander and Harbourmaster. The committee was advised by Banca Leonardo and Ashurst, whose fees were ultimately paid by SGD Group upon completion of the restructuring.

7.   Restructuring negotiation process

Following the appointment of the *mandataires ad hoc* and the presentation of the new management team's business plan in mid-July 2009, SGD's lenders were provided with the independent business review carried out by Deloitte in August 2009, which confirmed a high capex requirement, notably in the fragrance bottle division, which had endured the most significant underperformance.

In mid-August funds advised and managed by Oaktree LP, which had acquired a fraction of SGD's debt on the secondary market, expressed an interest in participating as a potential investor in a restructuring of SGD Group to implement the business plan presented to the lenders. The business plan and investment programme developed by SGD's management team in consultation with the *mandataires ad hoc* and other professional advisers (Bain) identified that SGD Group required a net 'new money' investment of up to €140 million over a two to three-year timeframe. Oaktree indicated to the *mandataires ad hoc* that, in principle, it would be willing to underwrite this new money need and allow all other senior lenders to participate on the same terms. Oaktree's proposal was subject to due diligence and negotiation and agreement of a consensual restructuring plan. At the time, SGD was anticipating restructuring proposals from the two most likely candidates: its equity sponsors and the committee.

The committee's proposal, submitted on September 4 2009, included a 40% writedown of the first-lien facilities and a total write-off of the second-lien and mezzanine debt. It would give subordinated lenders a small amount of equity and leave the first-lien lenders with a stake of more than 60%, while Sagard and Cognetas would have retained a 25% equity interest in exchange for a new money contribution. The first-lien lenders and SGD's equity sponsors would have shared board control of SGD.

The proposal submitted by Sagard and Cognetas on September 6 2009 contemplated a 'super-senior' €25 million new money injection from Sagard and Cognetas and a 70% writedown of senior debt. The proposal would have converted SGD Group's remaining facilities into bonds repayable in shares which could amount to a minority shareholding.

While both the committee's and Sagard-Cognetas's proposals acknowledged an

implicit need to inject €100 million into SGD Group, neither proposal fully financed the operational restructuring needs of the group.[1] The senior lenders were not keen to grant super-senior priority rights to the equity sponsors (as proposed in the Sagard-Cognetas proposal), but failed to identify readily available sources for financing their own plan given the likelihood that the sponsors would not participate in a lender-led plan.

As the two proposals were being assessed, SGD made a forbearance request in respect of an interest payment due on September 30 2009.

Unlike the other two proposals, the Oaktree restructuring plan, initially presented on September 15 2009, assumed a new money need of €140 million, in line with the business plan. Oaktree indicated that it was willing to backstop the plan in full, but was also prepared to syndicate to any other lenders or sponsors willing to participate. The proposal envisioned a new super-senior facility of €80 million and an additional €60 million of equity or quasi-equity. Oaktree would hold a controlling equity stake, with the first-lien lenders taking the remaining 30% in exchange for writing off €309 million of the first-lien facilities. As with the committee proposal, all second-lien and mezzanine debt would be written down.

An important aspect of Oaktree's proposal was the fact that it was conditional on receipt of 100% approval from all lender classes. Oaktree considered it essential to implement the plan *in bonis* (solvent) as any safeguard proceeding would need to be extended to operating subsidiaries of Cougard Investissement, which were borrowers under the senior facilities and could have been damaging to the underlying business given the potential reaction of trade creditors and customers. As senior debt from the LBO had been pushed down to operating subsidiaries, a 'pre-pack' safeguard strategy (such as that utilised in the *Autodistribution* restructuring completed earlier in 2009) was not a credible option. Indeed, management estimated that the opening of a safeguard proceeding would have had an impact of €30 million on the group's trade debt position.

Moreover, given the possibility that any individual dissenting lender could attempt to enforce a security interest, execution risk for the restructuring remained high in the absence of unanimity. It may have been possible to place the group's German and Spanish subsidiaries into a French law safeguard procedure under the applicable European regulation, with the active cooperation of the management teams of these subsidiaries. However, any such procedure would not have been binding on those lenders that held direct debt claims against SGD Group's US subsidiaries, unless further court proceedings were initiated in the United States. Such proceedings would have added further significant expense to the process and increased implementation risk as the outcome was highly uncertain.

Lastly, but no less importantly, any proposal would require the adherence of 100% of Cougard Investissement's direct and indirect shareholders, including employees who had invested fairly important sums alongside the equity sponsors of the LBO. The fact that SGD management would be reluctant to open a safeguard proceeding,

---

1   The Sagard-Cognetas proposal indicated that additional inventory and receivables-backed financings could have been made available.

especially since Oaktree's proposal would come off the table if they did, would inevitably strengthen the negotiating position of SGD's subordinated creditors.

Since the restructuring would give rise to a change of control in Cougard Investissement, the consultation process with SGD's works councils would need to be completed before the execution of any binding agreements with respect to the sale of shares in Cougard Investissement (and the process could be prolonged by the works councils for several weeks).

The one-month postponement of the September 30 interest payment (which the senior lenders had showed a willingness to extend further if an agreement on a restructuring would be reached within that initial period) would help to preserve SGD Group's cash position during the time necessary for Oaktree to conduct a limited high-level legal and risk assessment and to document any transaction. As of mid-September 2009, the cash-burn rate was not expected to result in a short-term liquidity crisis (ie, a cash insolvency situation), unless supplier credit became an issue.

The *mandataire ad hoc* backed Oaktree's proposal as the only "comprehensive solution" on the table. In this context, the committee requested that the process be opened to third parties in order to receive further proposals (or indications of interest in the lender-led plan) and to benchmark Oaktree's proposal. The equity sponsors, on the other hand, conceded and Sagard, which had taken the leadership role among shareholders, backed an Oaktree-led solution. By the end of September 2009, only Oaktree had submitted a binding and financed proposal.

Timing took on greater urgency when, on September 25 2009, an article[2] appeared in *Le Figaro* describing SGD's financial difficulties. In one of a series of crisis meetings and long negotiation sessions held under the auspices of a mediator from the *Comité Interministériel de Restructuration Industrielle* (CIRI) at the Ministry of the Economy, Finance and Industry, on September 30 SGD's CEO apprised the parties of the immediate adverse impact of the leaks, notably on dealings with suppliers. In this context, SGD Group indicated that it would have to proceed with the opening of either safeguard or judicial reorganisation proceedings, unless a restructuring agreement was reached within a short timeframe. During that meeting Oaktree, with the assistance of its financial adviser Rothschild & Cie, submitted a revised proposal taking into account certain comments received from various stakeholders.

Following the meetings with the CIRI and the *mandataires ad hoc* in early October 2009, negotiations reached their final stage. A key component of any successful restructuring is the availability of interim financing to address any liquidity issues ahead of the closing date of any restructuring. Oaktree's legal advisers at Willkie Farr & Gallagher faced the challenge of finding a mechanism by which Oaktree (which was not a credit institution for the purposes of the French banking regulations), could engage in a lending transaction with a non-affiliated party without violating

2   *"Une ex-filiale de Saint-Gobain en sursis"*, Anne de Guigné, highlighting the difficulties encountered by SGD's lenders and shareholders in reaching an agreement.

3   The banking monopoly is codified in Article L313-1 of the *Code Monetaire et Financier*; the characterisation of receivables-based financing as a banking transaction was established by two key judgments – one of the *Cour de Cassation*, France's highest civil jurisdiction, on February 20 1984 and one of the *Conseil d'Etat*, France's highest administrative tribunal, on July 8 1987.

France's banking monopoly,[3] and could benefit from priority and security for its new money which would be enforceable in the event of a subsequent insolvency of SGD.

As regards priority, in the absence of an ongoing conciliation proceeding, any new money lender to SGD would have to negotiate an *in bonis* priority right from all of its other lenders and that agreement would needed to be ratified by an order of the presiding judge of, or approved by an order of, the Nanterre Commercial Court to render the priority right enforceable. In the event of a subsequent recovery or liquidation proceeding and any adoption of an asset sale plan, the priority right would allow for the repayment of the new money before all other claims except certain employee claims (which benefit from a super priority right under French law), and the cost of the proceedings. Since the amount of any such recoveries would likely be insufficient to cover the priority claim, it was also essential to secure the new money injection by a 'bankruptcy-proof' lien (ie, a lien that transfers ownership of assets to the pledge). In France, the most effective type of bankruptcy-remote security is an assignment of trade receivables under the *loi Dailly* regime. Receivables assignments, however, can be made only to a credit institution and all receivables of SGD SA were already pledged to the senior lenders. Therefore, it was imperative that Oaktree make arrangements with a fronting bank and obtain a release of such security as a condition to its offer to provide interim financing.

The necessary interim financing was obtained through a factoring agreement with RBS Factor, which agreed to provide up to €50 million to SGD Group for the interim period before the closing date of the restructuring. The first-lien lenders agreed to release the assignment of commercial receivables granted by SGD so that they could be assigned to RBS Factor as security under the factoring agreement. Oaktree, through an affiliate, guaranteed RBS Factor through a cash collateral arrangement and a counter-guarantee entered into between the Oaktree affiliate, SGD and RBS Factor whereby any deduction by RBS Factor from the cash collateral would result in the Oaktree affiliate being subrogated in RBS Factor's position with respect to the same amount in regard to SGD.

As a result of negotiations with the committee, subordinated lenders and equity sponsors, Oaktree submitted a revised offer and term sheet on October 9 2009 (which was subsequently amended on October 23 and 30). The negotiations focused mainly on the quantum of reinstated senior debt, interest terms on that debt (notably the quantum of the cash component), the temporary moratorium of financial covenants and re-setting of covenant levels in later years and certain lender recovery issues. Oaktree was confronted by the challenge of reconciling the first-lien lenders' insistence on strictly adhering to the principles of subordination agreed to by all parties in the LBO with the need to give incentives to SGD Group's subordinated lenders to agree to an *in bonis* transaction (given that essentially they had nothing to lose in any safeguard proceeding or judicial reorganisation). Moreover, the shareholders of Cougard Investissement had to agree to walk away from their equity investment. The latter half of October was filled with intense discussions between:

- Oaktree and the committee;
- Oaktree and SGD;
- Oaktree and subordinated lenders (certain of which were insisting on being bought out rather than participating in the restructuring);

- the committee and the leading mezzaneurs;
- Oaktree and the various shareholders (each of which had a different agenda); and
- Oaktree and SGD employees, notably those that had invested in the LBO.

The mandataire *ad hoc* and the CIRI mediator each played pivotal roles: from cajoling through supporting to threatening the parties (or more than one at a time) to try to reconcile often irreconcilable positions until the right balance was struck. On the evening of October 30 2009, the revised Oaktree proposal had received adherence letters from 100% of SGD Group's key stakeholders. As the SGD works council had previously rendered the requisite opinion,[4] the first critical phase of SGD Group's restructuring was complete.

8.   Implementation of restructuring

On November 10 2009 the Nanterre Commercial Court (at the request of SGD) opened a conciliation procedure and appointed the two *mandataires ad hoc* as conciliators to facilitate the signing of a conciliation agreement. Because of the adherence letters that had already been signed, the parties had essentially signed onto the terms of the restructuring before the conciliation process was officially opened, and the conciliation was necessary only to have the court approve the contractual arrangements of the parties and ensure that the factoring arrangements and new money investment would benefit from a priority right in the case of a subsequent insolvency of SGD.

The conciliation agreement entered into on December 7 2009 and ratified by a judgment of December 18 2009 summarised the main terms of the restructuring, including the security to be provided to the new money providers, and obliged the parties to negotiate the final documentation in good faith.

In connection with the restructuring, which was fully reflected in definitive documentation entered into on February 4 2010:

- a syndicate of new money investors led by Oaktree extended to SGD Group €140 million, notably through a €40 million preferred equity certificate issuance by OCM Luxembourg Glasnost Holdings SCA, an entity incorporated for the purposes of acquiring Cougard Investissement, and a €90 million super senior operational facility comprised of:
  - operational facility A of €30 million, to be fully drawn at closing; and
  - operational facility B of €60 million, to be available for drawing up to three years (or, at the election of any lender, four years) after closing;
- the first-lien facilities were extended to December 31 2016 and reinstated within a €225 million facility comprised of:
  - facility A of a €150 million; and
  - facility B of a €75 million;

---

4   Despite an aversion to private equity firms, given their experience after the LBO, for the unions at SGD's plant in Mers-les-Bains the Oaktree-led restructuring was viewed as the best option in a worst-case scenario, as it at least contemplated much-needed capital expenditures at the site.

- €40 million of second-lien debt and €46 million in mezzanine bonds were effectively written down;
- OCM Luxembourg (controlled by Oaktree and in which the senior lenders hold a 20% equity stake) acquired each shareholder's stake in Cougard Investissement (post-conversion of the convertible bonds) for €1; and
- the warrants issued by Cougard Investissement in the LBO were cancelled.

To achieve the economic objective of the restructuring (ie, writedown of 63% of the first-lien facilities), the remaining amounts under the first-lien facilities were upstreamed through a series of *délégations imparfaites* under French law (where the corresponding intercompany receivable was then capitalised) or transferred by lenders to OCM Luxembourg in exchange for deferred consideration. The *délégation imparfaite* mechanism was vital, as had indebtedness under the reinstated debt facility been deemed novated, the lenders would have faced a risk of having the security granted for such indebtedness invalidated under certain circumstances.

In addition, the second-lien lenders and mezzanine bondholders accelerated their debt and transferred the resulting receivables to OCM Luxembourg for deferred consideration.

The deferred consideration was then utilised to subscribe to certain preferred equity certificates and warrants as regards the first-lien lenders, and warrants as regards the second-lien lenders and mezzanine bondholders. The warrants (which allowed subordinated lenders ultimately to recover a portion of their initial investment in the LBO) would be exercisable on a sale of substantially all of the assets and business of SGD Group to a third-party purchaser ('exit') or an initial public offering (IPO), but only to the extent that an applicable recovery for the first-lien lenders of 61% (as regards the second-lien lenders) or 63% (as regards the mezzanine bondholders) was satisfied. The first-lien lenders were also entitled to warrants entitling the holders to up to €13 million upon an exit or IPO.

9. Final closing structure

Under the new structure, OCM Luxembourg is the sole owner of Cougard Investissement. The rest of SGD Group's corporate structure was unaffected, as Cougard Investissement (now known as SGD Group SAS) continues to hold 100% of the share capital of SGD SA, SGD Inc, and SGD Germany GmbH. These three entities continue to hold their pre-restructuring subsidiaries, with the exception of the Russian entities, which were sold in July 2011 as had been contemplated shortly after the closing of the restructuring.

The post-restructuring corporate structure of SGD Group is illustrated in Figure 2 on the next page.

10. Conclusion

SGD Group's restructuring illustrates the beneficial – and often necessary – role that a long-term distressed asset investor can play in finding a solution for stakeholders of a troubled company. The timely injection of new money allowed SGD Group to deploy a capital spending programme of €293 million in order to modernise its

Figure 2. SGD post-transaction structure

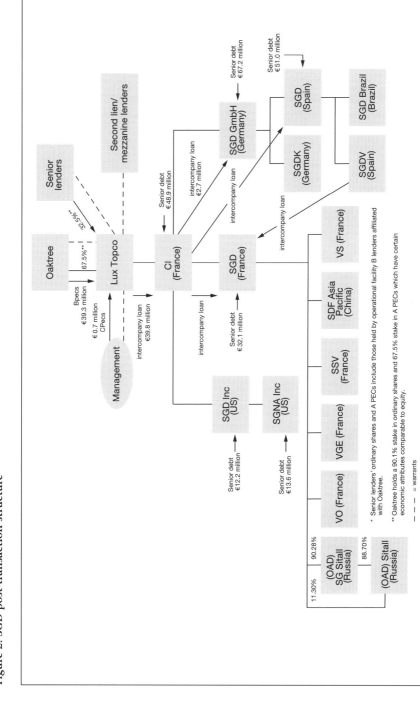

production capabilities, notably at its French sites, thereby improving its attractiveness to demanding clients and preserving employment. The financial covenants negotiated in the new loan agreements are intended to provide sufficient headroom so as to avoid a breach by SGD Group even in the case of significant underperformance in earlier years where the capital spending programme is being deployed.

Without Oaktree's ability to assess the operational and industrial aspects of SGD Group and its willingness and ability to backstop the group's new money financing needs, SGD Group would likely have been unable to obtain capital needed for a successful reorganisation *in bonis*. Oaktree's successful negotiations with SGD's stakeholders allowed SGD to avoid a safeguard procedure that would have taken several months to implement and would inevitably have led to a significant deterioration in the value and prospects of its business. The difficulties which SGD Group encountered in trying to implement its restructuring procedure, notably in obtaining unanimous consent among recalcitrant subordinated lenders, may have been a consideration in the French Parliament's decision to adopt an accelerated financial safeguard procedure. The new procedure, which came into effect on March 1 2011, provides for a fast-track implementation of plans negotiated within the context of a conciliation proceeding and affecting only financial creditors that would be entitled to participate in either the credit institutions committee or the bondholders committee of a traditional safeguard procedure, where the relevant commercial court concludes that the proposed restructuring plan enjoys sufficient support from such financial creditors so as to be approved by a two-thirds majority (calculated on the basis of value) within a one-month period.

The authors are grateful to Jared Jamesson, associate of Willkie Farr & Gallagher LLP, for his contributions to this chapter.

La Seda de Barcelona SA

Carlos Gila
Oaktree
Richard Tett
Freshfields Bruckhaus Deringer LLP
Alan Tilley
Bryan Mansell & Tilley LLP

---

1. Synopsis

La Seda de Barcelona SA is a leading manufacturer of food and beverage packaging and plastics, with operations across Europe and over 2,000 employees. In May 2010 it became the first Spanish company to use an English scheme of arrangement to restructure its syndicated debt. The scheme, combined with the injection of significant additional capital through a successful rights issue, a debt-for-equity swap and the careful rescheduling of the company's trade debts (all undertaken under considerable time pressure), saved a business that was perilously close to insolvency.

For the wider European restructuring market, the most significant aspect was that a non-English company restructured using an English scheme and, crucially, did so without moving its centre of main interests from Spain to England. Instead, the company relied on having a sufficient connection with England and an English establishment to use an English scheme to restructure its English law-governed debt. At the time, the effectiveness of such a strategy was doubted due to uncertainties as to the recognition in Germany of the Equitable Life English scheme. While the issue there concerned German law obligations being restructured by an English scheme, for some in the market those concerns also tainted the use of an English scheme to restructure English debt borrowed by non-English companies.

La Seda was seen as a watershed. It has since been followed by the restructurings of German companies Telecolumbus, Rodenstock and Primacom and a second Spanish company, Metrovacesa – none of which moved their centres of main interests to England or, going one step further, had an English establishment. In other words, they relied solely on a sufficient connection with England.

With so many European companies borrowing under English law loan agreements, the issue is particularly important for the European restructuring market. Accordingly, the restructuring of the company has become a template for the use of an English scheme to restructure non-English companies with English law debt obligations. The advisers on the restructuring were Gila & Co, Bryan, Mansell & Tilley LLP and Freshfields Bruckhaus Deringer LLP.

2. Background

La Seda, and the group which it heads, is one of the leading manufacturers of purified terephthalic acid (PTA), polyethylene terephthalate (PET), packaging materials, PET recycling products, resins and polyester fibres. These materials and products are used primarily in the production of food and beverage packaging. At the

time of the restructuring, the company had 22 production sites and more than 2,000 employees. The group also had operations and subsidiaries in a number of other countries, including Portugal, Greece, Italy, Turkey, Romania, the United Kingdom, Belgium, Germany and France.

From 2005 the group grew significantly through a series of acquisitions within the European PTA, PET and PET packaging sectors. These acquisitions were intended to transform the group from a fibre producer to one of the largest integrated PTA, PET and PET packaging groups in Europe. The goal of this growth strategy was to achieve scale and become the leader in the PET production and PET packaging markets in Western Europe.

3.   Pre-restructuring corporate structure

Figure 1 sets out a simplified corporate structure chart for the group before the restructuring.

Figure 1   La Seda de Barcelona, SA

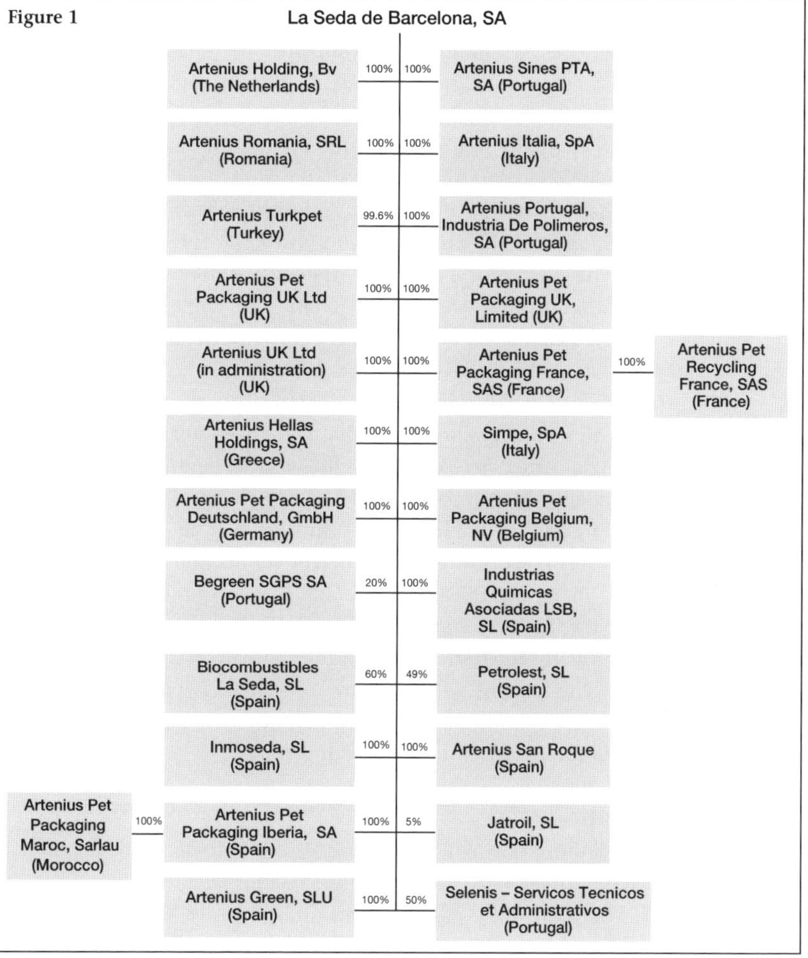

At the time of the restructuring, the La Seda board was made up of six directors. Three of the directors were the companies – or were directly related to the companies – that ultimately made the new capital investment into the company as part of the restructuring. Of the three remaining directors, two were company executives and the third, Mr Carlos Gila, was appointed to assist with the restructuring.

4. Pre-restructuring capital structure

Figure 2 sets out a simplified diagram of the group's capital structure before the restructuring.

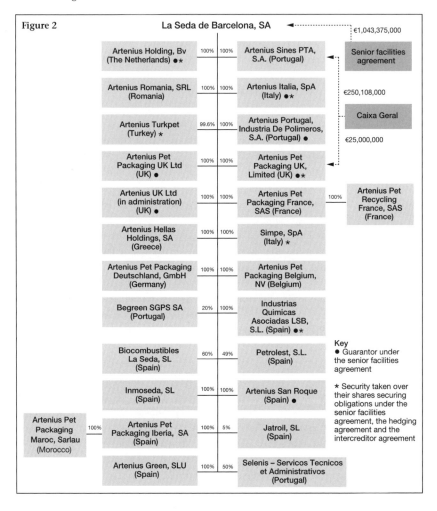

In summary, by a senior multi-currency term and revolving facilities agreement of June 8 2006 between the company and Deutsche Bank AG (acting as arranger, agent and security trustee), the lending institutions under the facilities provided the company with the following facilities of up to €603.3 million. (of which €578.6

million had been drawn when the scheme was launched):

- Facility A – a term loan of up to €163.3 million, which amortised every six months commencing on December 31 2007 and matured on June 30 2013. At the time of the restructuring, the principal amount outstanding under Facility A was approximately €145.8 million.
- Facility B – a term loan of up to €265 million, which matured with a bullet repayment on June 30 2014. At the time of the restructuring, the principal amount outstanding under Facility B was approximately €257.8 million.
- Facility C – a term loan of up to €100 million, which amortised every six months commencing on December 31 2010 and matured on June 30 2013. At the time of the restructuring, the principal amount outstanding under Facility C was approximately €100 million.
- Revolving facility – a revolving credit facility of up to €75 million. At the time of the restructuring, the principal amount outstanding under the revolving facility was approximately €75 million.

The senior facilities agreement was governed by English law.

In addition, the following documents were entered into in relation to the senior facilities agreement:

- a hedging agreement between the company and the hedge counterparty, under which those parties entered into a number of interest rate swap agreements to hedge part of the interest rate liabilities under the senior facilities agreement; and
- an intercreditor deed, under which, among other matters, it was agreed that the liabilities that were owed under the senior facilities agreement and the hedging agreement would rank equally.

Additionally the obligations under the senior facilities agreement (together with any obligations under the hedging agreement and intercreditor agreement) were secured by the company granting security over the shares of a number of its subsidiaries (see Figure 2).

The obligations under the senior facilities agreement were guaranteed by a number of the company's subsidiaries (see Figure 2). There were also share pledges over key subsidiaries; however, no asset level security was given by those subsidiaries.

In addition to the senior facilities agreement, the following main bilateral facilities were granted by the Portuguese state bank Caixa Geral de Depósitos, SA to:

- Artenius Sines PTA, SA and the company as guarantor, in respect of a number of bridging loans relating to the construction of a petro-chemical industrial plant in Sines, Portugal – at the time of the restructuring, €250,108,000 had been drawn under these facilities; and
- two UK subsidiaries to provide working capital – at the time of the restructuring, €25 million had been advanced under this facility for short-term liquidity purposes, as the group was running out of cash.

5. Restructuring triggers

In 2008 the company experienced severe trading difficulties as demand for its finished products weakened, oil price-related raw material costs rose and low-cost competition from the Far and Middle East significantly eroded its margins. These factors had a serious negative impact on the group's operations, causing it to suffer a severe lack of liquidity.

By the fourth quarter of 2008, these difficulties resulted in the company breaching a number of its financial covenants under the senior facilities agreement. Further breaches occurred during the course of the following year and the debt ceased to be serviced, resulting in payment defaults.

In April 2009 the audit revealed significant past accounting malpractice and, as a result, the preliminary 2008 results were significantly downgraded from an operating loss of €153 million to €561 million. A KPMG report uncovered questionable trades and other irregularities which became the subject of investigations by the authorities. The chairman and the chief operating officer resigned and a new chairman and Carlos Gila were appointed to lead the company's turnaround efforts. At the same time, Bryan, Mansell & Tilley LLP was appointed as restructuring and turnaround adviser to the group.

Difficulties for the group continued to increase throughout 2009. For instance:

- in July 2009 one of the group's UK subsidiaries, Artenius UK Limited, (AUK) was placed into administration in the United Kingdom – this was prompted by a winding-up petition that was issued against AUK by a creditor;
- two of the group's largest production plants in Spain were temporarily closed due to liquidity problems;
- the large-scale Sines project in Portugal was halted, with the contractors leaving the site and the construction project management company threatening legal action; and
- claims against the group by overdue trade creditors had reached approximately €130 million.

In June 2009 the company agreed to a standstill agreement with the senior lenders. This standstill was extended a number of times. With the protection of the standstill, the company focused on maintaining liquidity while identifying the group's viable core business and preparing a business plan and restructuring programme with the aim of attracting new capital.

6. Composition of lending syndicate and syndicate dynamic

The syndicate consisted of a mixture of funds and banks, many of which were Iberian. There was secondary trading and some special situations and distressed debt investors bought into the debt. However, no secondary fund built a significant stake and the majority of the debt remained with the primary par lenders.

A steering group of senior lenders with a significant proportion of the debt under the senior facilities agreement was constituted to handle preliminary negotiations. This included agent bank Deutsche Bank, HSBC Madrid and Caixa Geral, plus other Spanish and London-based banks. The significance of the steering role varied

throughout the process and many of the fees were paid only at the end of the restructuring.

7. Restructuring negotiation process

The key aim of the restructuring was to secure a stable and sustainable platform to allow new money to be invested into the group.

Midway through 2009, negotiations took place to identify potential parties to inject new investment into the group. Caixa Geral, which was a significant shareholder in the company as well as a lender to it, introduced BA Vidros SA, a Portuguese glass packaging manufacturer, as a potential new investor. BA Vidros SA, along with Liquidambar Inversiones Financieras SL and Caixa Geral, indicated that together they were prepared to invest €100 million into the company. However, before they made such an investment, these new equity investors required the company, among other matters, to restructure its financial debt, address some of the ongoing problems at its subsidiaries (AUK in particular) and enter into reasonable agreements with its unpaid trade creditors.

In relation to the restructuring of the financial debt, being primarily the amounts owed under the senior facilities agreement, meetings between the company, the equity investors and representatives of the senior lenders took place from September to November 2009 in Madrid, Lisbon and London. In addition, a number of all-party senior lender conference calls were held over the same period. These meetings and calls resulted by mid-November in a preliminary agreement for a rescheduling of part of the sums owed under the senior facilities agreement, together with a proposed debt-for-equity swap.

7.1 The restructuring

The proposed restructuring comprised the following components:
- group operational changes, which included:
  - a refocusing of the business on PET applications;
  - divestment of the raw materials part of the business;
  - a major cost-cutting programme; and
  - a wholesale change of senior management;
- new investment into the company of at least €150 million; and
- the restructuring of the company's debt under the senior facilities agreement.

7.2 New equity investment

The equity investors stated that, subject to the fulfilment of certain conditions, they would invest a total of €100 million in the company. To facilitate these investments, the company proposed to increase its share capital. However, the company additionally sought money from other sources in order to obtain a further €50 million investment.

In summary, it was proposed that there be an equal distribution of equity between the new equity investment of €150 million (which would in part comprise the €100 million investment proposed by the equity investors) and the senior lenders. Thus, it was proposed that €150 million of the debt under the senior

facilities agreement be converted into equity in the company. This would mean that both the senior lenders and the new equity investment would each own 41.4% of the company's equity, which left existing shareholders with 17.2% of the company. Such a high amount was unpopular with some of the senior lenders, which felt that 5% was more in line with similar recent restructurings. This issue contributed to delays and the subsequent failure to achieve unanimity of senior lender support.

At an extraordinary general meeting (EGM) in December 2009, it was put to the shareholders that, among other matters, the share capital of the company be increased by €300 million through the issue of new shares. These new shares would have the same financial and voting rights as the shares already issued by the company. KPMG was commissioned by the company to prepare a fairness report that supported the equity dilution. This was presented to the shareholders at the EGM and, after protracted debate, the proposed equity issuance was accepted by shareholders.

7.3 The financial restructuring

In broad summary, it was proposed that the claims of each senior lender against the company under the senior facilities agreement be settled by:

- the allotment and issuance of shares pursuant to the debt-for-equity swap;
- an allocation of debt under Facility A;
- an allocation of debt under a new payment-in-kind (PIK) facility; and
- cancellation of Facility B, Facility C and the revolving facility.

7.4 Other challenges

Throughout the period in which the restructuring was negotiated, talks continued to reschedule the €130 million that was overdue to trade creditors. This involved a number of separate but linked initiatives, including:

- putting in place much stricter cash-flow discipline for all members of the group;
- contacting critical vendors and stopping hostage payments;
- managing cash prioritisation centrally to ensure that critical suppliers were paid and maintained their supply;
- negotiating repayment programmes that were consistent with the restructuring, many of which were signed to become effective when the capital increase was completed; and
- avoiding litigation through negotiation, despite missed deadlines and extended timelines caused by delays in the implementation of the restructuring.

The most pressing challenge during the negotiation period was presented by AUK in England. As previously noted, it had been placed into administration in July 2009. According to the company's records, AUK was owed over €30 million by the company and various members of the group. The administrators also had potential claims against the company and members of the group in respect of a further possible €50 million of multilateral group netting transactions which had relatively

recently pre-dated the administrators' appointment, making an aggregate of over €80 million of potential claims by AUK. On the other hand, AUK owed a substantial amount to the company and members of the group, some of which had the potential to be offset, although it would have necessitated a complex analysis of where set-off would have been permissible. Netting these amounts would benefit both AUK and the company by avoiding a claim by AUK against various group companies, which would have resulted in their insolvency – which itself could have triggered an insolvency of the company at group level.

Pursuant to a settlement agreement of March 25 2010, it was agreed that AUK would release virtually all debts that were owed to it by the company and the group, and that the administrators would not pursue legal claims against the company or its subsidiaries in respect of the netting transactions. Essentially, it was a 'drop hands' between AUK and the group on agreed terms. Without reaching an agreement, it is likely that the company would have had to file for Spanish insolvency. This would have in turn led the senior lenders to claim against AUK as a guarantor under the senior facilities agreement, which would have caused the return to AUK's other unsecured creditors to be reduced significantly. The settlement was made subject to completion of the restructuring.

In June 2009 it had been forecast that €20 million of bridging finance would be required to fund the group through the restructuring, assuming a January 2010 completion. This was obtained in two tranches: the first from Caixa Geral (€5 million in October 2009) and the second from the Catalan State Funding Agency, the ICF (€15 million in February 2010).

7.5 Options for the group's business

The company believed that, in the absence of a successful restructuring, part or all of the group was likely to enter into insolvency proceedings. If that occurred, the board believed that it was likely that the proceeds available to the group's and the company's respective creditors (including the senior lenders) would be reduced to a level that was considerably lower than if the restructuring, of which the proposed scheme formed a part, were implemented.

This view was supported by a draft report that the company obtained in October 2009 from PricewaterhouseCoopers which, among other matters, estimated the recovery for scheme creditors if the company were placed into an insolvency procedure in Spain. This report was provided in draft form at that time and was not finalised because of issues surrounding the settlement of fees. In summary, the report concluded that on an insolvency of the company, the senior lenders would recover approximately €212.5 million. This equated to a recovery of less than 40% of the sums owed to them under the senior facility agreement (as of June 2009). Moreover, the report concluded that such recovery was likely to take a minimum of two to three years and estimated that if the restructuring were implemented, the percentage of recovery for senior lenders was likely to be between 69% and 94% by December 2014.

8.   Implementation of the restructuring

8.1   Lock-up agreement

In early 2010 the company entered into a lock-up agreement with some of the
scheme creditors. Appended to the lock-up agreement was a debt term sheet that set
out the agreed restructuring of the company's indebtedness under the senior facilities
agreement. The lock-up creditors agreed, subject to certain conditions, to support the
restructuring on the terms set out in that debt term sheet. By the time that the
scheme was proposed, over 75% of the scheme creditors had signed the lock-up
agreement.

However, not all of the conditions precedent to the lock-up agreement had been
achieved by the time that the scheme was proposed. Furthermore, the terms of the
debt term sheet appended to the lock-up agreement differed from the terms
appended to the scheme following continuing negotiations between certain senior
lenders, the company and the equity investors.

For the above reasons, the lock-up agreement was not binding on the senior
lenders at the time of the scheme meeting.

8.2   Implementing the financial restructuring

There was not unanimous senior lender support for the restructuring. As a result, the
financial restructuring was implemented pursuant to a scheme of arrangement under
Part 26 of the Companies Act 2006. The main advantage of such a scheme – which
allows for a court-enforced compromise between a company and its creditors – is
that, in very basic terms, it permits a minority of dissenting creditors to be dragged
along with a proposal provided that a sufficient majority of creditors support it.
Under Spanish law, such a 'cram-down' procedure is not available to companies
outside a formal insolvency process.

In an innovative move, it was suggested that the company, despite being
incorporated in Spain, could implement a scheme in England that bound
its creditors where they were located. The group benefited from having a UK
subsidiary which was a substantial operating business with significant employees in
the United Kingdom. Further, one of the company's employees was based in the
United Kingdom. Consideration was given to whether the company's centre of main
interests could be moved to England. However, as a listed Spanish company with
Spanish tax residency, this was impossible. Accordingly, a plan was developed to use
an English scheme, based on the company having a sufficient connection with
England and an English establishment. Some parties questioned this in light of issues
in Germany, where the effectiveness of the Equitable Life English scheme to bind
German creditors was being challenged. However, the company believed that its
situation was different, with English law obligations being subject to the scheme
rather than non-English law obligations (in Equitable Life, the challenge in Germany
related to German law-governed obligations).

After discussions with the interested parties, the company proceeded with the
English scheme and became the first Spanish company to implement such a scheme.

The scheme set out the restructuring proposals for the company's debt under the

senior facilities agreement. It proposed that, provided certain conditions were met (the most important being that the company obtain at least €150 million of new investment), the restructuring of the debt under the senior facilities agreement would take place as follows:

- The company would issue and allot new shares with a total value of €150 million to the senior lenders in return for the partial settlement of the claims of the senior lenders against the company with respect to their participation in the debt under the senior facilities debt.

If, during the rights issue, more than 150 million new shares were subscribed for by the existing shareholders of the company, the equity investors or any third party, then the scheme lenders' entitlement to receive the new shares as part of the debt-for-equity swap would be reduced on a pro rata basis. Instead, scheme lenders would receive a cash sum equal to the value of the new shares that they would have otherwise received.

- Amounts due under Facility B, Facility C and the revolving credit facility would be automatically converted into either new Facility A loans (with the principal amount of the new Facility A increased to €235,730,000) or into sums due under a new PIK facility.
- The terms and conditions of Facility A would be amended.
- The scheme lenders would release various members of the group (see Figure 3).
- All security interests securing any obligation of the company or the group in the company would be released.
- A number of additional members of the group would accede to become guarantors of the company's performance of the senior facilities agreement (see Figure 3).
- Facility B, Facility C and the revolving facility would be automatically cancelled.

If all the preconditions to the restructuring were not satisfied or waived by October 31 2010, the scheme provided that the restructuring would not take place and the scheme would cease to have effect.

8.3 Implementation of the scheme

At a hearing on April 30 2010, the English court gave the company permission to convene a meeting of the senior lenders to vote on the scheme.

The scheme meeting was held on May 21 2010. The notice period for the meeting was truncated due to severe liquidity issues and on the basis that the senior lenders had been aware of the broad commercial terms and proposed scheme for several months. Forty-one of the senior lenders voted at the meeting, representing 76% of the syndicate by value. Of those 41 senior lenders, 37 voted in favour of the scheme and four voted against it. Of those that voted, 95.54% of the senior lenders (by value) voted in favour of the scheme and 4.46% voted against it.

Under the Companies Act 2006, for a scheme of arrangement to be passed at a

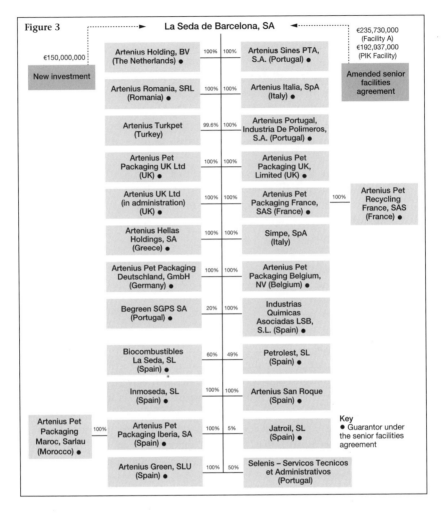

Figure 3

scheme meeting, a majority in number representing 75% by value of those creditors attending and voting at the meeting must vote in favour of the scheme.

Accordingly, on the basis of the above voting figures, the scheme achieved these statutory majorities and was successfully approved.

The sanction hearing of the scheme was held on May 26 2010. No senior lenders appeared at the hearing to object to the scheme and the scheme was sanctioned by the court at the hearing.

8.4   Issuance of new shares

In order to issue the new shares, the company had to follow the Spanish procedure for a share capital increase. In accordance with what was agreed at the EGM, there was an initial 15-day pre-emption period to allow existing shareholders in the company to subscribe for new shares. This pre-emption process raised €83.2 million, exceeding the target by €33.2 million. Under the terms of the scheme, this meant

that the senior lenders received €33.2 million in cash, thereby reducing their entitlement to equity by the same amount.

Once the allocation of new shares under the pre-emption process was completed, the company was permitted to allow the remaining shares to be subscribed for by new investors for cash (eg, the equity investors) or by way of set-off of debt.

Once all conditions under the scheme had been achieved, the company allotted and issued each scheme creditor with its share of the new shares in accordance with the provisions of the scheme and paid cash in place of such shares to the extent necessary.

On August 10 2010 it was confirmed that at least €150 million of the company's shares had been subscribed for in the share issues. The following day it was confirmed that all conditions to the restructuring becoming effective had been fulfilled. The restructuring, in accordance with the terms of the scheme, became effective on that date.

9.   Final closing structure
The group structure, including the new debt structure, is set out in Figure 3.

10.   Comment
As mentioned, the company was the first company incorporated in Spain to use an English scheme of arrangement to restructure its English debt obligations. It was subsequently followed by the Spanish company restructuring of Metrovacesa, with many billions' worth of debt, using an English scheme.

The impact has stretched further across Europe, as seen by the use of English schemes to restructure the English law debt obligations of German companies Telecolumbus, Rodenstock and Primacom. Furthermore, the use of English schemes by non-UK companies has prompted other European countries to review their insolvency regimes to consider implementing similar restructuring mechanisms in their own jurisdictions.

The authors would like to thank David Bryan from Bryan, Mansell & Tilley LLP and Nick Stern from Freshfields Bruckhaus Deringer LLP for their help in preparing this chapter.

Schoeller Arca Systems

Holly Neavill
Latham & Watkins
Teun Struycken
NautaDutilh

1.   Synopsis

In December 2009 Schoeller Arca Systems Services BV – in cooperation with its senior lenders and existing shareholders – completed a financial restructuring, which was implemented by way of a Dutch court-permitted private enforcement sale procedure. It was the first-ever Dutch pre-pack pursuant to which the existing shareholders reinvested in order to maintain ownership of the business, the senior lenders remained whole and the 'out-of-the-money' portion of the junior debt was released using contractual release provisions set out in an English law governed intercreditor agreement.

This case is interesting not only for the novelty of the local law procedure used to implement the restructuring, but also because it is a rare example of a pre-packaged enforcement and contractual release of junior claims where all parties accepted that the group's value broke, to some extent, into the junior debt. In other high-profile cases at around the same time (eg, IMO Carwash) and since, pre-packs and contractual releases have typically been used by companies and senior lenders where value has been shown to break conclusively into the senior debt.

The Schoeller precedent focused awareness on what was, at the time, a little-known restructuring procedure, but which could:

- potentially provide a viable (and even more flexible) alternative to an English pre-packaged administration;
- avoid the stigma associated with restructuring inside a formal insolvency regime; and
- save time, money and, in certain cases, the additional risk associated with shifting the centre of main interests of a non-UK entity to England.

Given the vast number of leveraged buy-outs that have been structured using Dutch holding companies, including Endemol, Premier Foods, Bulgaria Telecom and European Directories, it is unsurprising that this case has received widespread attention.

2.   Background to group operations

Schoeller Arca Systems is a global market leader in the field of plastic packaging systems. It has operations in more than 50 countries, including in Europe, America and Asia, with its head office located in the Netherlands. The group has its own production facilities and has formed local partnerships/joint ventures in various countries. It

provides products and services to a range of industries, including agriculture, automotive, beverage, fluid handling and processing, postal services and retail.

The group was created as a result of a merger between Dutch company Schoeller Wavin Systems and Swedish company Arca Systems. Schoeller Wavin Systems had been established in 1999 after a merger that united two of the industry's leading companies in plastic solutions for logistics and product branding: the German/Swiss Schoeller Plast Group and the Dutch Wavin Trepak Group. It led the European crate and tray market for the beverage industry and pooling companies. Arca Systems was a division of the Perstorp AB Group, which was, at the time, quoted on the Stockholm stock exchange.

In 2009 the group's aggregate turnover was approximately €490 million and it employed some 1,000 employees.

3. Pre-restructuring corporate structure

At the time of the restructuring, management owned a 10% stake in the group, with the remaining 90% owned by the ultimate holding company, Magnum SAS Investments BV, in which a private equity sponsor (and an affiliate of one of the bridge lenders) owned 60% and the Schoeller family owned the remaining 40%. The Schoeller family was the original founder and owner before a significant investment made by the sponsor in December 2007.

4. Pre-restructuring capital structure

The group raised €142 million of senior secured debt in December 2007. At the same time, it raised €180 million of subordinated secured bridge financing from two international financial institutions with the intention of refinancing this with a high-yield bond issuance. This refinancing did not occur, principally due to the significant macro-economic events that took place in 2008. The senior and subordinated loan agreements were governed by English law. In addition, one of the holdco entities owed approximately €11 million to the Schoeller family, representing a vendor loan, which was subordinated to the senior debt and the bridge debt.

The group's obligations in respect of the senior and bridge debt were secured by certain asset and share pledge securities that were held by a common security trustee (which was also one of holders of bridge debt). Among the security package was a first-ranking Dutch law governed right of pledge granted by Magnum SAS Acquisition BV over shares in Schoeller Arca Systems Services BV, both Dutch companies.

The relationships between the senior lenders, bridge lenders and vendor loan noteholders, and the contractual ranking of the group's obligations to those lenders, was documented by an English law governed intercreditor agreement. As is typical in English law leveraged finance documentation, the intercreditor agreement contained provisions authorising the security trustee to release all of a group member's liabilities to its lenders, as well as any security interests it had granted in favour of those lenders, in connection with any sale of shares of a member of the group which had been undertaken as part of a security enforcement process (ie, following an event of default under the senior/bridge loan agreements). The proceeds from security

Figure 1. Pre-transaction structure

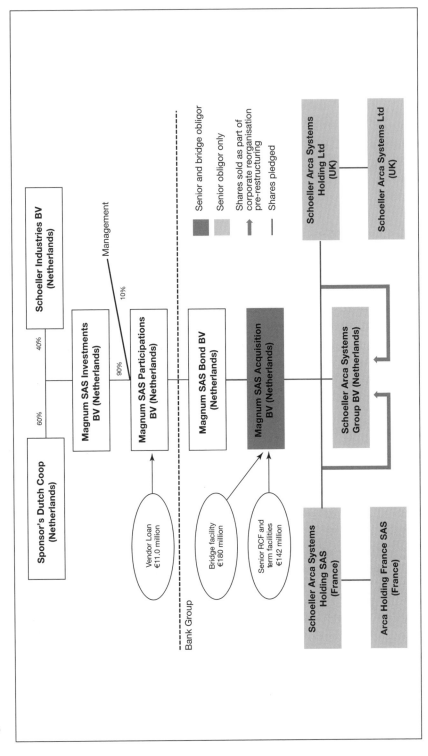

enforcement were to be applied first to repay the senior debt. Once this was repaid in full, they would be directed towards the bridge debt and then, following full satisfaction of this, to the vendor loan noteholders.

5.   The group's financial situation in the lead-up to restructuring

Before the restructuring, the group's financial situation was tenuous in light of the global economic downturn. The group's liabilities exceeded the value of its assets on a going-concern valuation (ie, it was balance-sheet insolvent). There had also been financial covenant breaches and the group had several liquidity shortages, despite the sponsor having contributed additional equity and financing over the previous 12 months using a variety of available baskets under the loan agreements, including the qualified receivables financing basket.

6.   Composition of the lending syndicate and syndicate dynamic

The senior lender syndicate included numerous collateralised loan obligations (CLOs), funds and banks and, during the course of the restructuring, some of the senior debt traded to distressed investors. An *ad hoc* committee of senior lenders was eventually formed to facilitate the negotiations and implementation of the restructuring. The bridge debt was held by, and remained throughout the restructuring process with, the original mandated lead arrangers.

The two bridge lenders were also holders of senior debt, which created a tense dynamic in the senior syndicate. This itself predominantly comprised senior lenders, which were in favour of a restructuring plan that involved a write-off of the entire amount of bridge debt. Naturally, the economic interests of the two bridge lenders would incline them to vote against any such plan. As a consequence, the restructuring had to be capable of implementation, notwithstanding at least two dissenting senior lenders.

Complicating matters further, one of the institutions that arranged the bridge finance also acted as a security trustee, whose cooperation would be an essential part of implementing the non-consensual restructuring. Much faith was placed in the efficacy of the internal walls between the agency and lending divisions of that institution.

7.   Restructuring negotiation process

Lengthy discussions between the company and its senior and bridge lenders took place from late 2008 to mid-2009, with the aim of reaching a fully consensual solution to the group's over-indebtedness. Numerous restructuring proposals – all of which involved a write-down of the bridge debt to some extent – were tabled, but all were ultimately rejected by the bridge lenders. Offers of settlement were made to the bridge lenders up to and after commencement of the enforcement proceedings in July 2009. One of the bridge lenders eventually accepted a settlement, but the other did not, and ultimately no unanimous agreement was reached.

At the same time that discussions with the lenders were ongoing, the company commissioned two independent valuations and its financial adviser conducted a market-testing process to solicit bids from third-party purchasers, including the

junior creditors. Ultimately, the valuations showed that value broke partially into the bridge debt and the market-testing process yielded no serious interest.

By July 2009, the company had entered a lock-up agreement with the shareholders and the senior lenders holding at least 85% of the total senior commitments, pursuant to which the parties agreed to implement a fully consensual restructuring if both of the bridge lenders acceded to the lock-up or a non-consensual 'plan B' restructuring if they did not. The principal terms of the fully consensual restructuring were as follows:

- The senior debt would be left unimpaired, but amended and restated with an uplift in interest, additional covenant headroom and so on;
- All bridge liabilities save for an amount of up to €60 million would be written off; and
- The shareholders would contribute interim bridge funding of €10 million and new money of €50 million once the restructuring was completed.

The principal terms of the plan B restructuring were identical to those above, save that the entire amount of bridge liabilities (other than the in-the-money portion of those liabilities, which would be repaid in cash) would be contractually released by the security trustee in connection with a share pledge enforcement sale, pursuant to which the company's shares would be sold by way of a Dutch court-permitted private enforcement sale procedure to a sponsor/shareholder-owned vehicle (Bidco). This was the plan that was ultimately implemented.

Because Bidco's offer would need to equal or exceed the total amount of the senior debt plus the in-the-money portion of the bridge liabilities, obtaining a reliable determination of where value broke into the capital structure was essential to the success of the offer and thus survival of the group as a going concern.

8. Implementation of the restructuring

8.1 Choice of jurisdiction

While commercial negotiations were ongoing between the company and its stakeholders, counsel to the company considered in which jurisdiction the restructuring should be implemented. One option was to implement the transaction in England by way of a pre-packaged administration sale in combination, if necessary, with a scheme of arrangement to effect the necessary amendments to the senior debt. The other option – the one ultimately pursued – was to implement the restructuring by way of a Dutch law governed share pledge enforcement process in the Netherlands.

An English pre-packaged administration sale process appealed mainly because:

- it offered a more certain outcome (tried and tested process);
- unlike the Dutch court-permitted sale process, which affords any interested party the opportunity to object to the enforcement sale, there is less likelihood that a dissenting creditor would bring an *ex ante* challenge to the sale and no public court forum for it to do so, in each case assuming clear valuation evidence; and

- unlike the Dutch court-permitted sale, which can be appealed (albeit on procedural grounds only) up to three months after it has been granted, there is no formal appeal period in a pre-pack that could lead to relatively higher indemnification liabilities.

Despite this, there were two principal commercial reasons why the company opted to implement the restructuring in the Netherlands. First, the requirement for a robust market-testing process in the United Kingdom worried the management and the sponsor/shareholders, which were reluctant to allow potential strategic bidders – including the group's main competitors – to review its financial information and commercially sensitive contracts. Second, potential negative tax consequences were associated with shifting the obligor group's relevant members' centre of main interests to England.

8.2 Enforcing a pledge in the Netherlands

The statutory framework for enforcing a pledge in the Netherlands is designed to ensure that any sale proceeds are maximised. The legislature assumed that this is best achieved by a public sale, usually by way of auction. Consequently, public sale is the rule and alternative enforcement methods are treated as exceptions that require special checks and balances, usually in the form of permission from the court.

A private enforcement sale is allowed in one of three circumstances, each designed to protect the interested parties from a sale being made at an undervalue.

The first is with consent of the pledgor and all other interested parties, such as those with a second-ranking pledge over the asset. The pledgor can validly give its consent to a private sale only after the pledgee has become entitled to enforce. Consent at the time of the pledge's creation is deemed insufficient because the pledgor must be able to take an informed decision at the time of enforcement about whether the specific offer maximises the proceeds of sale. This method of private sale will not be viable where the company is not on-side with the secured parties.

Second is with permission from the court. The court must determine whether the private sale will yield more than a public sale, taking into account the price offered by the purchaser, the nature of the collateral, the special circumstances at that time and the likelihood of a successful public sale. In order to obtain permission, the pledgee (in this case, the security trustee) submits a request to the judge entrusted with special measures, setting out the details of the intended sale and the value of the collateral. Although not legally required, it is customary and prudent to submit one or more independent valuations. The court will then set a date for a hearing, usually within three or four weeks, and render a decision within a week of the hearing. Where an urgent decision is needed, such as when there is an imminent risk of insolvency, the time between submitting the request and the court's decision can be reduced to a week, as was demonstrated in a later case concerning the Selexyz bookshops (Court of Utrecht, March 30 2012, LJN BW0487).

The third is a sale by the pledgee to itself with permission from the court and at a price determined by the court on the basis of valuation evidence. The secured obligations owed to the pledgee are reduced by the amount of the purchase price set

by the court, which in effect amounts to a combination of appropriation and credit bidding. Appropriation of collateral on the basis of a contractual power only is null and void and the legislation implementing the EU Financial Collateral Directive in the Netherlands applies to cash and publicly traded shares only.

In any private enforcement sale process in the Netherlands, the pledgee is in control of the process. Notwithstanding court supervision, via a bailiff or a notary, it is the pledgee that acts as seller and remains ultimately responsible for the manner in which the enforcement sale and the distribution of the proceeds is carried out. There is no need to appoint a special administrator and enforcement can be carried out inside or outside insolvency proceedings. It is still a basic premise of security laws in the Netherlands that a secured creditor is free to act without intervention from an administrator or bankruptcy trustee, and that the proceeds of enforcement of a security interest are fully available to satisfy the secured obligations.

8.3 Implementing a Dutch pre-pack by way of private sale

In the case of Schoeller Arca, the chosen method for enforcing the share pledge was a private sale with permission from the court. The security trustee as pledgee had to act as seller and request permission from the court to effect the private sale. This necessitated lengthy negotiations regarding the scope and quantum of the indemnification provided to the security trustee by the senior lenders and ultimately the sponsor, which provided the principal indemnification and back-to-back indemnities for the senior lenders.

This raises the question of why the parties did not implement this enforcement using an out-of-court private sale with the consent of the pledgor and other interested parties (see the second option in section 8.2 above), given that the group and the sponsor were orchestrating the restructuring. There were two reasons. First, the security trustee and the senior lenders, which were focused on minimising the risk of liability to the bridge lenders, considered that a sale permitted by a Dutch court would reduce the likelihood of success for any potential claims, including claims that the security trustee had sold at an undervalue. Second, it was not entirely clear, as a matter of Dutch law, which parties qualified as 'interested' and whose consent to an out-of-court sale would be needed for such sale to be valid.

More specifically, it was – and is – uncertain whether the beneficiaries of the proceeds of security (eg, all senior lenders and bridge lenders) would qualify as interested parties. There is no Dutch case law supporting the proposition that only parties with an economic interest qualify as interested, although this uncertainty was irrelevant in this case because all parties agreed that the bridge lenders were to some extent in the money.

The enforcement sale in Schoeller Arca resembled an English-style pre-pack in several ways. The terms of sale were entirely pre-agreed and Bidco's financing arrangements were in place. The type of valuation evidence used to support Bidco's offer was the same type of evidence that an administrator would require before effecting a sale. To that end, in addition to obtaining two independent valuation reports, the security trustee and many senior lenders were eager to follow the English approach on market testing, despite the fact that there was no such requirement in the Netherlands.

8.4   Valuation issues – value determiners in Dutch courts

In contrast to the abundant market practice and case law in England – which gives practitioners confidence as to the types of, and relative weight attached to, valuation evidence needed in connection with an English pre-packaged administration sale, a UK scheme of arrangement or an enforcement of security under English law – none of the practitioners knew with certainty what importance a Dutch judge would assign to the various types of valuation evidence that would be proffered by the security trustee and Bidco in connection with the first-ever court-permitted private enforcement sale in the Netherlands.

In addition, the implementation of a pre-packaged enforcement sale and contractual release of junior claims in circumstances where value did not conclusively break into the senior part of the capital structure placed a sharp focus on the importance of reliable valuation evidence. If the court was to accept that Bidco's offer represented the best price for the asset, then in the absence of a better bid, it seemed likely that such acceptance would be given only on the basis of reliable desktop valuations and sufficient evidence that efforts had been made to find the highest bidder. In the end, this proved to be correct, although the scrutiny of such evidence was not as rigorous as it would have been in an English court.

A limited market-testing process was conducted by the company's financial advisers and produced only one indicative offer, which was less than Bidco's offer. In addition, and as explained in section 8.6 in more detail, one indicative offer was submitted by a former owner of the group on the eve of the hearing, which was arguably better than Bidco's. In light of this second offer, the court adjourned the hearing and granted the bidder a brief period to complete its diligence and to remove all conditions attached to its offer. When the hearings reconvened, the alternative bid was still subject to approval by the bidder's investment committee; the court therefore rejected it on the basis that it was not deliverable. It is understood that one of the bridge lenders was the alternative bidder's principal relationship bank.

Two desktop valuations were commissioned by the company and relied upon by the security trustee. Those valuations were prepared using discounted cash-flow (DCF) analysis, comparables and leveraged buy-out methodologies. Bidco's purchase price for the company's shares comprised:

- the assumption of all senior debt owed by the pledgor; and
- approximately €13.5 million in cash, which represented that portion of the bridge liabilities that were in the money using the top end of the narrow range of valuations indicated by the independent valuations.

As mentioned previously, Bidco would also be capitalised with €50 million of new money, which would benefit the post-restructured group; the judge took this into consideration when considering whether to approve Bidco's offer.

The bridge lenders obtained their own independent valuation, which suggested that Bidco's offer was less than the group's lower range of value. Similar to the behaviour of the junior creditors in the IMO Carwash case, the bridge lenders' valuation was not made available to the company or the senior lenders until a couple of days before the court hearing. However, in stark contrast to the junior lenders'

valuation in the case of IMO Carwash, the valuation commissioned by the bridge lenders was produced using customary and accepted valuation methodologies (including DCF analysis). In theory, their valuation could not be dismissed out of hand by the Dutch court.

As the junior creditors to IMO Carwash had done only a few weeks earlier, the bridge lenders argued that there was intrinsic value in the business, which meant they could recover more or even all of their claims over time. Accordingly, they petitioned the court to withhold permission for the sale to Bidco because it would deprive them of their residual claim/interest in the business and wrongfully and unfairly transfer this potential value/upside to the existing sponsor and shareholders, which were contractually and legally subordinated to the bridge lenders. The Dutch judge ultimately rejected these arguments on essentially the same grounds as the judge in the IMO Carwash case: the finance documents gave the senior lenders a right to enforce their security and sell the business for what it was worth on the date of enforcement and to release any residual out-of-the-money claims of the bridge lenders. There was no obligation on the senior lenders to wait to see whether the group's value would increase in the future.

In its final judgment, the court stated: "In circumstances where no unconditional and better offer is made than the offer of [Bidco], and the pledgee and pledgor are in agreement with the offer of [Bidco], it cannot be determined that in the current circumstances the proceeds for which the shares are being sold do not at this time represent the maximum possible proceeds."

The valuation reports and the market-testing process seem to have been of limited significance to the court. Remarkably, the court's judgment in no way discusses the reports or its methods for valuing the group. The judge indicated that he did not want to enter into discussions about valuation methodology as actual bids matter more to determine the market value of an asset than a valuation report. With a clear bid on the table, which was not entirely off the mark set by two valuation reports, and an alternative bidder on the scene, no further attention was paid to the valuation reports.

8.5   Structuring issues

Because the two bridge lenders were also holders of senior debt, the restructuring needed to be capable of implementation, notwithstanding the existence of at least two dissenting senior lenders and the dissenting bridge lenders. To address this, implementation was designed in a way that would trigger the company's ability to replace the two dissenting senior lenders through the use of so-called 'yank-the-bank' provisions in the senior facilities agreement.

To achieve this, the restructuring had to incorporate an element that would require unanimous senior lender consent. If this was supported by senior lenders holding at least 85% of the senior commitment, it would then give the company the right to require the dissenting senior lenders to transfer their senior commitments to a third party at par plus accrued. In this case, implementation was structured to include a novation by the pledgor of its rights and obligations under the senior facilities agreement to Bidco as the element requiring unanimous senior lender

consent, and therefore triggering the yank-the-bank provisions. The senior debt held by the dissenting bridge lenders was acquired by the sponsor and ultimately rolled into the amended and restated senior facilities as a separate tranche of term debt carrying a higher rate of interest than the other tranches, but with no voting and limited information rights. Timing the replacement of the dissenting senior lenders was critical – the sponsor would be willing to purchase the debt of dissenting lenders only if it had sufficient certainty that the restructuring would be implemented, yet such a purchase could not, for various other reasons, occur as the final step in the restructuring. It was ultimately completed six business days before the final restructuring effective date.

The novation served a second important purpose – following novation of the pledgor's senior obligations to Bidco, the cash portion of the consideration for the purchase of the company's shares could be paid to the security trustee and applied to satisfy the bridge liabilities, which were, post-novation, the liabilities next in line for repayment in accordance with the intercreditor agreement. This avoided the need for an amendment to the waterfall provisions set out in the intercreditor agreement, which would have required the consent of bridge lenders.

8.6   Alternative bid

The bridge lenders aggressively contested the restructuring proposal, which involved the write-off of all but 7% of their claims. One of their strategies involved floating an alternative bid for the company. The bridge lenders never actually tabled a bid of their own, but continuously stated that there would be a much higher bid from a third party. Indeed, very late in the process, a former co-owner announced its interest in buying the group. The alternative bidder had co-owned the group until 2007, when it sold its 60% stake to the existing sponsor.

The new bidder wrote a letter to the court, requesting admittance to the hearing and setting out its intention to make a much higher bid for the company subject to a number of conditions, including completion of due diligence on the group and the approval of its internal investment committee. At the court hearing, the new bidder was allowed to set out its views on the value of the group and explain its offer and the conditions to which it was subject. The court explicitly stated that the new bidder was admitted not as an interested party in the statutory sense, whose interests must be protected, but as a party whose views and proposals were relevant for determining whether it could allow the private sale to Bidco as proposed by the security trustee.

The court adjourned the initial hearing for a brief period and ordered the company to provide information needed by the new bidder to finalise and deliver an unconditional offer. An exchange of information took place and protracted discussions and debates were carried out in the following days about whether the company had provided sufficient information. The court was informed about the status by means of letters from the different parties. On September 2 2009 (eight days after the hearing was adjourned), the court ended the discussion and announced that it would issue a decision on September 10 2009. In the Netherlands, when a court rules that discussions are closed, no party may address it further, except with the

consent of all parties. Nevertheless, the alternative bidder instructed its English solicitors to write a letter to the Dutch court on September 8 2009 which contained a more detailed offer, albeit still subject to some conditions. The company, the security trustee and the senior lenders all took the view that the offer:

- was not firm and committed;
- wrongly assumed the senior lenders would be willing to provide staple financing; and
- was merely a sham in order to prevent the release of the bridge liabilities (recall that the alternative bidder was an entity with ties to one of the bridge lenders).

Although the court had previously declared that discussions were closed, it decided that it could neither allow nor reject the proposed enforcement sale to Bidco without hearing further the views of all parties on this more detailed offer. It therefore ordered a second hearing for this purpose. At the time, this decision caused some concern among the parties advocating a restructuring. Upon further reflection, however, it seems that this was a clever way of ensuring that no party could reasonably argue that it had not been heard properly. A violation of the fundamental right to due process would have created an exceptional possibility to appeal the court's decision. Appealing the grant of a private sale would otherwise be impossible as the statute itself provides that such grants are not appealable. In fact, the second hearing gave the bridge lenders a second chance to substantiate their claims that the bid accepted by the security trustee did not constitute the best offer available. The bridge lenders did not seize this second chance, which was expressly mentioned in the court's final judgment set out below.

8.7 Identifying and minimising the potential liability of the security trustee

The enforcement process in the Netherlands, unlike an administration sale in England, does not involve nominating an administrator who would exercise discretion, take responsibility for the sale and shield the security trustee from virtually all risks of liability towards any party. In the Dutch court-permitted private enforcement sale process, the security trustee is responsible for requesting permission from the court to sell the shares and for carrying out the sale to the extent allowed. As a result, a full liability analysis was undertaken by company counsel with counsel to the security trustee in order to identify and quantify the potential liability under both Dutch law (in relation to the restructuring process itself) and English law (in relation to the contractual duties and obligations contained in the English law governed finance documents). The security trustee required, as a condition to its willingness to perform its central role as seller of the pledged shares, an indemnity from the sponsors that included cash held on account with an undertaking to fund additional amounts requested. This cash-collateralised amount was escrowed until the expiration of the statutory limitation periods on the potential Dutch and English claims (the longest of which was 12 years).

As a result of the alternative bid having been tabled by the group's former co-owner, the security trustee increased the amount of cash collateral required to be held on account in support of its indemnity.

8.8   Court's decision

In a judgment dated September 29 2009 (LJN BJ8848), the court in Amsterdam allowed the private sale by the security trustee to Bidco. The judgment contains valuable guidance on the powers and duties of the parties involved in a private enforcement sale in the Netherlands, and on the criteria which courts should use to determine whether a private sale is a permissible way of enforcing a pledge.

(a)   *Timing of enforcement*

It was undisputed that the pledgee had the right to enforce the pledge as a result of the pledgor being in breach of the finance documents and ultimately in default of a payment obligation, as required under the laws of the Netherlands for enforcement of security. However, the bridge lenders did ultimately question whether the group was in severe financial difficulties and argued that there was sufficient time for the pledgee to arrange a public auction, which would be fairer on all creditors, or to allow alternative bidders more time to come up with a higher price. The court explicitly ruled that upon a payment default, it is up to the pledgee to decide whether and when to enforce its security interest. In this regard, the court said: "This means that the debate about the cash flow of the company is not relevant for the question whether the exercise of the right of summary execution is necessary on short term. It is at the discretion of the pledgee to determine the timing of enforcement, which it has done by filing the request for approval."

The mere fact that enforcement at a certain time may not be to the advantage of junior creditors does not preclude the pledgee from exercising its enforcement rights, as junior creditors have chosen to accept a subordinated pledge. The court went on to say that this does not mean that a pledgee is entirely free to disregard the interests of creditors with a subordinated pledge or interest. According to the court, if the chosen method of enforcement creates unnecessary prejudice to junior creditors – which will be the case only if there is sufficient evidence to suggest that the enforcement will not result in the maximum, or most optimal, proceeds with loss of value for the other creditors as a consequence – then such method/timing of enforcement would be precluded.

(b)   *Public versus private enforcement sale*

Despite the widely held view that a public auction of shares can almost never be successful, the bridge lenders argued that the enforcement should take place by public auction instead of a private sale because it would result in a higher purchase price and greater return to the bridge lenders. The Dutch court said that "it can be assumed that a private sale will result in a higher purchase price than a sale of the shares by an auction, taking into account the structure and complexity of the Schoeller Arca Systems group and the necessity of further financing thereof."

(c)   *Purpose of refinancing*

In its summary of the facts, the court made clear that it was well aware that the share pledge enforcement amounted to a financial restructuring in which:

- neither the sponsors nor the senior lenders would lose their economic

interests in the group;
- no actual satisfaction of the senior secured obligations would occur; and
- the bridge lenders would be the parties taking a substantial loss.

It is significant that the court did not rule that enforcement of the share pledge should be prohibited for this reason; instead, the court stated that in these circumstances it should proceed with great caution with respect to the procedures to be followed. On this basis, the court justified giving the bridge lenders and the alternative bidder a second chance by ordering a second hearing before it decided whether to allow Bidco's offer.

(d)   The alternative offer from Stirling

The court focused on determining whether the alternative offer made by the former co-owner of the group was 'real' by considering whether it was an 'unconditional' and 'better' offer. It concluded that the alternative offer was not unconditional because, among other things, it remained subject to the bidder's investment committee approval, despite the bidder having been provided with additional time to satisfy or remove this condition. The court further concluded that the alternative offer could not be seen as better because some of the senior lenders had confirmed during the hearing that they would not agree to provide staple financing to the bidder's offer. Therefore the court ruled that "because it was established at the hearing that no agreement was reached with all senior lenders in respect of the alternative offer, the feasibility of the alternative offer could not sufficiently be established". It would seem that the Dutch court saw it as entirely within the senior lenders' gift to elect or refuse to provide staple financing to any particular bidder (although the senior lenders did have commercially reasonable grounds for refusing the alternative bidder). More recently, where senior lenders lock up to a certain bid and refuse to offer staple financing to alternative bidders, they are often accused by junior creditors of chilling the market (ie, discouraging other potentially better bids).

(e)   Conclusion

The judgment ended with a surprising quirk. The court held that the uncertain macro-economic conditions and unrest in the financial markets necessitated that it set a long-stop date on its grant, which would be valid until December 1 2009. After that date, the pledgee would have to seek new permission. This unexpected and unrequested decision proved problematic to some of the parties involved for the following reason. When negotiating the share purchase agreement, the security trustee insisted on a three-month window for effecting the share transfer following permission by the court. This was because, in the unlikely event that an appeal was made on exceptional procedural grounds (the only available grounds), it would need to be lodged within three months.

However, the timeframe set by the court meant that the grant would expire before the end of the three-month appeal period. It took extra effort and additional promises to get the security trustee and the senior lenders to agree to complete the transfer of the company's shares to Bidco before the expiry of the appeal period. Most

probably, the court was unaware of this concern when setting the time limit and took the view that no extraordinary appeal was likely, thus not imagining that the parties would want or need to wait for the expiry of the appeal period to effect the share transfer.

9. Final closing structure

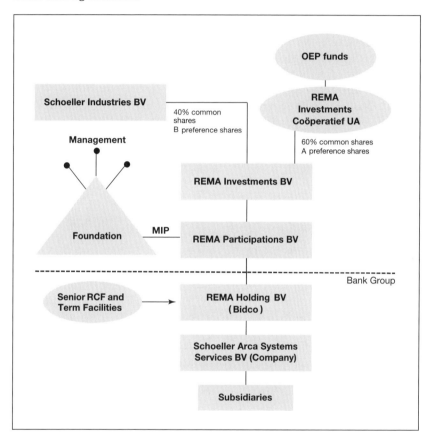

10. Conclusion

The Schoeller Arca restructuring set an important precedent and paves the way for subsequent restructurings to be implemented by way of a Dutch share pledge enforcement procedure.

The decision has shown that a court-permitted enforcement of a share pledge in the Netherlands is a viable implementation option. The procedure offers an incremental degree of protection for secured parties against liability by virtue of there being a court-permitted process, which lends legitimacy and credibility to the underlying offer.

In addition, to the extent that conclusions can safely be drawn from a single precedent, the Schoeller case establishes that the Dutch court-permitted sales process

affords some additional flexibility to stakeholders, which may be unavailable in traditional English administration sales, where management buy-out or senior loan-to-own strategies accompanied by the release of junior claims have typically been carried out only where value has been shown to break conclusively into the senior debt. In that respect, it was an interesting test case, which supports the general proposition that a secured party is free to exercise its contractual rights of security enforcement at the time and in the manner it so chooses. So long as there is no alternative deliverable bid and the valuation evidence is reasonable, it appears possible for secured parties to effect pre-packaged sales even where valuations are on the cusp or break into the junior part of the capital structure.

Risanamento

Bruno Cova
Paul Hastings

1. Synopsis

Risanamento SpA[1] is a real estate company listed on the Milan stock exchange. Certain investment decisions and the worldwide financial crisis have led it to the brink of insolvency. In July 2009 the public prosecutors of Milan started bankruptcy proceedings against Risanamento. However, Risanamento successfully fended off the risk of bankruptcy by entering into a restructuring agreement under Article 182*bis* of the Bankruptcy Act,[2] one of a series of restructuring tools introduced in Italian insolvency law only a few years ago. Risanamento's restructuring was finally approved by the Tribunal of Milan in a landmark decision on October 15 2009.

Risanamento's restructuring resulted in an extraordinary outcome for the company's bondholders, highlighted the uncertainties inherent in the execution of contractual arrangements in a jurisdiction governed by a foreign law and demonstrated the impact that external factors – in this case, the initiative of the public prosecutors – may have on complex restructurings.

The economics of the restructuring involved, among other things, the restructuring of debts of €1.25 billion, a €130 million share capital increase in cash, a €20 million debt-to-equity swap and the issuing of a €350 million convertible bond.

2. Background

2.1 Factual background

While the company's operational activities date back to 1888, Risanamento was first incorporated on September 23 1998 as Domus Italica SpA, a company into which was incorporated Società pel Risanamento di Napoli SpA (established in 1888 in Naples). Domus Italica subsequently changed its name to Risanamento Napoli SpA and then to its current denomination, Risanamento SpA. The company is listed on the Milan Stock Exchange.

In its early years, Risanamento's core business was the management of properties in the south of Italy and, on behalf of financial institutions, other properties in Italy. In 2000 Risanamento sold a significant part of its assets to another major Italian real

---

1   This chapter is based on publicly available information. Most relevant documents are available at the following websites: Consob, www.consob.it/main/emittenti/societa_quotate/index.html?codconsob= 182990#; Borsa Italiana, www.borsaitaliana.it/borsa/azioni/scheda.html?isin=IT0001402269&lang=it; and Risanamento, www.risanamentospa.com/bilanci-e-relazioni/.

2   Royal Decree No 267 of March 16 1942 (the Bankruptcy Act).

estate player, Pirelli RE (now Prelios), and then, under the leadership of Luigi Zunino – Risanamento's *dominus*[3] – set about expanding its activities into property development and other real estate businesses, such as buy-to-rent investments and acquisitions of smaller real estate groups and their associated assets.

Between 2002 and 2006 Risanamento continued its usual business activities, but starting in 2007 the company entered into the following material transactions that later became important factors in the company's restructuring:

- the Santa Giulia project;
- the ex-Falck project;
- the issuance in 2007 of €220 million in convertible bonds, due in 2014 and listed on the Luxembourg stock exchange (Euro MTF);[4] and
- the company's increased presence abroad with, in particular, material investments in luxury buildings in New York (24,000 square metres on Madison Avenue) and Paris (*Champs Elysées* and the *Triangle d'or*).

Risanamento became a major real estate player, active mostly in Italy, but with significant investments in other jurisdictions (eg, United States and France).

Risanamento was subsequently described by the *Financial Times* as:

Italy's biggest real estate casualty of the financial crisis. The Risanamento saga is a classic example of over-indulgent banks extending cheap money to an over-ambitious property developer in the middle of a bubble with predictable results.[5]

The company was structured as a multinational group that materially leveraged its financial resources and focused on three main areas of the real estate business: development, trading and management.

2.2 Legal background

Since an *ad hoc* law was introduced in December 2003 to assist the restructuring of Parmalat, Italy has seen several reforms of its insolvency law, all aimed at facilitating out-of-court and in-court restructurings. Risanamento's restructuring was implemented using one of a series of new pre-insolvency restructuring instruments that were introduced in Italian bankruptcy law (or significantly reformed) only in 2005 – namely, the Article 182*bis* proceeding, of which the Risanamento restructuring is the most notorious application to date. Article 182*bis* of the Bankruptcy Act is intended to prevent bankruptcy and simultaneously facilitate the bail-out of corporations that face financial or industrial crisis.

---

3   Risanamento's pre-restructuring activity was often described as a 'one-man show'. This is probably due to the fact that from 2000 to 2009, Luigi Zunino controlled more than 70% of Risanamento's shares and held the position of chairman and CEO. Please see the chart of Gruppo Zunino, updated as of January 26 2006 (the last one publicly available), in Figure 1 ('Zunino Group Structure in 2006').

4   The author and his restructuring colleagues at Paul Hastings represented a group of holders of these bonds in the pre-restructuring phase, during the restructuring and bankruptcy proceedings at the Milan Tribunal and in the post-restructuring phase. While this bondholders' group changed in size over time due to ongoing trading activities, it represented up to 60% of the outstanding bonds.

5   The *Financial Times*, November 11 2009, at www.ft.com/cms/s/0/5bc994e2-cef0-11de-8a4b-00144feabdc0.html#axzz1aZ5NLbgA. Copyright: The Financial Times Limited 2011. The relevant paragraph continues: "*Milan prosecutors sought to make Risanamento insolvent. But in the first major application of new Italian bankruptcy legislation, the court approved a debt restructuring agreement between the distressed company and its creditors.*"

Figure 1 – Zunino Group structure in 2006

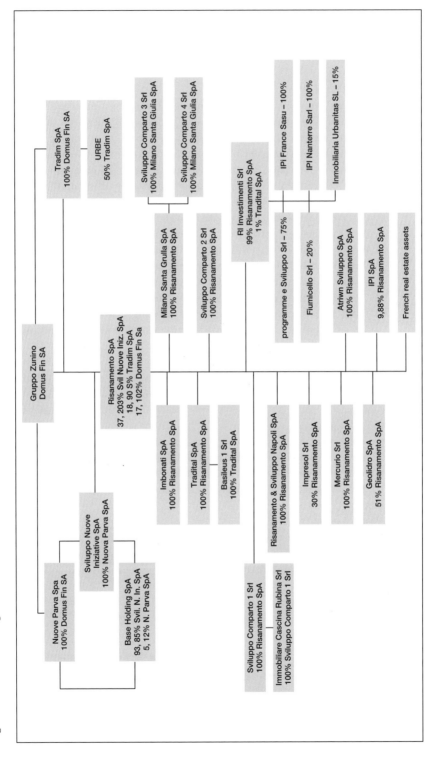

In 2012 material amendments were introduced to the Italian Bankruptcy Law by the Italian government and Parliament. The restructuring tools have been strengthened and new legal tools are available to creditors and debtors.[6]

(a)   ***Article 182*bis**

Under this proceeding, the debtor negotiates and then executes a restructuring agreement on a reorganisation plan, with creditors holding no less than 60% of the outstanding claims. The 60% figure takes into account all outstanding claims of the debtor (including intercompany debt), without regard to the nature (secured or unsecured) of the claims. An agreement under Article 182*bis* must ensure that the creditors not party to the restructuring agreement are paid in full when due.

Once executed, the agreement must be filed with both the Companies Register and the court, along with the assessment of an independent expert (appointed by the debtor) for the verification and confirmation that the proposed agreement is financially feasible and that it complies with the requirements of Article 182*bis* – that is, that at least 60% of the outstanding claims are party to the agreement and all creditors not party to the agreement will be paid in full when due.

The filing with the Companies Register, held at the Chamber of Commerce, is intended to publicise the envisaged restructuring. Creditors or other interested parties (eg, a public prosecutor) may file an opposition against the restructuring in the 30 days following publication in the register. Foreclosure proceedings against the debtor company are barred for 60 days following publication in the register.[7]

The filing with the court is intended to provide a court's supervision over the process, as it is the court's approval that closes the restructuring proceeding. However, the court evaluates only whether all Article 182*bis* requirements are met and whether the expert opinion and restructuring agreement are reasonable overall; it assesses neither the merits of the restructuring agreement nor the merits of the underlying financial or industrial plans. The Risanamento case provided useful guidance as to the scope of the court's review.

The assessment of the industrial and financial plan is made by an independent expert, who will also confirm that the finances upon which the restructuring is based are accurate and reliable.

From a practical standpoint, Article 182*bis* is often used when a debtor (one that is in a reversible crisis and intends to restructure its debt and business) can negotiate with financial creditors holding a significant portion of the debtor's total debt. Hence, the financial creditors (banks) are usually involved, but not the commercial creditors. The generally small number of financial creditors makes it possible to conduct negotiations with them and reach the 60% threshold.

---

6   For more information on these new legal tools, please see the short alert memorandum available at http://www.paulhastings.com/publicationdetail.aspx?publicationId=2216 (July 2012).

7   A material amendment of Article 182*bis* was made in 2010, adding Paragraph 6, which allows the debtor to seek an additional 60-day window during the negotiations stage (before any agreement is filed or even executed), during which any foreclosure proceeding would be barred. In theory, therefore, a debtor could obtain 120 days of protection from foreclosure proceedings: 60 days during the negotiations plus 60 days after the publication of the agreement. However, this (and other) provisions were not available when the Risanamento proceeding was pending.

While in the period immediately after its introduction Article 182*bis* was very seldom used, recently it has become more popular. Its increased use is due to the influence of the Risanamento case and certain additional amendments of the Bankruptcy Act.

Other pre-insolvency procedures were available to Risanamento: namely, a restructuring plan pursuant to Article 67 (3)(d) of the Bankruptcy Act or a *concordato preventivo* under Article 160 of the Bankruptcy Act.[8] While Risanamento elected not to resort to them, their description might be helpful.

(b)   ***Article 67***

Article 67 is an out-of-court proceeding that allows a distressed company and its creditors to carry out a restructuring plan without incurring the risk of claw-back actions, because payments and securities over the debtor's assets granted in execution of an Article 67 plan are not subject to claw-back actions, provided that such payments and securities are suitable for the restructuring of the debts and can ensure the debtor's forthcoming financial recovery.

The only independent review of an Article 67 restructuring is carried out by an expert called to assess the feasibility of the proposed financial and industrial plan. Therefore, Article 67 is a relatively swift procedure which may nonetheless need time to be negotiated and completed.

The main advantages of an Article 67 restructuring are that the company continues to operate on a regular basis, as it is a debtor-in-possession proceeding and the whole restructuring can remain confidential because there are no disclosure requirements (unless the debtor company is listed). The terms of an Article 67 restructuring are binding only on the debtor and the creditors that are party to it.

As a consequence, Article 67 is usually applied as a precautionary measure to be used in a distressed situation, rather than as the remedy of a fully developed crisis. Risanamento considered an Article 67 restructuring, but resorted to an Article 182*bis* scheme when the public prosecutors and a creditor requested the Tribunal of Milan to declare the insolvency of the company.

(c)   ***Concordato preventivo***

Concordato preventivo is an in-court procedure (ie, the court supervises from beginning to end) that is normally used either when the company is facing a crisis that cannot be solved through the other pre-insolvency proceedings or to transfer assets to a buyer that intends to insulate those assets from past liabilities.

In a *concordato preventivo*, the debtor makes a proposal to its creditors and, if the proposal is approved by creditors representing the majority of the company's debts, the proposal becomes final and binding on all creditors. The creditors may be

---

8   The Bankruptcy Act was further amended in summer 2010 – after the Risanamento case – introducing certain material amendments. Among these, two are particularly significant: Article 182quater grants a super-priority ranking to financing granted by financial institutions and shareholders pursuant to either a *concordato preventivo* or Article 182*bis*, while Article 217*bis* grants an exemption from certain bankruptcy-related criminal law crimes that may potentially be triggered from payments or transactions if performed pursuant to Article 182*bis* or a *concordato preventivo*.

divided into different classes depending on their economic position (eg, their ranking in terms of security). While *concordato preventivo* is a debtor-in-possession procedure, the law provides for deep court scrutiny of a debtor's actions and business decisions; for example, a judge delegated by the court is empowered to authorise certain transactions.

From a formal point of view, a *concordato preventivo* can be proposed only by the debtor. However, creditors may try to influence the debtor by making their own proposal and, in practice, the debtor usually negotiates the terms of the proposal with its main creditors (ie, institutional creditors) before filing for a *concordato preventivo*.

Concordato preventivo has a number of advantages (eg, no risks of claw-back actions, no third-party foreclosures allowed and the delegated judge may authorise a bridge financing), but the strong court involvement, publicity of the proceedings and the debtor's limited control over the proceedings have limited the appeal of *concordato preventivo* as a turnaround tool. It is therefore often used as a tool of last resort.

3. Pre-restructuring corporate structure and corporate governance

Risanamento's group had (and still has) the typical structure of international real estate players, where there is a clear vertical command structure of the holding company and a number of special purpose vehicles (sometimes as many as one for each building owned by the group). See the 2009 group charts in Figure 2a, 'Risanamento Structure in 2009 (Italy)'.

In the pre-restructuring Risanamento, Zunino played a key role in the governance of the company as the main shareholder, chairman and CEO.

The global financial crisis of 2008 and 2009 had a dramatic impact on many markets and strongly affected the real estate markets in the countries in which Risanamento operated. The company was not unique in facing severe distress, and several other Italian real estate players went through a restructuring process in those years, with some filing for insolvency.

The restructuring of the company took place in 2009 and was implemented in 2010 and 2011. Risanamento's board of directors changed materially, first to address the crisis and subsequently as a consequence of the restructuring agreement. The market, financing banks and relevant public authorities needed a clear signal of change, which Risanamento addressed by introducing changes to the composition of the board of directors. The shareholders' meeting that was held on April 30 2009 elected the following directors: Luigi Zunino (chairman and CEO), Umberto Tracanella, Oliviero Bonato, Matteo Tamburini, Luigi Ragno, Carlo Peretti and Angelo Tesori.

On July 20 2009 Zunino returned all his proxies to the board and on July 27 2009 the board of directors co-opted Professor Vincenzo Mariconda to replace Matteo Tamburini, who in the interim had resigned. Moreover, on August 3 2009 Professor Mario Massari was co-opted to replace Zunino, who had resigned from the board.

Following the filing of the restructuring agreement under Article 182*bis* with the Tribunal of Milan, on September 14 2009 the entire board of directors (with the exclusion of Mariconda and Massari) resigned.

Following the court's approval of the restructuring agreement, the shareholders' meeting was held on November 16 2009 and elected the new board of directors, with

Figure 2a – Risanamento Structure in 2009 (Italy)

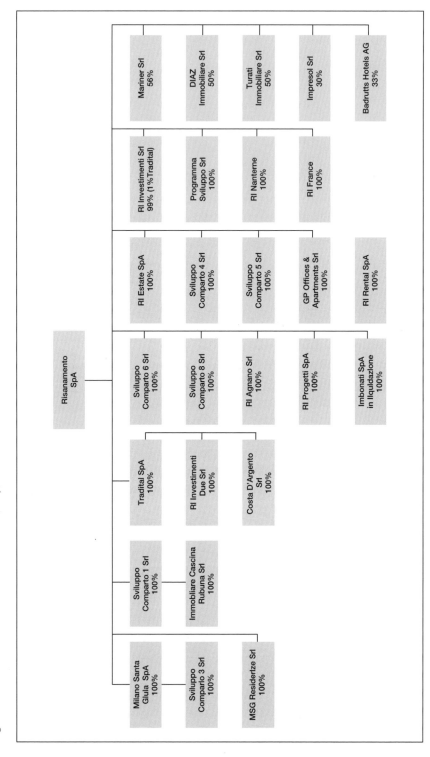

Figure 2b. Risanamento Structure in 2009 (other juristictions)

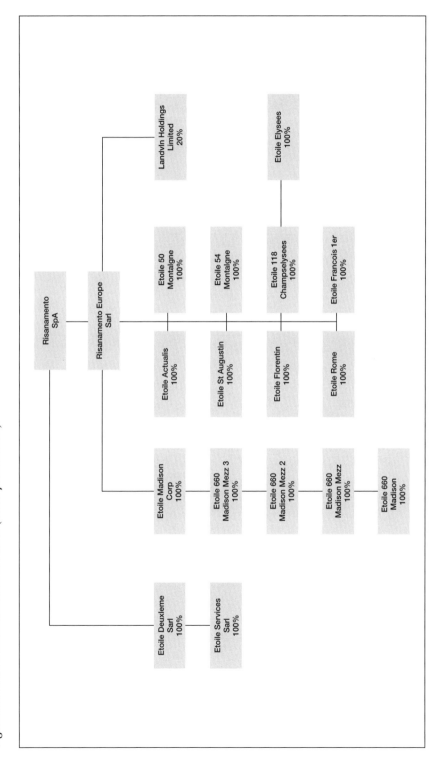

a mandate for the years 2009, 2010 and 2011. The current members of the board of directors are:[9]

- Daniele Discepolo,[10] chairman;
- Mario Massari, vice chairman;
- Claudio Calabi, CEO;
- Fabio Faina;
- Ciro Piero Cornelli;
- Alessandro Cortesi;
- Luigi Reale;
- Carlo Pavesi;
- Franco Carlo Papa;
- Sergio Schieppati; and
- Matteo Tamburini.

4.   Capital structure and financial situation

Risanamento's financial plan, dated September 2 2009, was attached to the restructuring agreement and set out the group's debt situation.

As of December 31 2008 the Risanamento group had a net financial debt of approximately €2.9 billion, of which about €1.8 billion consisted of Italian investments and about €1.1 billion consisted of investments abroad (approximately €900 million in France and €200 million in the United States). At the time, the assets (real estate) owned by the group were valued at €3 billion. As of June 30 2009 the financial net debt was calculated to be €3 billion.

In its review of May 20 2008, Merrill Lynch described Risanamento's financial situation before the restructuring:

After substantial losses in FY07A (€92m) and in 08Q1A (€39m), the book equity in Risanamento has been substantially eroded. At 12/06A Risanamento had a book value of €1.65, but by 3/08A this had reduced to €1.22. Risanamento has now been forced to sort out its balance sheet and Banca Intesa has provided an (interim) loan for €150m.

The following is a snapshot of the structure of Risanamento's debt at the time of the restructuring (with rounded figures), as included in the expert opinion:

- bank and leasing financing – €617 million;
- intragroup claims – €261 million;
- other debts – €372 million;
- total debts – €1,252 million;
- debts party to the restructuring – €879 million (equal to 70% of total debts); and
- debts not party to the restructuring – €372 million (equal to 30% of total debts).

---

9   For an up-to-date snapshot, please see Consob's website at http://www.consob.it/main/documenti/ organi_sociali/semestre1-2012/182990_OrgSoc.xml?filedate=24/09/2012&sem=/documenti/organi _sociali/semestre1-2012/182990_OrgSoc.xml&docid=0&link=&xsl= organisociali.xsl&nav=false for

10   The former chairman was Vincenzo Mariconda.

These figures refer to Risanamento alone, as a similar analysis was conducted with respect to the other companies which were party to the restructuring agreements and led to similar percentages. Please see the capital structure before the restructuring in Figure 3 on p42.

5. Lending syndicate

The banks that held the debt and were therefore involved in the restructuring were Intesa Sanpaolo SpA, Unicredit Corporate Banking SpA, Monte dei Paschi di Siena SpA, Banco Popolare Società Cooperativa, Banca Popolare di Milano Soc Coop a rl (known as Bipiemme) and Banca Italease SpA. Through the implementation of the restructuring agreement, the banks ultimately became shareholders of Risanamento, with the exception of Banca Italease, which did not join in the recapitalisation of the company.

Having only banks as parties to the restructuring agreement provided the benefit of not having major creditor ranking issues or lengthy negotiations on contractual and structural subordination of receivables and guarantees (as often happens when mezzanine or junior creditors are involved).

The negotiations among Risanamento and its lenders proceeded at a slow pace until July 2009, when the public prosecutor asked for the declaration of Risanamento's insolvency; this prompted a dramatic acceleration of the decision-making process of Risanamento and its creditors.

6. Restructuring negotiations, lead-up to restructuring and restructuring triggers

Risanamento's management had accepted that, due in part to the worldwide crisis that spread across markets in 2008, a restructuring of the company's financial structure was needed. Until the beginning of 2009, Risanamento negotiated a possible restructuring of its debts with its main financial creditors, with the ultimate goal of reaching a private agreement that would not need court approval. To this end, in April 2009 Risanamento appointed Giovanni La Croce as the expert called to validate a restructuring plan pursuant to Article 67 of the Bankruptcy Act. The complex negotiations went on for several months, without visible progress, until the situation became dramatically urgent during the summer of 2009 due to a string of pressing events.

Since February 2009, there had been press-reported rumours concerning investigations into environmental law violations on the Santa Giulia project. Such rumours increased and in July 2009 it was even hinted that allegations of money laundering were being considered.[11] Santa Giulia was a core project and a material investment for Risanamento.

On July 14 2009 Consob (the Italian securities exchange commission) requested

---

11   See the Milan newspaper *Il Corriere della Sera* articles of February 3 2009, available at http://milano.corriere.it/milano/notizie/cronaca/09_febbraio_3/santa_giulia_truffa_bonifica_cantiere_m ontecity_zunino-150964504273.shtml?fr=correlati, and of July 27 2009, available at http://milano. corriere.it/milano/notizie/cronaca/09_luglio_27/santa_giulia_procura_processo_lampo_riciclaggio-1601607859808.shtml?fr=correlati.

that Risanamento review and update its financial statements – especially the balance sheet as of June 30 2009 – while taking into account the matured debts, and provide disclosure of both its compliance with the contractual covenants and the gap between its actual results and the forecasts of the industrial plan.[12]

On July 15 2009 the public prosecutors[13] of Milan filed a claim for the insolvency of Risanamento with the Tribunal of Milan.[14] This initiative had a dramatic effect on the negotiations and the overall decision-making process. Risanamento was notified of the public prosecutors' claim on July 17. The board of directors was suddenly called either to take urgent action in a very limited amount of time or face bankruptcy; either an agreement with the company's lenders and main shareholders was to be agreed upon and signed in a matter of days or the company would be bankrupt.

On July 27 2009 Risanamento's board of directors resolved to resort to an Article 182*bis* proceeding to restructure the company. On July 29 Risanamento issued a press release indicating that the judge of the insolvency proceedings acknowledged that Risanamento had communicated its will to submit a restructuring agreement under Article 182*bis* and had set September 1 2009 as the term for filing the restructuring agreement. This term was later postponed to September 8 2009.

On August 3 2009 Risanamento engaged two certified accountants, Giovanni La Croce and Marco Giulio Sabatini, with the mandate to provide an opinion on the financial feasibility of the restructuring agreement.

On August 20 2009 certain banks (Intesa Sanpaolo SpA, Unicredit Corporate Banking SpA, Banco Popolare scarl, Banca Popolare di Milano scarl and Banca Monte dei Paschi di Siena SpA) filed a request of clarification with Consob on the possibility of obtaining an exemption from the mandatory bid provisions of the Finance Act[15] (the tender offer exemption request). More precisely, the terms of the restructuring agreement contemplated a share capital increase and the issuance of a convertible bond, and it was predicted that the implementation of the restructuring agreement would have led the banks to hold jointly more than 30% of Risanamento's shares; one of the banks alone could have reached such a percentage threshold at the end of the restructuring. Therefore, pursuant to the Italian laws and regulations concerning tender offers, the banks would have run the risk of being forced, as a consequence of the implementation of the restructuring agreement, to make a public tender offer for the entire share capital of Risanamento. Such a risk was increased by the fact that the banks intended to execute a shareholders' agreement concerning Risanamento's governance, which would have also triggered tender offer obligations.[16]

---

12 Pursuant to Article 187*decies* of the Finance Act, Consob and the public prosecutors are empowered (and in some ways even expected) to join forces when a listed company is involved in a criminal proceeding. The law allows both Consob and the public prosecutors to share information with each other, and both are allowed to obtain information on the respective investigations.

13 Under Article 6 of the Bankruptcy Act, a claim for insolvency can be filed by the debtor, a creditor or a public prosecutor.

14 Also, one trade creditor filed a claim for the insolvency of Risanamento on July 27 2009. However, this creditor (Munters Italy SpA) formally desisted from its request on September 25 2009 and its claim therefore did not affect the procedure.

15 Legislative Decree 58/1998 (the Finance Act), Article 106 in particular, and Consob Regulation 11971/99.

16 In particular, Article 101*bis* (4)(a) of the Finance Act.

Figure 3. Risanamento capital structure before restructuring

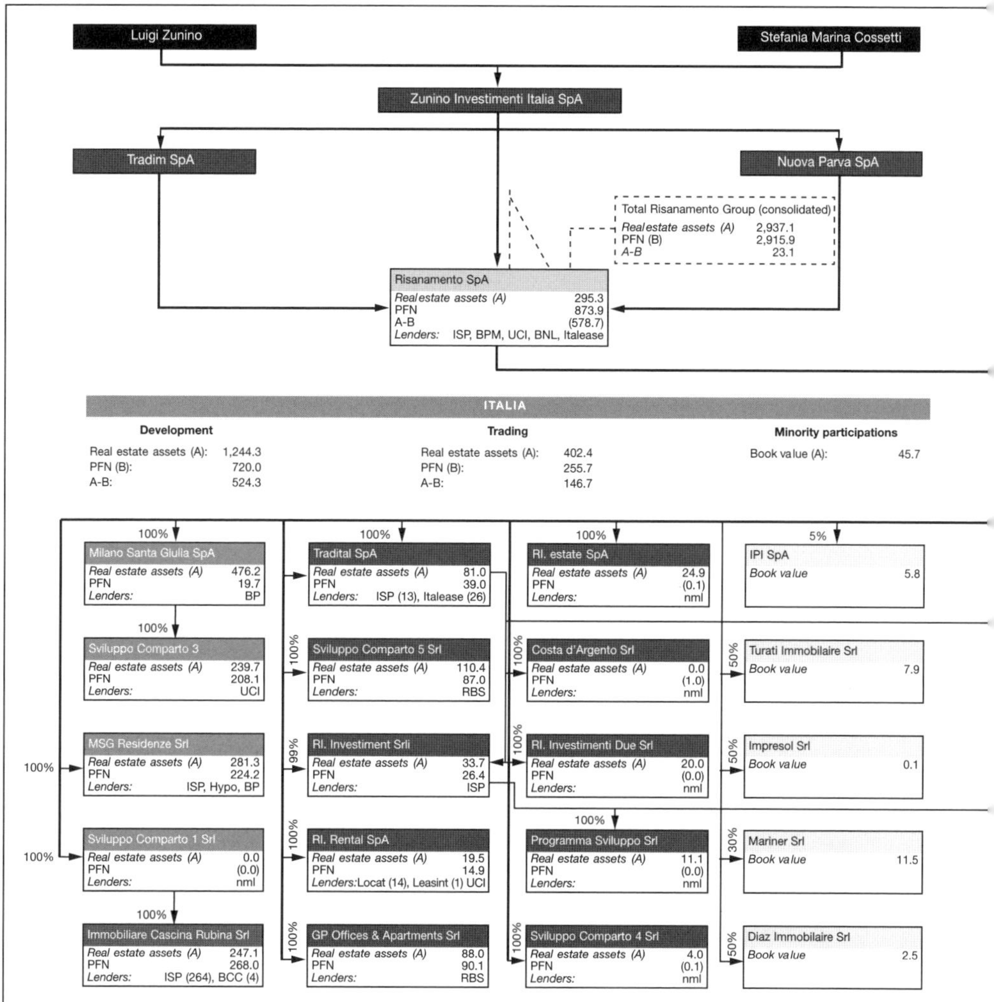

Source: Risanamento (Restructuring Agreement and its attachments).

Notes:

(1) Realestate Assets: values as at December 31 2008.

(2) Figures based on the financial statements.

(3) The chart does not include minor companies.

(4) Book value as at December 31 2006 from Madison Corp. financial statements.
Change rate $/€ 1.39.

(5) Capital value of the convertible bonds issued by Risanamento in 2007.

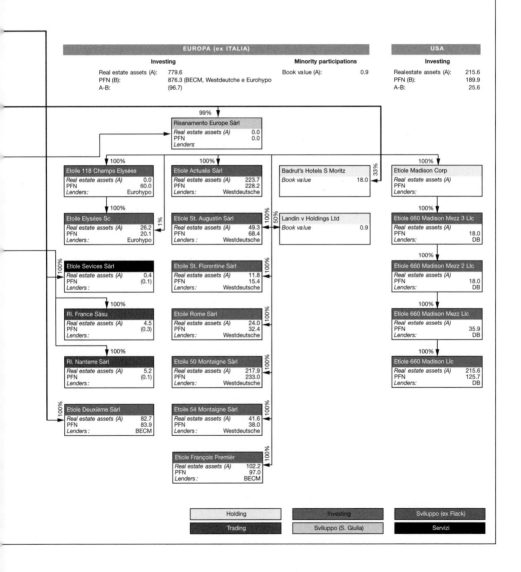

Risanamento SpA

Debt	Amount	Bank
New Unsecured	75.0	ISP, UCI, MPS, BPM
Old Unsecured	291.6	ISP, UCI, BPM, MPS, BNL, BCC
Development	51.7	BPM
Trading	280.9	Italease, Meliorbanca, BNL, ISP
POC (5)	220.0	
Cash	(45.3)	
Total	**873.9**	

EUROPA (ex ITALIA)

Investing
Real estate assets (A): 779.6
PFN (B): 876.3 (BECM, Westdeutche e Eurohypo)
A-B: (96.7)

Minority participations
Book value (A): 0.9

USA

Investing
Realestate assets (A): 215.6
PFN (B): 189.9
A-B: 25.6

The banks' request addressed the issue of a possible exemption to be granted by Consob to shield the banks from such a mandatory tender offer obligation. Consob was therefore called to evaluate whether the parameters to grant such exemption were met and particularly to assess whether Risanamento was 'in crisis',[17] whether there was a restructuring plan to address such crisis and whether the tender offer threshold would be triggered by such restructuring. Consob's exemption in favour of the banks was a key factor in making the overall transaction acceptable to the banks. On August 27, September 1 and September 2 2009, amendments to the tender offer exemption request were filed with Consob.

On September 2 the expert opinion was delivered to the board of directors. On the same day, Risanamento first approved the industrial and financial plan for 2009 to 2014 and then, along with certain controlled companies, executed the restructuring agreement with the banks. Also on that day and pursuant to Article 182*bis* of the Bankruptcy Act, the main shareholders of Risanamento (Zunino Investimenti Italia SpA, Nuova Parva SpA and Tradim SpA, jointly holding about 73% of Risanamento) executed another restructuring agreement with certain banks (Intesa Sanpaolo, Unicredit and Banco Popolare) called the 'holding agreement'.

On September 3 2009 Consob issued its favourable opinion[18] (*Comunicazione No DEM/9079430*) to the tender offer exemption request. The banks, which were acting in concert and would have jointly obtained control of Risanamento, were therefore exempted from launching a mandatory tender offer.

On September 8 2009, as soon as the restructuring agreement was executed by all the creditors involved, Risanamento filed the restructuring agreement with the Chamber of Commerce and the Tribunal of Milan.

Any opposition to the restructuring agreement had to be filed with the Tribunal of Milan within 30 days. The public prosecutors, who had previously filed the insolvency claim, opposed the approval of the restructuring agreement substantially on the same grounds upon which the insolvency claim was based.

The filing of a restructuring agreement under Article 182*bis* while the insolvency claim was already pending prompted a debate as to the effects of the Article 182*bis* restructuring proceeding (triggered by the filing of the restructuring agreement) on the bankruptcy proceeding (triggered by the insolvency claim). One interpretation of the law stated that the bankruptcy proceeding would have been automatically barred by the restructuring proceeding. Such interpretation, which was indeed favourable to the parties of the restructuring agreement, was supported by a *pro veritate* legal opinion issued by a prominent university law professor, which was filed as Attachment 19 to the restructuring agreement. According to a second interpretation supported by the public prosecutors, the two proceedings (insolvency and restructuring) were to be examined independently.

However, in its decree the court elaborated on a third interpretation of the law, according to which the restructuring proceeding did not bar the insolvency

17   This expression, which is also used in the Bankruptcy Act, is not defined. It is believed to refer to a company in the zone of insolvency but technically not yet insolvent.
18   The full text of Consob's decision is available at: www.consob.it/main/documenti/ bollettino2009/ c9079430.htm.

proceeding; rather, the two proceedings should be examined jointly,[19] because they were tied by an inseparable connection. In other words, the two proceedings would be incompatible with each other and should therefore be addressed at the same time.

On October 15 2009 a hearing was held before the Tribunal of Milan, chaired by the president of the insolvency section of the tribunal, Judge Lamanna. The public prosecutor, Risanamento and the attorneys involved discussed the matter with the court. At the end of the hearing, the judges reserved their decision without giving any indication as to the likely outcome of their review. Only on November 10 2009, when the court decree was notified, did the parties discover that the court had already decided on October 15 to approve the restructuring agreement, thus rejecting the public prosecutors' claim for insolvency.

Pursuant to Italian procedural and substantive law, the tribunal's decree became final and binding on December 19 2009 (ie, after the 15-day term for the filing of oppositions against the decree expired with no opposition having been filed).

The validity of the restructuring agreement (and of the parallel holding agreement) was subject to the tribunal's decree becoming final and binding. Technically speaking, it was not a condition precedent but rather an automatic termination clause that would have been triggered if the court decree had failed to become final and binding. From a practical standpoint, the automatic termination clause had the same effect of a condition precedent, but provided greater legal certainty for the court's approval of the agreement.

7. Implementation of the restructuring

The overall restructuring process was intended to rebalance the financial situation of the Risanamento group. The restructuring agreement set forth the following main terms and conditions:

- The recapitalisation of Risanamento was to be achieved through:[20]
    - a share capital increase to be paid, with an option right in favour of those entitled by law (the shareholders controlled by Zunino assigned their option rights to the banks and the banks committed to subscribe them), for a total of €150 million, including principal and premium, with the simultaneous issuance of new ordinary shares; and
    - the issuance of bonds with mandatory conversion into ordinary shares (a *convertendo*), newly issued, with the option rights in favour of those entitled by law (the shareholders controlled by Zunino assigned their

19 An insolvency petition is in summary based on the assumption that the debtor is insolvent. 'Insolvency' is defined as the moment when a debtor is no longer able to fulfil its payment obligations when due. On the contrary, restructuring proceedings such as Article 182*bis* and Article 67 are based on the assumption that the debtor is 'in crisis', but such crisis is not defined by the law. Being in crisis does not necessarily entail being also insolvent. Technically, a company goes through a restructuring proceeding to recover from a crisis (not an insolvency), thus never reaching the complete insolvency status (if the restructuring takes place and is successful, of course). Therefore, when the court decided that it had to evaluate the two proceedings at the same time, a substantive and procedural law issue was raised. Interestingly, the court simply stated that the insolvency claim had to be rejected because the company had proved that the restructuring agreement was fit, in the short term, to turn around the company's crisis – therefore bypassing the 'crisis' and 'insolvency' definition debate.

20 The price for the issuing of the new shares that resulted from the share capital increase was set at €0.45 per share.

option rights to the banks and the banks committed to subscribe them), for a total of €350 million, expiring December 31 2014, and the subsequent share capital increase by issuing new ordinary shares. On March 23 2011 Risanamento's board resolved to issue such convertible bonds. These *convertendo* convertible bonds are subject to a sort of automatic mandatory conversion into shares at maturity (ie, in 2014).

- In addition to the recapitalisation of Risanamento, the restructuring agreement provided for certain additional material commitments, including in particular:
  - the banks' commitment to subscribe the share capital increase up to a maximum of €150 million by using the option rights that had been previously assigned to them (obligations undertaken and option rights assigned pursuant to the holding agreement). Such commitment was to be met by €130 million in cash and €20 million in debt-to-equity swaps;
  - the banks' commitment to subscribe in full the *convertendo* convertible bonds, in the overall amount of €350 million;
  - the banks' commitment to provide a financing agreement for up to €272 million that was exclusively addressed to guarantee the repayment (at maturity or in case of early repayment) of the amounts due under the convertible bonds issued by Risanamento on May 10 2007 and due on May 10 2014, denominated as "Euro 220,000,000 1.0 per cent convertible bonds due 2014";
  - the rescheduling of certain banks' receivables with Risanamento and other companies of the group. Such rescheduling obligation also provided that the repayment of these receivables would be contractually subordinated to the entire repayment of the bonds described in the previous point, due no earlier than December 31 2014;
  - the rescheduling of all intercompany receivables until December 31 2014;
  - the banks' waiver of certain receivables in favour of the companies of the Risanamento group, with an express termination clause in case any of the companies of the Risanamento group committed a serious breach[21] of contractual obligations; and
  - Risanamento's commitment to proceed with the disposal of certain assets and to assign the proceeds of such disposals to the repayment of certain receivables, including the receivables of the banks.

On July 20 2010 the public prosecutors notified Milano Santa Giulia SpA (a special purpose vehicle wholly controlled by Risanamento) of the seizure of the Santa Giulia assets due to criminal and environmental law charges. The Santa Giulia site turned out to be polluted and its ground water poisoned. As a consequence, Risanamento requested a private consultancy to assess the potential costs arising out

---

21   Article 1455 of the Civil Code is recalled by the wording of the agreement, which provides that a breach of contract will not cause the termination of the agreement if such breach is irrelevant or of little relevance.

of the possible clean-up of the Santa Giulia site and also requested a new external adviser to prepare an overall updated property valuation of Risanamento's assets. The clean-up costs of the site were estimated at around €80 million and as a result, a provision was made in the draft updated financial statement.[22]

Risanamento's shareholders' meeting was held on October 30 2010 to resolve upon, among other things, the interim financial statements as of June 30 2010, which reported a loss of €451,076,783. That loss was more than one-third of Risanamento's share capital and therefore, under Article 2446 of the Civil Code, the company had to take appropriate measures. The shareholders' meeting resolved to approve such interim financial statements.

The shareholders' meeting also resolved to revoke the shareholders' resolution of January 29 2010 concerning the €150 million share capital increase and at the same time resolved to approve (substantially) the same share capital increase but on slightly different terms: 536,714,338 new shares were to be issued, each at a price of €0.28, for an overall amount of €150,280,014.64. The resolution for the issue of the convertendo convertible bonds followed a similar path: the previous resolution was revoked and a new resolution was taken authorising the issuance of *convertendo* convertible bonds for a maximum of €255 million.

On that same day (October 30 2010), the parties – Risanamento, the banks as creditors and the shareholders (which included the banks)[23] – executed additional agreements that substantially confirmed the terms and conditions of the restructuring agreement, updated certain provisions and aligned the terms with the company's new financial situation. Such agreements could have been construed as new obligations, and therefore a new Consob exemption from mandatory tender offer was requested. On January 13 2011 Consob confirmed its opinion and the exemption that it had granted on September 3 2009.[24]

On January 13 2011 Consob[25] authorised Risanamento to publish the prospectus for the €150 million share capital increase. On the same day, Risanamento filed and published the prospectus.[26]

By February 24 2011 the share capital increase had been fully implemented, thus modifying the shareholding structure. The final step of the restructuring implementation – on the financial and capital consolidation side – took place over the summer of 2011, while the industrial side is ongoing. More precisely, on May 18 2011 Consob approved the publication of the prospectus relating to the offering of a total of 254,816 *convertendo* convertible bonds, each with a nominal value of €1,000, with a compulsory and automatic conversion into Risanamento's shares at maturity. All such bonds had been fully subscribed by June 21 2011.

---

22 See Risanamento's press releases of September 7 2010 and October 30 2010.
23 On October 30 2010 Risanamento's board of directors also approved the procedure for related parties transactions, pursuant to Consob Regulation 17221/2010, as amended by Consob Resolution 17389/2010.
24 Consob Resolution DEM/9079430.
25 Consob Decision 11002118 (January 13 2011).
26 The prospectus was filed with Consob, Borsa Italiana and the Luxembourg Stock Exchange, and is available at Risanamento's registered office.

Material factors affecting the restructuring agreement

Role of bondholders

The holders of the convertible bonds that were issued by Risanamento on May 10 2007 and due on May 10 2014 created an *ad hoc* committee that played a significant role in Risanamento's restructuring. The committee intervened in the court proceedings to support Risanamento's request that the Tribunal of Milan approve the restructuring agreement by writing a letter to the tribunal and the public prosecutors and by participating in the hearing of October 15 2009. The bondholders stressed how their position, and that of other creditors that were not parties to the restructuring agreement, would have been materially impaired had the tribunal declared the insolvency of Risanamento.

The terms of the restructuring agreement were very favourable to the bondholders, as in practice their claim was treated as senior to those of the secured creditors (ie, the banks that were parties to the restructuring agreement). As previously mentioned, the bondholders obtained a commitment from the banks to guarantee the repayment of the bonds at maturity or, if triggered, in case of early repayment. The banks' commitment was provided in the form of a term-sheet attached to the restructuring agreement that described the main terms of a financing agreement that the banks provided to Risanamento to be used exclusively to repay the bonds.

The bonds were governed by a trust deed which contained, among other things, customary provisions as to the acceleration of the repayment of the bonds in case of certain events, including cross-defaults and change of control. The trust deed was governed by English law, but the restructuring agreement was under Italian law and the bonds were issued in Italy, and there were conflicting interpretations of the terms of the trust deed, particularly of the change-of-control provision, which caused uncertainty among the parties involved (Risanamento, the bondholders and the banks party to the restructuring agreement). The issue highlighted the risks inherent in the implementation of contractual provisions governed by a foreign law in the context of a different legal regime – an issue which is not uncommon in cross-border restructurings and that has been seen in other high-profile Italian restructurings.

Criminal proceedings

Another material issue that put the restructuring agreement under stress was the criminal investigation that concerned the Santa Giulia assets. Santa Giulia, a real estate property of Risanamento that was intended to be developed and sold, was seized by the public prosecutors for alleged violations of environmental law. Such seizure had a financial impact due to the clean-up costs of the site and to the devaluation of the assets' portfolio. However, Risanamento obtained confirmation of the banks' commitments under the restructuring agreement and, in amendments executed in October 2010, substantially confirmed its restructuring plan.

8.   Final closing structure

The group structure in 2011 was as follows on the next pages.

Figure 4a – Risanamento Structure in 2011 (Italy)

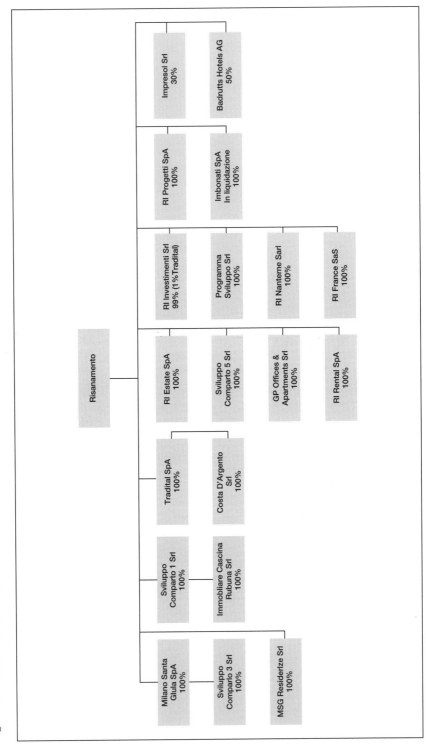

Figure 4b – Risanamento structure in 2011 (other jurisdictions)

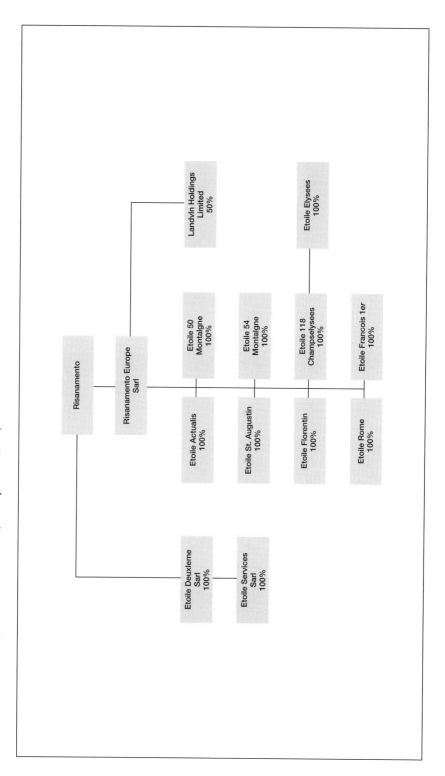

Figure 5 – Shareholding structure in 2011

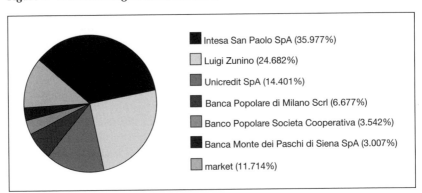

Intesa San Paolo SpA (35.977%)

Luigi Zunino (24.682%)

Unicredit SpA (14.401%)

Banca Popolare di Milano Scrl (6.677%)

Banco Popolare Societa Cooperativa (3.542%)

Banca Monte dei Paschi di Siena SpA (3.007%)

market (11.714%)

Risanamento's group structure remained substantially the same as it had been before its restructuring, while the shareholding structure changed materially – not only because Intesa Sanpaolo SpA and the other banks were now the reference shareholders (rather than Zunino), but also because the free-floating share capital was reduced.

In the prospectus of the new *convertendo* convertible bonds issued in 2011, Risanamento pointed out that with an agreement executed on October 30 2010, Risanamento had received a representation from the banks concerning each bank's best effort to ensure that Risanamento's free-floating share capital remained sufficient to not interrupt trading activities (ie, to avoid a delisting of the company).

9. Conclusion

Risanamento's restructuring has been a landmark case in Italy for a number of reasons.[27] The restructuring produced the unusual consequence of a *de facto* inversion of the priority of the claims, with the unsecured creditors (in particular, the bondholders) having their claim fully recognised and the secured creditors converting a significant part of their claims into company equity. This was due to a number of unusual circumstances, chief among them the banks' desire to avoid Risanamento's insolvency and the tight timeline dictated by the public prosecutors' initiative.

The Risanamento case was the first major test of an Article 182*bis* restructuring.[28] Such a test is especially meaningful because this restructuring proceeding was used to forestall the public prosecutors' request for a declaration of insolvency. From a procedural point of view, there were therefore two parallel proceedings that were

---

27   An analysis of the procedural and substantive law implications of the Risanamento case is available in the articles (in Italian) of Franco Bonelli and Ugo Molinari, published in *Crisi di imprese: casi e materiali* (Giuffré, Milan, 2011). In the same book, Bruno Cova contributed the chapter on multinational corporations' restructurings in Italy. At the end of the book is a copy of Risanamento's restructuring agreement, the court decree approving the restructuring agreement and the minutes of the Risanamento shareholders' meeting in which the restructuring agreement was approved and implemented.

28   Please see footnote 6 for more information on the new restructuring tools available under Italian law, some of which were introduced in 2012.

incompatible with each other, as the Article 182*bis* procedure was aimed at restructuring the company, while the public prosecutors' initiative was aimed at a declaration of insolvency of the company. The bankruptcy proceeding was activated before the restructuring proceeding,[29] and it was less complex from both a documentary and burden-of-proof point of view. The court decided to unify the two proceedings and ultimately ruled in favour of the restructuring, thus rejecting the insolvency claim.

The court also stated some important principles that have clarified certain aspects of Article 182*bis* proceedings. In particular, the tribunal determined the following:

- The court will rely on the expert's opinion assessing the feasibility of the restructuring plan and the accuracy of the financial information upon which the restructuring is based and of the expected turnaround. Therefore, the expert (along with the external auditors that review the company's financial statements) will carry the burden of the responsibility of such assessments.
- The court will evaluate whether all the Article 182*bis* requirements are met, and whether the expert opinion and restructuring agreement are reasonable overall, without becoming involved in the merits of the financial or industrial arguments.
- In conducting its reasonableness assessment, the court will evaluate from a period of about one year after the date of the restructuring agreement, without necessarily assessing the viability of the restructuring plan in the medium to long term, as such a forecast would be subject to too many variables (eg, the restructuring agreement set forth terms, conditions and forecasts from 2009 to 2014, but the court limited itself to a one-year forecast, stating that the conclusions reached in the restructuring agreement and in the expert opinion seemed reasonable enough as a one-year forecast).
- The court will evaluate the merits of the restructuring agreement or plan only insofar as any opposition against it is filed by a dissenting party (eg, a creditor not party to the agreement or the public prosecutor) and only to such a degree as is commensurate with the level of opposition against such agreement or plan. Therefore, the degree of the court's scrutiny is variable.
- There was a prejudicial connection between the bankruptcy proceeding and the Article 182*bis* proceedings, because an Article 182*bis* restructuring is *per se* an alternative to bankruptcy, expressly comparing it to a *concordato preventivo* procedure. Therefore, the court stated that when a bankruptcy proceeding is pending and an Article 182*bis* restructuring is filed, the two proceedings must be examined jointly.

The author would like to thank Anteo Picello for his assistance in preparing this chapter, and his colleagues Antonio Azzarà, Paolo Manganelli and Anteo Picello for their work in representing a group of international investors on the Risanamento matter.

---

29   However, it should be taken into account that in August in Italy there is almost no business or legal activity, and even court proceedings and the running of legal terms are suspended.

Almatis

Kon Asimacopoulos
Kirkland & Ellis International LLP
Justin Bickle
Oaktree
Adam Paul
Kirkland & Ellis LLP

1. Introduction

In the middle of the global financial crisis, Almatis BV and its affiliates faced financial issues that were common among many companies in cyclical industries at the time: a downturn in operations and revenue, an over-leveraged balance sheet and an inability to find financing alternatives. However, what made Almatis unique was how – as a Dutch and German company – it resolved these issues.

The Almatis Group's operations consisted primarily of alumina manufacturing. Headquartered in the Netherlands, it maintained significant operations in Germany and the United States, as well as smaller operations in China, India, and Japan. As a consequence, its capital and corporate structures were extremely complex. Following a swift and sharp drop in steel consumption during the global recession, the group found itself in dire financial straits and in mid-2009 it received the first of nine forbearances from its lenders. Over the next 10 months the group negotiated the terms of a restructuring with the assistance of its senior lenders, led by Oaktree. The restructuring allowed Almatis to emerge as a much stronger and more competitive company, having significantly deleveraged its balance sheet. This restructuring was achieved through the filing of a US Chapter 11 bankruptcy case and swift confirmation of a plan of reorganisation by a US bankruptcy court. The use of the US Bankruptcy Code and a Chapter 11 filing to reorganise such a large and complex non-US company was a watershed moment for European restructuring, which continues to be viewed as precedential by non-US companies in search of restructuring options that may be impossible under local regimes.

In addition, Oaktree managed to leverage its 'loan-to-own' strategy into a proposed Chapter 11 plan that resulted in a nine-digit profit for its investors and a 74% internal rate of return. This success has provided other distressed funds with a blueprint for analysing whether and how to invest in troubled companies with multiple European operations.

2. Background to group operations

At the time of its restructuring and Chapter 11 cases, the Almatis Group was a global leader in the development and production of speciality alumina materials, employing around 900 people worldwide. Originally, the group was a division of Alcoa Inc. In 2007, following a spin-off from Alcoa to private equity firm Rhone Capital – on what were, in hindsight, very attractive terms – the group was acquired by a Dutch acquisition entity, DIC Almatis Bidco BV, which was indirectly controlled

by Dubai International Capital LLC (DIC), the ultimate shareholder. The purchase price for the group was $1.2 billion and the acquisition was financed by a combination of the secured financings that existed at the time of the restructuring and equity contributions made by DIC. At the time of DIC's buyout, the business's headline earnings before interest, taxes, depreciation, and amortisation (EBITDA) were said to be around $150 million, although this was inflated by the favourable feedstock contract historically provided by Alcoa to Rhone when it purchased the company.

In 2009 the Almatis Group generated approximately $400 million in revenue and $81 million in EBITDA. At the time that the group filed for Chapter 11, the group was projecting revenue of approximately $530 million for the following year and EBITDA of $96 million.

3. Pre-restructuring corporate and capital structure

The Almatis Group was headquartered in the Netherlands. Its ultimate parent was a cooperative entity incorporated under Dutch law. The group included Dutch, German, US and other foreign subsidiaries. The ultimate ownership interests in the Dutch cooperative – and therefore the group – were held by DIC.

The relationship between the members of the Dutch cooperative, including those that were also officers and directors of other group subsidiaries, was governed by an investment agreement. Although German law applied to the investment agreement, it was also expressly stated that nothing in the agreement would override Dutch mandatory law, which imposes fiduciary duties similar to those imposed by Delaware law in the United States.

At the time of its restructuring, the group's capital structure consisted primarily of the senior lender claims, the second-lien lender claims and the senior and junior mezzanine lender claims. In total, the group owed approximately $1.044 billion to these lenders. The senior lenders were owed approximately $681 million, the second-lien lenders $77 million and the senior and junior mezzanine lenders approximately $200 million and $80 million, respectively.

4. Restructuring: lead-up and triggers

The global financial crisis in 2008 and 2009 took a significant toll on the group's operations and financial outlook, which ultimately led to its Chapter 11 filing.

4.1 Global recession and deterioration in group trading performance

The group's operations were most significantly affected by two factors: the slowdown of the global economy in general and the steel industry in particular, and an increase in the cost of commodities. Ultimately, these deteriorating market conditions led to a drop in sales of the group's alumina product from 310,000 metric tons in the first half of 2008 to 160,000 metric tons in 2009 – a year-on-year decline of more than 50%. As a result, the group's revenue fell from approximately $311 million in the first half of 2008 to approximately $162 million in the first half of 2009, and EBITDA fell from $86 million to $27.2 million over the same period – a year-on-year decline of almost 70%.

4.2 Payment defaults, waivers and forbearances

In the face of this deterioration in financial performance, the group undertook a series of restructuring and cost-alignment efforts, but to no avail. In June 2009 the group was unable to make certain scheduled principal and interest payments under the senior lender facilities or interest payments due under the senior mezzanine facility. These payment defaults put the group at risk of violating certain cross-default terms in its other loan agreements.

Following the defaults, the group succeeded in obtaining certain waiver and forbearance agreements with its lenders which prevented the premature acceleration of its debts. Specifically, the group entered into waivers and forbearances in June 2009; these subsequently lasted for almost a year, until May 2010.

5. Lending syndicate: composition and dynamic

Based on all reasonable valuations of the group in the run-up to the Chapter 11 filing, the senior lenders were the fulcrum security, meaning that value broke in that class and the more junior creditors were out of the money. The senior lenders were a disparate group, consisting mainly of European and Middle Eastern relationship banks of DIC and various collateralised loan obligations. Given the state of the markets during the global recession, most of these lenders were unwilling to write off any of the loans held on their books; thus, the senior lenders to the group that did not sell their debt stakes entirely were particularly passive throughout much of the process. Nevertheless, the senior lenders understood the issues surrounding the operations and capital structure of the group. Therefore, they organised a coordinating committee to engage in negotiations with the group and other parties over a restructuring of the group and its capital structure.

Private equity firm Oaktree stepped into the breach. Oaktree liked the group's leading market position and the fact that it was in a highly cyclical industry, whose performance was closely linked to global steel trends. Oaktree was prepared to own the business and invest in it, provided that its balance sheet was properly deleveraged. Oaktree had no interest in a 'zombie' restructuring in which the company retained too much debt; moreover, the firm believed that the group could not protect its historically strong market position without investing in a new $50 million facility in China.

Initially, Oaktree decided to work its position as a small, but influential member of the coordinating committee. Once it was clear that the other committee members had no appetite for a full-scale balance-sheet restructuring, Oaktree resigned from the coordinating committee and sought to agree terms for a consensual restructuring with sponsor DIC. This relationship proved short-lived, as DIC was intent on preserving its equity stake in the company and ensuring smooth relations with its relationship banks and CLOs, given the preponderance of lenders to the Almatis Group that also had exposure to DIC's other stretched European portfolio companies.

Oaktree ultimately came to own approximately 46% of the senior lender claims, having built its stake at a substantial discount in the secondary market. The increase in its holdings reflected Oaktree's belief that the group's balance sheet had to be fit

for purpose, and that it was important to continue to invest in the business to ensure its long-term survival. Furthermore, the size of Oaktree's senior lender claim meant that the firm could effectively block a restructuring proposal based on a US Chapter 11 or other alternative implementation mechanism under the financing documents, since it would have sufficient votes to reject any proposed Chapter 11 plan that it did not support.[1]

All of the parties – including the Almatis Group, the coordinating committee, Oaktree, the other lenders and DIC – engaged their own legal advisers.

6. Restructuring negotiation process

6.1 Competing restructuring proposals and agreement on Oaktree's plan

Given the reluctance of the remaining senior lenders to write off any portion of their debt, the restructuring process dragged on and resulted in significant professional fees – to the consternation of both the Almatis Group and Oaktree. Since the company also had over $100 million in cash, there was no immediate liquidity crunch and thus no natural catalyst to expedite the restructuring talks.

As restructuring talks continued, a number of other options were considered, including:

- multi-jurisdictional insolvency filings in the Netherlands, the United States and Germany;
- an Oaktree/DIC proposal to deleverage the capital structure in return for an infusion of new equity into the group;
- the sale of the group to DIC as a stalking-horse bidder under Section 363 of the US Bankruptcy Code;
- multiple proposals by Oaktree to forgive a significant amount of the funded debt and allow the senior lenders to retain the equity in the group; and
- alternative proposals by DIC and the mezzanine lenders to deleverage the capital structure, in return for the majority of the shares of the group and an infusion by DIC of up to $100 milllion in new equity, or proposals that would result in the long-term forbearance of existing defaults.

In early 2010 the group, the coordinating committee and Oaktree finally agreed on the framework of a restructuring proposal that:

- significantly deleveraged the group;
- provided a feasible plan that could be effected through a Chapter 11 filing in the United States; and
- left the senior lenders with the majority of the equity.

Oaktree's support was crucial, given the blocking position that it held with respect to any future vote to accept a plan proposed by the group in a US Chapter 11 case. The Oaktree-led plan was as follows:

---

1   Under US bankruptcy law, a class of creditors votes in favour of a plan if it is supported by more than one-half (in number) and two-thirds (in amount) of those creditors that vote.

- The group's debt would be reduced from approximately $1.044 billion to approximately $410 million, consisting of approximately $273 million in new senior debt and approximately $137 million in new junior debt.
- The senior lenders could choose between distributions that provided either a larger portion of debt (Option A) or equity (Option B). Those that chose Option A were slated to receive $0.80 in new senior debt and $0.065 in cash for each $1 in principal held by the senior lender, and up to 13.5% of the equity. Those that chose Option B were slated to receive $0.45 in new junior debt for each $1 in principal held by the senior lender, and up to 86.5% of the equity.
- Second-lien lenders and senior mezzanine lenders were slated to receive warrants. The junior mezzanine lenders were not entitled to a distribution.

The group, the coordinating committee and over 60% of the senior lenders supported the Oaktree-led proposal. Thus, the group was able to propose a feasible plan that deleveraged its capital structure and, given the support of the majority of senior lenders, could be effected through a US Chapter 11 proceeding. Chapter 11 was being used because it was almost impossible to consummate a consensual plan using court processes in either the Netherlands or Germany. Given the meagre distributions (if any) to junior lenders and equity, this proposed plan attracted significant opposition.

The group's management would remain in place during the Chapter 11 process. Furthermore, in order to ensure that its management was properly incentivised, its chief executive officer and chief financial officer would each receive customary bonuses if the restructuring were successful, if the group achieved certain performance metrics and if it could participate in a management incentive plan, consistent with other US Chapter 11 cases.

6.2   Litigation in the Netherlands

The complex, tax-driven corporate structure of the group was characterised by numerous holding companies and operating entities – many sharing the same board of directors – in various jurisdictions. The group's ultimate parent had a two-tiered board structure that included a supervisory board. The members of the supervisory board of the Dutch cooperative included an independent director, the group's management and representatives of DIC. The relationship between the members was governed by an investment agreement that allowed the members to look to Dutch mandatory law for their fiduciary obligations. Thus, the members could take actions consistent with their fiduciary duty to act in the interest of creditors, as opposed to shareholders, if the group was insolvent.

In light of these fiduciary duties and the fact that the Dutch cooperative would not participate in the restructuring, the group and its advisers concluded that the members of the management of the group's subsidiaries did not need the consent of the cooperative's supervisory board in order to authorise the Chapter 11 filing and implement the Oaktree-led proposal. Nevertheless, a conservative decision was made to consult the supervisory board before initiating the Chapter 11 cases.

The supervisory board met twice in March 2010 and, after rejecting last-minute restructuring proposals by DIC, the group's management decided to proceed with the Oaktree-led proposal and the Chapter 11 filing. However, before the filing commenced, DIC filed a petition with the Enterprise Chamber of the Amsterdam Court of Appeal to enjoin the group from commencing the restructuring and related Chapter 11 cases. On April 12 2010 the Dutch court rejected DIC's petition.

7. Implementing restructuring through Chapter 11 filing

The restructuring of the group presented a number of issues: its corporate interrelations were complex, the jurisdictions were diverse and the restructuring proposal was contested. Therefore, the group decided to implement the restructuring through a US Chapter 11 process – the near-impossibility of a consensual restructuring in Europe made this the 'least worst option'.

7.1 Benefits of Chapter 11 filing

One significant factor in the group's decision to file a Chapter 11 proceeding was the global scope of the automatic stay. When a Chapter 11 petition is filed, a worldwide injunction is automatically issued which, among other things, enjoins any actions taken by parties to enforce their debt or recover the property of the Chapter 11 debtors. Creditors often refrain from actions in jurisdictions outside the United States if they would violate such an automatic stay, given the punitive penalties associated with violations and the ability of a US bankruptcy court to assert jurisdiction over such creditors if they have property in, or significant connections with, the United States. The company considered that over 90% of the creditors had some nexus to the United States, either by virtue of trading or having offices there or because their ultimate owners were based there. Therefore, the company believed – correctly, as it proved – that the creditors would not violate the court's order.

The group filed for an order confirming the extraterritorial scope of the automatic stay. This motion was granted by the US bankruptcy court and allowed the group to provide a copy of a US court order when faced with a recalcitrant creditor that demanded support for the proposition that the automatic stay applied in non-US jurisdictions.

Another benefit of a Chapter 11 proceeding was the authority of the US bankruptcy court to approve a plan and 'cram down' non-consenting junior creditors. The US Bankruptcy Code provides that creditors may be forced to accept a plan of reorganisation if:

- the plan complies with certain other elements that apply to Chapter 11 plans; and
- at least one 'impaired' (ie, not fully paid) class of claims at each entity accepts the proposed plan (ie, by more than one-half in number and two-thirds in value of the creditors voting).

7.2 Pre-packaged plan

In order to expedite the restructuring, the decision was made to file a pre-packaged bankruptcy case. Unlike the more traditional Chapter 11 proceedings, a pre-

packaged bankruptcy is characterised by the fact that the company proposes a plan of reorganisation and solicits votes on it before initiating the formal Chapter 11 proceeding. Since votes have already been cast in favour of the plan, a company can typically exit Chapter 11 within 60 days of filing for Chapter 11. In this instance, the delay associated with the proceedings before the Dutch court allowed the group to finalise the requisite plan of reorganisation and associated papers before filing, in order to accelerate its emergence from Chapter 11. Thus, the group began the process of solicitation on the proposed plan on April 23 2010, seven days before filing for Chapter 11. Ultimately, the senior lenders voted overwhelmingly in favour of the proposal; unsurprisingly, the second-lien lenders and mezzanine lenders voted overwhelmingly against it.

7.3 Other motions to promote US bankruptcy cases and reorganisation plans

US bankruptcy courts have broad discretion to fashion relief that better enables a Chapter 11 debtor to restructure. The group took advantage of this discretion and obtained a number of orders that furthered its restructuring.

(a) *Authorisation to pay non-US creditors*

Generally, a company that files a Chapter 11 bankruptcy case cannot pay amounts owed to creditors that arose before the company filed for bankruptcy. An exception applies if a company can demonstrate a true need and show that a failure to pay would imperil the reorganisation. On this basis, the group sought and received authority to pay certain claims held by foreign creditors that arose before the group filed for Chapter 11, thereby avoiding the possibility that these creditors would take adverse actions that would disrupt the group's operations. This was particularly important in respect of creditors with little or no connection to the United States, which might have considered themselves and their actions to be outside the scope of the automatic stay.

(b) *Limitations on transfer of claims*

There was also a concern that certain recalcitrant lenders which were opposed to the Chapter 11 case would transfer their claims to a holder with few or no US ties, and that the new holder would then take enforcement actions outside the United States which would imperil the group's operations and its ability to restructure. Thus, the group sought and received authority to institute certain procedures that applied to proposed transfers by its lenders. These procedures provided the group with notice of a potential transfer to a non-US transferee and the opportunity to object to it. The order entered by the US bankruptcy court also provided that any transfers made in violation of the procedures were void.

(c) *Litigation in the bankruptcy court*

Given the stark differences in recovery between the senior and more junior lenders, and the fact that DIC – the existing equity holder – would have its interests wiped out, the initial pre-packaged plan met with significant opposition. Given the litigation threat, it was clear that the process was likely to exceed the 60-day period

for most pre-packaged Chapter 11 cases. Nevertheless, since the filing was pre-packaged, the US bankruptcy court set a hearing on confirmation of the plan for July 19 2010 – just over 80 days after the filing of the Chapter 11 petition.

Over the next eight weeks the group, the senior lenders and the parties opposing the proposed plan exchanged millions of pages of documents and conducted depositions of no less than 14 witnesses in multiple jurisdictions. Nevertheless, the plan's proponents and the US bankruptcy court kept the confirmation schedule in place and multiple requests by the junior lenders to delay the confirmation hearing were denied.

The litigation was an attempt by the junior lenders to play for time while DIC continued its efforts to refinance the senior lenders and thereby avoid losing control of the business.

(d)   *New sponsor offer, subsequent agreement and amended Chapter 11 plan*
Despite the Chapter 11 filing by the management against their wishes, DIC continued to propose restructuring options. As none of the proposals seemed both credible and feasible, each was rejected by the group. However, on July 2 2010, shortly before the plan confirmation hearing, DIC finally made a proposal that was feasible, credible and deliverable in the eyes of the management team. It included a $100 million equity infusion by DIC. As a result, and in keeping with its fiduciary duties, the group engaged with DIC in extensive negotiations in an effort to reach a consensual agreement on a new restructuring proposal.

These negotiations culminated in the Almatis Group, DIC and the junior lenders entering into a new agreement to support a plan based on the most recent DIC proposal. The main terms of the proposal were as follows:

- The senior lenders would be paid in full. This payment included principal and interest, along with default interest from the date on which the group filed for Chapter 11 to the date on which the senior lenders were paid under the plan of reorganisation.
- Each second-lien lender would receive a *pro rata* share in senior unsecured payment-in-kind (PIK) notes in the principal amount of approximately €52 million. The PIK notes accrued 2% a year of PIK interest. The second-lien lenders would be able to receive certain warrants if the PIK notes remained outstanding five years after the effective date of the plan of reorganisation.
- Each senior mezzanine lender would receive a *pro rata* share of approximately 35% of the group's equity and certain junior preference shares. Each junior mezzanine lender would receive a *pro rata* share of approximately 5% of the group's equity and certain junior preference shares.
- In exchange for its equity contribution of $100 million, DIC would receive approximately 60% of the group's equity and a possible cash payment if the group's shares were sold or offered on an exchange.

All of the remaining creditors of the Almatis Group remained unimpaired under the DIC proposal. In addition, the management incentive plans remained in place.

The DIC plan left the business with much greater debt than would have been the

case under the Oaktree plan, and with a much higher annual cash interest burden. Ultimately, the management decided that the DIC plan would keep more stakeholders happy and therefore decided to support it based on its fiduciary duties.

The proposal of a plan that satisfied all of the senior lenders' claims in full represented a great economic recovery for secondary lenders, such as Oaktree, that bought into the capital structure in an attempt to own the company – that is, following a 'loan-to-own' strategy. If the DIC proposal failed, the group would revert to the original Oaktree-led plan that distributed the group's equity to the senior lenders. However, if the DIC proposal succeeded, these lenders would profit handsomely by receiving payment in full, along with default interest, since such lenders had bought their interests at well below par value. The essence of the strategy is that one's downside is covered by buying senior debt claims at a discount. From there, one either takes control of the company to make an equity-like return or is paid out at par-plus accrued interest, making an attractive risk-adjusted return through debt ownership.

The bankruptcy court confirmed the amended Chapter 11 plan on September 20 2010.

8.   Conclusion

The Almatis Group restructuring demonstrated that European companies can and should look to a US Chapter 11 process as a viable restructuring alternative where a consensual European restructuring is impossible to achieve, either because of the locations of operating assets or because of shortcomings in the local bankruptcy laws or the underlying financing documents. As European restructuring schemes continue to develop and become more uniform, it is particularly useful to be able to consider Chapter 11 as a viable scheme to restructure a large European company, especially when faced with possible uncoordinated filings in multiple jurisdictions, all with disparate restructuring laws.

Furthermore, the benefits of the Chapter 11 process are manifest from the perspective of company counsel. The worldwide scope of the automatic stay, the ability to obtain certain unique forms of relief to promote the restructuring, the bias in favour of management retaining control and the company's ability to reorganise, and the experience and sophistication of the specialist Chapter 11 courts are only a few of the reasons why companies like to have a US Chapter 11 proceeding as an alternative restructuring method.

For these reasons, the Almatis Group restructuring strategy is likely to continue to be used by restructuring professionals both in Europe and in the United States.

WIND Hellas

Ben Davies
White & Case LLP
Mark Glengarry
Morgan Stanley

1. Introduction

The restructuring of WIND Hellas Telecommunications SA in 2009 was expected to herald a new dawn by relieving financial pressures on the company and freeing up significant cash flows for an aggressive repositioning of the business. It was also a landmark restructuring, in that the centre of main interests (COMI) of Hellas Telecommunications (Luxembourg) II SCA, a Luxembourg-registered holding company, was established in England, which resulted in an English pre-packaged administration process, reducing the group's liabilities by more than €1 billion. However, the anticipated turnaround did not happen, as a severe deterioration in macroeconomic conditions in Greece led to a continued decline in performance. This chapter considers the second financial restructuring of the group, which closed in December 2010 and was notable for its complex nature and an innovative approach that employed a combination of the tools available to English law insolvency practitioners.

2. Background to group operations

WIND Hellas is a Greek telecommunications business that supplies fixed-line and mobile telephony services, as well as internet access and broadband services. The company received its inaugural Global System for Mobile Communications licence in September 1992 and launched commercial operations in June 1993. In April 2007 WIND Hellas was acquired subject to existing debt by Weather Investments SpA, the private investment vehicle of Egyptian entrepreneur Naguib Sawiris, from Texas Pacific Group and Apax Partners in a deal worth €3.4 billion.

At the end of 2008 the Greek mobile market was estimated to be worth €4.15 billion, with penetration rates of 78% and a mobile spend of 1.79% of gross domestic product (GDP) per head. WIND Hellas's two national competitors were Cosmote (a subsidiary of OTE) and Vodafone Greece. Cosmote's market share had grown from 36% to 41% in the three years to the end of 2008, mainly benefiting from Vodafone Greece's drop from 39% to 33%, with WIND Hellas steady at 25%. WIND Hellas's main competitors in the fixed-line and internet services market were OTE, Forthnet and Hellas Online. At the end of 2008 WIND Hellas had a mobile customer base of approximately 5.193 million with a fixed-line and internet customer base of approximately 783,000.

In the three years to the end of 2008 WIND Hellas had grown its total customer numbers by more than 15% each year on the basis of a successful non-premium

pricing model. However, at the start of 2009 it experienced the first signs of a deteriorating performance driven by competitive, operational and market pressures. In terms of the competitive environment, WIND Hellas was suffering from an aggressive price war which affected the whole mobile market as each of the three players slashed prices with a view to increasing their market shares. The main operational concern presented itself in the form of a network in need of rapid modernisation – low signal quality, lagging coverage with both 2G and 3G technology and significant site availability issues all contributed to the company's growing inability to attract and retain new customers. In addition, WIND Hellas had begun to experience a fall in its average revenue per user due to the recent introduction of new mobile taxes, as well as regulatory changes such as the reduction of termination and roaming charges.

A number of cost-reduction initiatives were initiated by the WIND Hellas management team in the first quarter of 2009, but these proved insufficient to offset the erosion of revenues. Against the backdrop of an increasingly weak economic climate in Greece, it became apparent that the company was generating insufficient cash to support the group's debt structure or to enable sufficient investment in its network and brand in order to remain competitive. The company soon began to consider measures to reposition the business and reverse performance – the expectation was that operational efficiencies would be achievable and competitive pressures would ease on a reduction in debt levels, given that WIND Hellas had a clear and defensible share of the market, but this would likely entail a fair and transparent restructuring of the capital structure. In November 2009 a financial restructuring of the group concluded in the reacquisition of WIND Hellas by Weather.

The 2010 Greek economic crisis occurred at a time when WIND Hellas was seeking to recover from the events of the previous year and consolidate its market position. The 2009 restructuring had left the company with a leveraged capital structure, but one that the management team had considered to be supportable in its business plan projections. However, that business plan had been prepared on the basis of an assumption that the macroeconomic conditions in Greece would remain stable. Greece's budget deficit had reached 13.6% of GDP at the end of 2009, with government debt totalling 115% of GDP. With the global economy moving into a recession, economic activity slowing and unemployment levels rising, Greece's financing costs rose and began to transform an already high debt burden into an unsustainable one. Following negotiations with the European Union, the European Central Bank and the International Monetary Fund, in April 2010 Greece announced agreement on a €110 billion financial assistance programme that was conditional on the implementation of strict austerity measures.

At the start of 2010 WIND Hellas's corporate credit rating with Standard & Poor's was CCC+, with the rating agency expressing concern about:

- the company's leveraged capital structure and aggressive financial policy;
- its limited financial flexibility;
- its exposure to a depressed Greek economy;
- its weak operating performance; and
- the tougher regulation of telecommunications operators in Greece.

The negative impact of the Greek economic crisis exacerbated the unfavourable operating conditions, in which aggressive levels of competition continued, with multiple price reductions from WIND Hellas's competitors. Downward pressure on consumer spending as a result of the government austerity measures soon led to a heavy reduction in business revenues and sustained the financial distress at the company.

The weakening fundamentals at WIND Hellas were evident in its falling subscriber numbers, and by September 2010 the company's mobile customer base had shrunk to approximately 3.88 million, with the fixed-line and internet customer base totalling approximately 556,000. The WIND Hellas management team had taken significant steps to reposition the business in the aftermath of the 2009 restructuring, such as a renewed focus on customer retention, a headcount reduction and other cost-cutting initiatives, but those measures were unable to compensate for the decline in revenues. The company's year-on-year decreases in revenues and earnings before interest, taxes, depreciation and amortisation were 18.5% and 31.4%, respectively, in the first quarter of 2010, 27.5% and 52.4% in the second quarter and 28.8% and 44.8% in the third quarter.

3. Pre-restructuring corporate structure

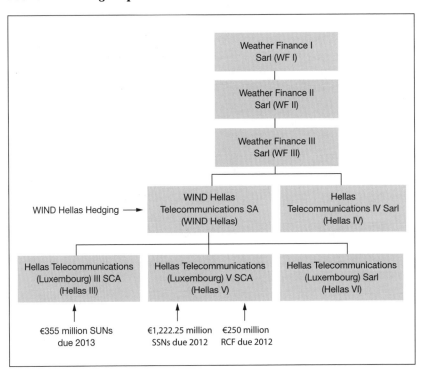

At the top of the WIND Hellas group structure before the 2010 restructuring was Weather (Italy) in its capacity as ultimate parent of the group. Weather owned Weather Finance I Sarl (Luxembourg) (WF I), which in turn owned Weather Finance

II Sarl (Luxembourg) (WF II). Weather Finance III Sarl (Luxembourg) (WF III), the next intermediate holding company in the group, was owned by WF II and itself owned WIND Hellas (Greece), the operating company and principal asset in the group, and Hellas Telecommunications IV Sarl (Luxembourg) (Hellas IV). In addition, WIND Hellas owned Hellas Telecommunications (Luxembourg) III SCA (Luxembourg) (Hellas III), Hellas Telecommunications (Luxembourg) VSCA (Luxembourg) (Hellas V) and Hellas Telecommunications (Luxembourg) Sarl (Luxembourg) (Hellas VI). Each of the Luxembourg entities in the group was a finance company with no trading activities.

4. Pre-restructuring capital structure

The 2009 restructuring of the WIND Hellas group left in place the existing financing under:

- a €250 million super senior revolving credit facility maturing in 2012;
- €1.225 billion in senior secured floating rate notes due in 2012;
- €355 million in 8.5% senior notes due in 2013; and
- super senior hedging liabilities at WIND Hellas.

The revolving credit facility provided for revolving credit facilities up to an amount of €250 million to be drawn by Hellas V. The revolving credit facility lenders received guarantees from WF III, Hellas IV, Hellas V, Hellas VI and WIND Hellas, and benefited from first-ranking security over substantially all assets of Hellas II, Hellas III, Hellas IV, Hellas V, Hellas VI and WIND Hellas.

The senior secured floating rate notes were issued by Hellas V and traded on the Luxembourg Bourse. The senior secured floating rate note holders received guarantees from WF III, Hellas IV, Hellas VI and WIND Hellas and benefited from security over substantially all assets of WF III, Hellas III, Hellas IV, Hellas V and WIND Hellas.

The 8.5% senior notes were issued by Hellas III and traded on the Luxembourg Bourse. The 8.5% senior note holders received guarantees from WF III, Hellas IV, Hellas VI and WIND Hellas and benefited from security over the WIND Hellas shares, all intercompany debt claims of Hellas III and the bank accounts of Hellas III.

The WIND Hellas hedging related to interest rate swap agreements designed to mitigate risk derived from the variable interest rate under the senior secured floating rate notes.

A new intercreditor agreement was put in place following the 2009 restructuring between certain members of the WIND Hellas group and the creditors under the revolving credit facility, the senior secured floating rate notes, the 8.5% senior notes and the WIND Hellas hedging. The intercreditor agreement provided that the transaction security granted by the various members of the WIND Hellas group ranked and secured the debts owed, and the proceeds of its enforcement ranked in right and priority of payment, in the following order:

- the revolving credit facility and the WIND Hellas hedging;
- the senior secured floating rate notes;
- the 8.5% senior notes; and
- certain intercompany debt.

The intercreditor agreement also set out the parameters within which any enforcement sale could occur, stating that the security agent would be permitted to release all security granted by and claims against WIND Hellas (to facilitate a sale of the WIND Hellas business free and clear of the debts owed to its financial creditors) if a purchaser of the WIND Hellas shares offered all-cash consideration for sale at a price supported by a fairness opinion from an internationally recognised investment bank.

5. Financial situation of group in lead-up to restructuring and restructuring triggers

As described above, the financial distress experienced by WIND Hellas before the 2009 restructuring continued into 2010 with the onset of the Greek economic crisis. At the heart of the company's fragility was an acute liquidity position that remained unaffected by the management team's efforts to renegotiate supplier terms, defer capital expenditures and reduce operating costs. It was soon apparent that the group's capital structure remained unsustainable, notwithstanding a reduction of more than €1.5 billion in its debt burden as a result of the 2009 restructuring. Crucially, the ongoing decline in revenues would ensure that at some stage in the course of 2010, the WIND Hellas group would have insufficient funds to service its debts. Immediate pressure points included a €17.5 million step down in the revolving credit facility at the end of June 2010 and interest payments due under the senior secured floating rate notes and the WIND Hellas hedging in July 2010.

The revolving credit facility was fully drawn, there were no baskets available to the company under its finance documentation for raising additional secured debt and it was clear that short-term borrowing via various types of asset-backed or unsecured financing was not an option, due to poor credit market conditions and a lack of confidence in Greek borrowers.

With the prospect of imminent defaults and cross-defaults under the group's finance documentation, and bearing in mind the applicable directors' duties in Greece and Luxembourg, it was the WIND Hellas management's view that decisive action would be required to address the operating weakness in the business, restructure the debt in the group and restore customer and supplier confidence. In addition, any solution would almost certainly have to introduce new money to address the persistent liquidity issues.

Valuation evidence indicated that the 8.5% senior note holders were fully impaired and out of the money, with no economic value in the capital structure unless the model employed an unusually high valuation multiple. The 8.5% senior notes continued to trade at prices materially above their intrinsic value, apparently the result of:

- imperfect information in the market on WIND Hellas' earnings outlook; and
- a perception that 8.5% senior note holders would be legally difficult to disenfranchise due to ambiguities in the intercreditor agreement release provisions.

6. Composition of lending syndicate and syndicate dynamic

As the senior secured floating rate notes and the 8.5% senior notes were traded on

the Luxembourg Bourse, the respective creditor groups consisted of public noteholders. This introduced a number of challenges to the restructuring, such as low visibility of creditor identities, a limited willingness on the part of those creditors to receive material non-public information, a diversity of interests and attendant issues with organisation. All this could be contrasted with the creditors under the revolving credit facility and the WIND Hellas hedging, which were comprised primarily of European and international banks.

The senior secured floating rate notes and the 8.5% senior notes were both actively traded in the market in early 2010, with particular liquidity in the 8.5% senior notes. In particular, there were signs of an increased focus in the debt, notably from distressed debt investors, at around the same time as the full extent of the Greek economic crisis became known.

7.   Restructuring negotiation process

In May 2010 WIND Hellas and other members of the group appointed financial and legal advisers to begin considering restructuring options.

In June 2010, in the WIND Hellas first quarter of 2010 investor call, WIND Hellas announced the appointment of its advisers and the initiation of discussions regarding the group's situation with its key stakeholders, namely:

- the revolving credit facility lenders;
- an *ad hoc* committee of holders of the senior secured floating rate notes (the 'senior secured floating rate note holders working group'); and
- the WIND Hellas hedging counterparties.

The purpose of the initial discussions was to explore the possibility of:

- deferring the group's obligations towards those creditors so as to improve its liquidity position; and
- stabilising the group's capital structure via a number of potential strategies, including a reduction of overall debt levels, a sale of the group or the implementation of a second financial restructuring.

The outcome of the initial discussions and subsequent negotiations was the execution of a standstill agreement at the end of June 2010 between several members of the WIND Hellas group, the revolving credit facility lenders, the senior secured floating rate note holders working group and the WIND Hellas hedging counterparties. This was designed primarily to address the impending amortisation and interest payments, and to suspend defaults and cross-defaults under the finance documentation pending the implementation of a restructuring solution. The standstill agreement laid out a number of milestones to provide a clear framework for the subsequent conduct of the restructuring, at the centre of which was an extensive two-phase M&A process to identify prospective financial and strategic purchasers of the WIND Hellas business. The standstill agreement also mandated the appointment of a chief restructuring officer to assist with managing liquidity at the group and to act as the principal point of contact at WIND Hellas for all subsequent engagement and negotiations with creditors.

The two-phase M&A process was conducted over the course of July to October 2010. Any prospective purchaser was likely to view WIND Hellas as an overleveraged business and a genuine refinancing risk, particularly in light of the restricted access to the capital markets for Greek issuers for the foreseeable future, and would likely be reluctant to commit any new capital to the business due to the prevailing economic uncertainties. There were material change of control risks relating to the WIND Hellas telecommunications licence, the finance documentation and the potential need for competition clearances. However, notwithstanding these obstacles, the M&A process attracted high levels of interest and nine non-binding expressions of interest were received as part of the first phase, with six binding offers submitted at the end of the second phase. The successful bidder was ultimately identified as a newly incorporated entity (Bidco) within a group established by the senior secured floating rate note holders working group (the 'Bidco group'), with a final offer that had the support of the revolving credit facility lenders, the WIND Hellas hedging counterparties and senior secured floating rate note holders representing in excess of 75% of the senior secured floating rate notes.

On the conclusion of the M&A process at the beginning of November 2010, when Bidco was identified as the successful bidder, WIND Hellas and other members of the group executed a comprehensive restructuring agreement with the revolving credit facility lenders, the WIND Hellas hedging counterparties and senior secured floating rate note holders representing in excess of 75% of the senior secured floating rate notes. The restructuring agreement constituted formal consent for the commercial deal and obliged all parties to work towards a detailed implementation structure that had been developed and agreed upon by the parties' advisers. It was contemplated that an English law scheme of arrangement would have to be entered into between Hellas V and the senior secured floating rate note holders, under which the senior secured floating rate note holders would transfer ownership of the senior secured floating rate notes to a parent company of Bidco (Holdco) to facilitate the implementation of the broader restructuring. The scheme would be necessary to cram down and bind any dissenting senior secured floating rate note holders to the overall restructuring in order to prevent extraction of their *pro rata* entitlement to the proceeds of realisation under the intercreditor agreement waterfall provisions, and thereby avoid any cash leakage.

The scheme featured only one class of creditor –the senior secured floating rate note holders – and sought to bind each senior secured floating rate note holder to its terms. The main elements of the scheme were as follows:

- an instruction from the senior secured floating rate note holders to the senior secured floating rate note trustee to transfer 100% of the senior secured floating rate notes to Holdco in consideration for an initial allocation of 10% of the equity in the Bidco group structure and the right to subscribe for additional shares;
- an additional offering to allow the senior secured floating rate note holders to subscribe in cash for further equity in the Bidco group to part-finance the purchase price for WIND Hellas and to provide for the imminent cash needs of the business;

- an authorisation to Hellas V to enable it to enter into specified restructuring documents for and on behalf of the senior secured floating rate note holders; and
- a deed of covenant by which the senior secured floating rate note holders agreed not to take legal action against certain identified parties.

The scheme process was commenced at an initial hearing in the English High Court of Justice on November 4 2010, at which Justice Newey established that:

- Hellas V was a company liable to be wound up under the Insolvency Act 1986;
- Hellas V had sufficient connection to England (meaning that it was appropriate for the court to exercise its jurisdiction); and
- the creditor class proposed by Hellas V was correct.

On this basis, the judge was prepared to grant leave for Hellas V to convene a creditors' meeting for the purposes of considering and, if thought fit, approving the scheme. At the subsequent creditors' meeting held on December 6 2010, a majority of senior secured floating rate note holders representing 98.48% in value of the senior secured floating rate notes voted in favour of the scheme. The scheme approval hearing took place on December 8 2010; approving the scheme, the judge confirmed that a combination of the scheme procedure undertaken, the express support for the scheme and the absence of any opposition in the context of the overall proposed restructuring meant that it was fair and met the requisite conditions for approval.

On December 2 2010 the boards of managers or the general partner (as applicable) of each of WF III, Hellas III, Hellas IV, Hellas V and Hellas VI resolved to approve the making of applications to the High Court to place each of those companies into administration. In line with the detailed implementation structure set out in the restructuring agreement, an administration of WF III would enable a pre-packaged administration sale of the WIND Hellas shares to Bidco by way of an enforcement sale conducted by the security agent. Further, administrations of Hellas III, Hellas IV, Hellas V and Hellas VI would enable pre-packaged administration sales of various rights of these companies, including intercompany debts owed by WIND Hellas to those companies, as part of the same enforcement sale. The intercreditor agreement permitted the security agent to release guarantees and security immediately before any enforcement sale, but did not allow for the release of principal or interest liabilities. As such, the enforcement sale would be accompanied by the exercise of put options over the shares in Hellas III, Helas V and Hellas VI, which would see the shares in those companies transferred to WF II, and thereby enable WIND Hellas to be sold free of its subsidiaries and their principal and interest obligations. In granting the administration applications on December 10 2010, Justice Arnold was satisfied that each of the companies was or was likely to become unable to pay its debts in light of the overleveraged capital structure of the WIND Hellas group, and agreed that there was a real prospect of achieving one or more of the statutory purposes of administration, in that the joint administrators were likely

to realise property in order to make a distribution to one or more secured or preferential creditors and/or achieve a better result for the creditors as a whole than would be likely if each of the companies were to be wound up immediately: "In the present case, I am satisfied on the evidence before me that the proposed pre-pack administration, and in particular the proposed sale, is realistically the only way forward ... Moreover, if the pre-pack sale that is proposed does not go ahead, it seems perfectly clear that the only realistic alternative is going to be some form of liquidation or other insolvency process which is going to result in a drastic deterioration in the value of the group which will benefit no one."[1]

On December 17 2010 the joint administrators entered into the agreed form sale documentation to effect the anticipated pre-packaged administration sales on a same-day basis and bring the restructuring to a successful close. Bidco utilised a daylight loan to fund the purchase price in cash as per the requirement in the intercreditor agreement release provisions. The sale proceeds were applied by the security agent in accordance with the waterfall provisions in the intercreditor agreement, which saw the revolving credit facility lenders and the WIND Hellas hedging counterparties repaid in full with the balance of the moneys paid to Holdco in its capacity, following the scheme, as holder of 100% of the senior secured floating rate notes (which in turn enabled repayment of the daylight loan). As the amounts owing in respect of the senior secured floating rate notes far exceeded the moneys paid out to Holdco, the 8.5% senior note holders received no payment from the application of the sale proceeds. Ownership of WIND Hellas was transferred to Bidco free and clear of the debts owed to the group's financial creditors, including the 8.5% senior note holders. The senior secured floating rate note holders that opted to put forward new money via a participation in the €420 million additional offering by the Bidco group shared the 90% portion of the equity in the restructured group that had not been distributed in the initial allocation that was part of the scheme.

8.   Implementation of restructuring

From the early stage evaluations of potential restructuring solutions, it was clear that the complexity of the WIND Hellas capital structure and the presence of multiple stakeholders would create a number of challenges. The terms of the finance documentation, particularly the requisite voting levels, limited the number of viable alternatives and effectively ruled out the possibility of a consensual restructuring. Constant attention would have to be given to the directors' duties and filing obligations of the WIND Hellas group's management teams throughout the restructuring process.

A further challenge derived from the jurisdictions of the companies in the WIND Hellas group – namely, Greece and Luxembourg, both of which were considered to have an unfavourable insolvency regime. In the interests of gaining access to a jurisdiction with flexible insolvency laws that would be conducive to a timely and effective restructuring, the WIND Hellas group commenced steps to move the COMI of each of WF III, Hellas III, Hellas IV, Hellas V and Hellas VI from Luxembourg to

---

1   *Re Hellas Telecommunications (Luxembourg) 5 SCA* [2010] EWHC 3489 (Ch) at para 14.

England. This included implementation of the following measures at each of the companies:

- installation of independent management resident in England together with the engagement of independent advisers;
- establishment of a new head office and principal operating address in London, from which all future business activities and administrative procedures would be undertaken and all future correspondence would be sent;
- the transfer of all property (predominantly statutory books, records and corporate documents) from Luxembourg to the new London office;
- the opening of a bank account in London for the purpose of funding day-to-day operations;
- termination of existing contracts in Luxembourg;
- communication of the change of address to creditors, including those under the revolving credit facility, the senior secured floating rate notes, the 8.5% senior notes and the WIND Hellas hedging, via notices under the relevant finance documentation and announcements on the Luxembourg Bourse;
- the conduct of all future management meetings and negotiations with creditors in London;
- registration at Companies House in England as a foreign company and a UK establishment of an overseas company; and
- application to Her Majesty's Revenue and Customs to register for tax purposes.

The COMI shifts were necessary in order for the group to avail of UK law insolvency procedures for the purposes of implementing a restructuring or sale. These procedures, including the scheme of arrangement and pre-packaged administration sales, were considered to be much more flexible and conducive to a successful restructuring than those available in Greece or Luxembourg. In considering the steps taken in furtherance of the COMI shifts, the judge was satisfied that there were a sufficient number of objective factors in the public domain to ensure that it was ascertainable to third parties dealing with those companies in the ordinary course of business that their COMI was located in England. As such, the court reasoned that this would rebut the presumption that the COMI of WF III, Hellas III, Hellas IV, Hellas V and Hellas VI was in Luxembourg, the jurisdiction where each of those companies was incorporated and maintained its registered office.

The viability of the restructuring rested on the ability to transfer WIND Hellas to a new owner with the company's assets unencumbered by the claims of the group's financial creditors. To enable a release of the guarantees and security over WIND Hellas' assets, the pre-packaged administration sale had to comply with the intercreditor agreement release provisions. This necessitated payment of the purchase price in cash (assisted by Bidco's utilisation of the daylight loan) and delivery of an accompanying fairness opinion from an internationally recognised investment bank.

Further, it was crucial to ensure that the prospective administrators would be sufficiently comfortable to accept their appointment (bearing in mind applicable statutory and fiduciary duties, including their Statement of Insolvency Practice (SIP) 16 obligations) and execute the sale documentation once the administration orders had been granted. In particular, the prospective administrators had to be satisfied with the strength of the M&A process, mindful that the valuation evidence should support a conclusion that the best price had been obtained for the assets and confident that the restructuring was capable of implementation. At the administration hearing on December 10 2010, the judge confirmed his view that a robust M&A process had been undertaken and that the prospective administrators had complied with their SIP 16 obligations.

The scheme of arrangement was at the centre of this complex cross-border restructuring and, once it had become effective under English law, the WIND Hellas management team had to consider the group's ability to enforce the scheme in other jurisdictions. Overseas recognition of the scheme in these circumstances can be vital to avert the risk of damage or delay caused by dissident creditors launching a challenge to the restructuring in foreign courts. The key jurisdictions in this restructuring were Greece, Luxembourg and, as the senior secured floating rate notes and 8.5% senior note indentures were governed by New York law, the United States. In the absence of any formal recognition procedures in Greece and Luxembourg, defensive strategies were developed by the group and its advisers to combat any challenge resulting from dissident creditor actions in the local courts. In the United States, judicial recognition of the scheme was sought under Chapter 15 of the US Bankruptcy Code immediately after its approval by the English High Court, and such recognition was granted on December 14 2010, thereby installing an automatic moratorium in relation to actions against Hellas V and its property in the United States. Chapter 15 recognition of the scheme had been a condition precedent to closing the restructuring.

9.   Final closing structure

The restructuring, illustrated by the post-restructuring corporate structure chart on the next page, led to the transfer of WIND Hellas into the Bidco group free and clear of the debts owed to the financial creditors of the old WIND Hellas group. The revolving credit facility and the WIND Hellas hedging were fully discharged and the senior secured floating rate notes were transferred to Holdco as part of the scheme and partly discharged by the application of the sale proceeds by the security agent. The claims of the 8.5% senior notes remained outstanding, but were restricted to the companies left behind in the old WIND Hellas group as a result of the release of the WIND Hellas guarantee and all security over WIND Hellas's assets at the time of the enforcement sale.

10.   Conclusion

The second financial restructuring of the WIND Hellas group preserved the benefits of the first restructuring in 2009 by averting the threat of formal Greek insolvency proceedings, and thereby ensuring a continuation of the business as a going concern.

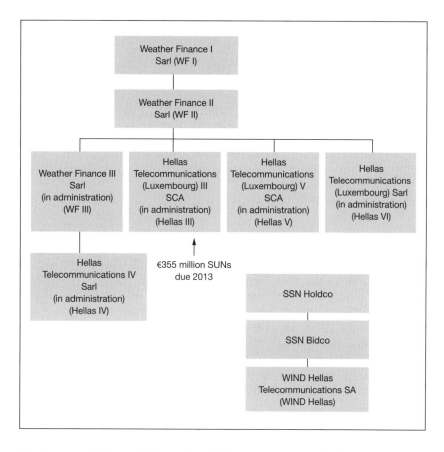

At its core, this avoided an inevitable termination of the WIND Hellas telecommunications licence and heavy losses for the group's creditors, as well as rescuing several thousand jobs in Greece at a time of unprecedented economic upheaval. Moreover, the provision of additional funding to the business via the €420 million additional equity offering represented the largest foreign direct investment into Greece since the onset of the country's financial crisis.

It has been suggested that the 2010 restructuring amounts to further evidence that the English law scheme of arrangement has come to prominence in recent years as a favoured tool in complex financial restructurings. Certainly, a scheme can be the mechanism to deliver a legal solution in scenarios where a 100% consensual arrangement cannot be implemented, the key advantage being that it can introduce a lower threshold for creditor support than would apply under the terms of the applicable finance documentation. In providing an alternative to the need for unanimous or prohibitively high levels of consent from a particular creditor group, a scheme can prove essential as a means of neutralising the hold-out value of dissident creditors that could otherwise frustrate a widely supported restructuring.

European Directories

Kon Asimacopoulos
Partha Kar
Elaine Nolan
Freddie Powles
Kirkland & Ellis International LLP

1.   Synopsis

The European Directories restructuring was implemented at the end of 2010 by means of a pre-packaged sale by UK administrators of the shares in one of the group's holding companies, originally incorporated in the Netherlands, together with certain other assets of that company, following a shift of its centre of main interest (COMI) for the purpose of the EU Insolvency Regulation (1346/2000) from the Netherlands to the United Kingdom.

The restructuring was extremely complex, given that the group consisted of companies in nine European jurisdictions.

Before completion of the restructuring, certain second-lien lenders brought a challenge in the United Kingdom – in the High Court and subsequently in the Court of Appeal. Their challenge concerned the proper interpretation of some common provisions in European leveraged finance documents that provide the ability to release debt, guarantees and security granted by obligors when lenders take enforcement action in certain circumstances. The successful conclusion of the litigation and the subsequent completion of the restructuring have provided welcome certainty in relation to the operation of these provisions, which are widely used in the European leveraged finance market.

2.   Background to group operations

Before the restructuring the European Directories group and its parent companies were owned by Macquarie Capital Alliance. Macquarie Capital Alliance acquired the group in a series of transactions, beginning with the acquisition of the Yellow Brick Road Group for approximately €1.8 billion from Veronis Suhler Stevenson LLC and the 3i Group plc in 2005. This was followed by bolt-on acquisitions, including the acquisition of the TDC Förlag Group's search and directory businesses in Denmark, Sweden and Finland in November 2005 and the acquisition of the Gouden Gids business from Truvo Nederland BV in September 2008.

European Directories has operating subsidiaries which conduct business in Austria, the Czech Republic, Denmark, Finland, the Netherlands, Poland, Slovakia and Sweden. The group offers advertising products through a variety of online and offline media, ranging from printed directories to internet directory services, affiliate marketing, search engine marketing and search engine optimisation and directory assistance. The group uses these media to generate leads for its customers (ie, advertisers). The focus of the group's business was originally the printing of yellow

pages directories; however, due to the structural decline of this business – largely as a result of competition from online alternatives, such as Google – the group is in the process of transforming and diversifying its business. Instead, it focuses on generating leads for the small and medium-sized enterprises (SMEs) which advertise in its online and offline media. The 700,000 SMEs that comprise its customer base typically operate in a limited geographical area and therefore look to local media as their primary form of advertising. Consequently, the advertisements that they place with the group are often critical to the marketing of their businesses. European Directories employs approximately 5,150 people, of whom approximately 4,800 are full-time employees.

3. Corporate structure before restructuring

The group's ultimate parent was a company incorporated in Luxembourg. This company's immediate subsidiaries were all private limited liability companies incorporated under the Dutch Civil Code. One of these Dutch companies in turn owned the shares in the various intermediate holding companies, through which the group operated in a number of European jurisdictions.

A simplified structure chart for the group, showing the position before restructuring, is shown on the right.

4. Pre-restructuring capital structure

The financing structure for the group comprised senior, mezzanine and payment-in-kind (PIK) facilities and certain hedging arrangements, representing a total of almost €2.3 billion outstanding at the time of the restructuring. This consisted of the €1.52 billion senior facilities, a €325 million mezzanine facility and a €155 million PIK facility; the total amounts outstanding under each of these were €1,483,565,781, €441,124,336 and €349,339,021, respectively.

The PIK debt was unsecured and structurally subordinated. The priority between the various lender groups was governed by an English law intercreditor agreement.

5. Financial situation of the group in the lead-up to restructuring, and restructuring triggers

In the second quarter of 2009, the group's London-based management identified the possibility that the group could be in breach of one or more of the financial covenants in its facilities agreements, at year end, when they came to be tested in relation to the 12-month period ending on December 31 2009. The deterioration in operating performance was largely a result of the global economic downturn, which had a negative effect on the advertising market generally and a specific impact on customer and sales retention rates in each of the group's operating territories. In addition, the performance of the European printed directories sector declined as a whole – a consequence of the acceleration of the structural change from printed directories to online advertising. These problems were exacerbated by operational difficulties in the Netherlands and Denmark. In the Netherlands, the group faced difficulties in integrating the Gouden Gids and De Telefoongids businesses, which had a negative impact on sales force efficiency and productivity, resulting in a loss of customers and

Pre-restructuring simplified group structure

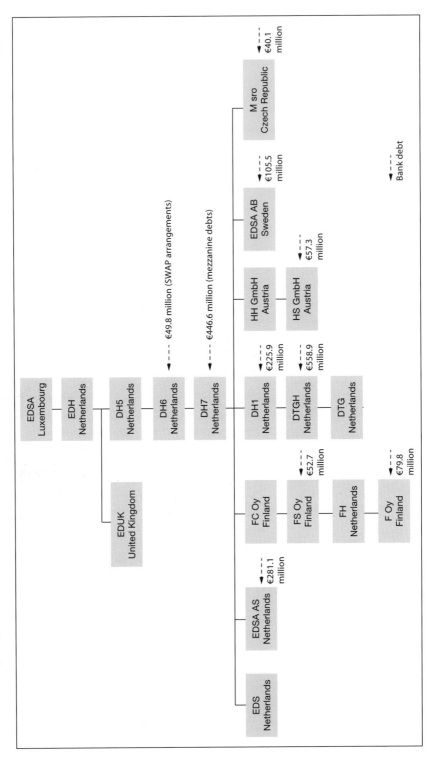

revenue. The Danish business also performed significantly below expectations, due to ongoing operational problems in the sales and back office departments.

The deterioration in performance resulted in a 10% reduction in total revenue for financial year 2009, compared with the previous financial year. The reduction in revenue was not accompanied by an equivalent reduction in costs, which contributed to a 6% reduction in reported earnings before interest, taxes, depreciation and amortisation for financial year 2009. On the basis of the group's forecast of a reduction in ongoing earnings and cash flow, the management predicted that the group would be unable to meet cash interest and amortisation obligations under its finance agreements or to meet upcoming covenant tests in the medium term.

In response to the deterioration in the group's operating performance, its management took action to reduce costs and attempted to halt the decline in sales. Its actions included:

- a reduction in headcount and associated employee costs;
- the development of working capital initiatives to maximise cash usage; and
- a focus on sales force productivity, which included the introduction of a dedicated sales force to sell specialist products, reductions in capital expenditure and deferrals of marketing initiatives.

The company engaged NM Rothschild & Sons Limited as its financial adviser and Kirkland & Ellis as its legal adviser, to advise on any potential restructuring that would be required. Alvarez & Marsal was also later engaged to advise on potential restructuring options.

In addition, the group requested that Deloitte Belastingadviseurs BV undertake certain tax analyses with respect to the group. Specifically, Deloitte Belastingadviseurs was engaged to produce a tax structure report, including an outline of the probable main tax consequences of the individual steps of the proposed restructuring (including steps designed to achieve the deleveraging of the group, the refinancing of the Dutch holding companies and their subsidiaries and the settlement of inter-company debts within the group).

On August 26 2009 the group engaged PwC London to undertake a financial and commercial review focusing on the key territories of the Netherlands, Austria, Denmark, Finland, Sweden, Poland, the Czech Republic and Slovakia. This culminated in the production of an independent business report, which was presented on December 11 2009, in relation to which PwC granted a limited duty of care to the group's lenders.

PwC's report identified three areas of challenge that had a material and detrimental impact on the group's performance. These were:

- the material deterioration of the economic environment in each territory;
- the acceleration of the pace of structural change from printed directories to online search tools; and
- significant challenges in integrating the merger of De Telefoongids and Gouden Gids in the Netherlands, and persistent operational issues in Denmark.

These conclusions indicated that the group was unlikely to be able to satisfy its debt service obligations in full with respect to amortisation payments (in particular those due in June 2010) and interest payments in respect of the senior debt and the mezzanine debt, which would cause an event of default under the respective facility agreements. In addition, without an alternative financing source or a refinancing, the group would be unable to satisfy its repayment obligations under the facilities agreements in full on their maturity.

On March 1 2010 a restructuring committee was established at the level of one of the Dutch holding companies, European Directories DH6 BV, to allow the board to consider the potential restructuring of the group and to liaise with the company's legal and financial advisers, who would attend meetings and advise on any restructuring proposals presented to the company. The restructuring committee was established in conjunction with the appointment of Peter Briggs as chief restructuring officer and a director of the group companies.

6. Lending syndicate: composition and dynamics

The senior lending syndicate was large and diverse, comprising CLOs, banks and funds. A representative senior coordinating committee – consisting of Alcentra Limited, Allied Irish Banks plc, Lloyds Banking Group, M&G Investment Management Limited and The Royal Bank of Scotland plc – was established on December 22 2009 to conduct restructuring negotiations on behalf of the senior syndicate. Moelis & Company UK LLP was appointed as the financial adviser to the committee and Linklaters was appointed as its legal adviser.

7. Restructuring negotiation process

7.1 Senior lender negotiations

In light of the anticipated event of default, the group initiated discussions with the senior coordinating committee and certain junior lenders at the end of 2009. In January 2010 an all-lender meeting was held in London, at which the group presented a review of its 2009 performance, the business plan and the strategy and outlook for the group, highlighting the liquidity and other constraints faced by the group that would culminate in an event of default under the facilities agreements.

The initial event of default occurred in mid-February 2010 as a consequence of a breach of one of the financial covenant restrictions contained in the facilities agreements in relation to the period ending on December 31 2009. Negotiations with the senior lenders after the all-lender meeting resulted in the senior lenders granting a waiver of the actual February event of default and future anticipated events of default, plus certain other potential events of default that might have ensued from the commencement of discussions between any member of the group and its creditors regarding a potential restructuring.

The initial expiry date of the waiver given by the senior lenders was extended on April 6 2010 to May 14 2010, and was later extended on May 14 2010 to July 15 2010. At the same time, the company requested that the senior lenders forbear from taking enforcement action in relation to non-payment of interest due on May 28

2010 and amortisation payments due on June 30 2010; this forbearance was also granted. A second and third event of default would have occurred in mid-May, in relation to the period ending March 31 2010, but for the waivers obtained.

The granting of a further waiver was not required from the senior lenders after July 15 2010, as the waivers addressed in the waiver letter of May 14 2010 were superseded by a lock-up agreement, which became effective on July 15 2010 and was later amended and extended on November 12 2010.

In addition to its negotiation with the senior lenders, the group negotiated with its hedging counterparties, two of which signed a forbearance letter on June 25 2010, which was amended and restated on August 3 2010. Under the terms of the amended and restated letter, the hedge counterparties agreed not to take any permitted enforcement action with respect to the prevailing events of default or additional termination events (as set out in the relevant swap documentation) relating to non-payment of the monthly swap payments due in April, May and June 2010 and the outstanding events of default under the facilities agreements.

The third hedging counterparty also executed a forbearance letter on similar terms on September 6 2010. As part of the restructuring process, the hedging arrangements were novated down the group structure so as to remain within the post-restructuring group.

7.2 Discussions with second-lien lenders

Initially the senior coordinating committee and its advisers acted for the senior lenders as a whole. Consequently, the second-lien lenders were privy to the same financial and other information as the senior lenders. However, on May 6 2010 the senior coordinating committee issued a notice on Intralinks to all senior and second-lien lenders, advising that from then on it would represent only the senior lenders.

Many of the senior lenders had cross-holdings in the second-lien debt. However, certain second-lien lenders, including Hastings Funds Management Limited and AMP Capital Investors Limited, had no senior cross-holdings. The two lenders held 14.5% of the second-lien debt and proceeded to engage Quinn Emanuel Urquhart & Sullivan to act as their legal counsel.

In May 2010 the senior facility agent, acting on behalf of the senior lenders, issued a notice to the second-lien lenders in accordance with the terms of the intercreditor agreement, suspending any payments due to the second-lien lenders. An updated stop notice was reissued in October 2010.

On May 20 2010 Quinn Emanuel wrote to Kirkland & Ellis and Linklaters. Quinn Emanuel confirmed its representation of Hastings Fund Management and AMP Capital Investors Limited, and suggested that those second-lien lenders had concerns regarding the valuation of the group that had been presented to the all-lenders meeting on May 6 2010. The firm expressed its clients' concern that the senior coordinating committee was seeking to implement a restructuring that improperly ignored or overrode the interests of the second-lien lenders, and sought additional information with regard to the restructuring proposal and the latest group valuation.

Kirkland & Ellis responded to Quinn Emanuel's letter, stating the company's position. It invited the second-lien lenders to share their analysis of the valuation

issue and to present a restructuring proposal to the extent that they believed themselves to have an economic interest in the group. The group received no valuation analysis or restructuring proposal from or on behalf of the second-lien lenders.

In response to this initial correspondence, the group also confirmed that, subject to timetable and process constraints, it would be happy to afford the second-lien lenders access to group information and senior management representatives.

Quinn Emanuel's initial letter was followed by two more, to which Kirkland & Ellis responded in detail following receipt of executed confidentiality undertakings by the second-lien lenders, enclosing a substantial amount of information requested and offering access to the group's management. Linklaters also wrote to Quinn Emanuel, addressing certain issues raised in its previous letters and including additional information that the second-lien lenders had requested.

Quinn Emanuel wrote further letters to Linklaters and Allen & Overy LLP (as counsel to the security trustee under the facilities agreements) questioning the security trustee's construction of, and reliance on, a clause of the intercreditor agreement. The clause, which was widely used in documents of that kind at the time that the initial acquisition of the group was completed, provided for an ability to release junior debt, security and guarantee claims on certain enforcement action taken by senior lenders. Quinn Emanuel asserted that the construction on which the security trustee relied was incorrect. Allen & Overy rejected this assertion in correspondence, and further correspondence ensued on this topic.

On September 7 2010 the company was served – by Quinn Emanuel through Kirkland & Ellis – with a claim form pursuant to Part 8 of the Civil Procedure Rules, requesting a number of declarations. The main tenet of the Part 8 claim was that certain implementation mechanisms which the security trustee would need to use to implement the restructuring, in particular the releases described above, were invalid and ineffective.

Justice Proudman heard the Part 8 claim at first instance on September 23 2010 and held in favour of the second-lien lenders. An appeal by the security trustee, the company and the senior coordinating committee was heard on an expedited basis in the Court of Appeal on October 21 2010 by Lords Justice Longmore and Jacob and Justice Kitchen. The appeal judges upheld the appeal, overturned the Proudman judgment and dismissed the claim, holding that the mechanisms that the security trustee proposed to use to implement the restructuring were valid and effective. The appeal judges refused the second-lien lenders permission to appeal to the Supreme Court.

The Court of Appeal decision was crucial to the European restructuring market because of the prevalence of the drafting mechanisms under dispute in a number of finance documents for leveraged acquisitions of this vintage.

7.3 Discussions with the junior lenders

On January 5 2010 the mezzanine lenders formed a junior *ad hoc* committee. The committee appointed Houlihan Lokey (Europe) Limited as financial adviser and Bingham McCutchen LLP, London as legal adviser. Before this date certain junior

lenders had availed themselves of the observer rights that they had on the boards of three of the group's holding companies, and informal discussions had been held as a consequence. The junior lenders were being advised by Goldman Sachs at that time.

Negotiations with the mezzanine lenders resulted in a waiver of the actual and anticipated events of default, plus certain other potential events of default, being granted by the mezzanine lenders until an initial expiry date of March 31 2010, and included a requirement to deliver the compliance certificate in relation to the financial covenants by March 1 2010.

The mezzanine lenders did not immediately grant an additional waiver on the expiry of the initial waiver; however, a further waiver was granted on May 5 2010, to expire on May 14 2010. During negotiations regarding this waiver, the group requested that the mezzanine lenders forbear from taking enforcement action in relation to non-payment of interest payments due on May 28 2010. The mezzanine lenders did not grant such forbearance. The subsequent waiver was not extended and expired on May 14 2010 in accordance with its terms.

The mezzanine lenders were given the opportunity to undertake due diligence in respect of the group and were given substantial information about its operations and business. The diligence period started in January 2010 and continued until May 2010. Mezzanine lenders were given full access to the group's management, as well as to the management teams of the operating companies. During this diligence process both Macquarie Capital Alliance (as incumbent sponsor) and the junior *ad hoc* committee made a number of restructuring proposals to the senior coordinating committee. However, these proposals were ultimately either rejected or withdrawn; the reason given for the withdrawals being the group's deteriorating financial results.

Stop notices suspending payment to the junior lenders were issued in May 2010 by the senior lenders, suspending any payments due to the mezzanine lenders, and an updated notice was reissued in October 2010.

8.   Implementation of restructuring

As holders of the highest-ranking liabilities in the financing structure, with first priority rights in respect of the transaction security, the senior lenders had a controlling position in any restructuring process in the circumstances facing the stakeholders – that is, where there was clear valuation evidence to demonstrate that the enterprise value of the group was lower than the total aggregate amount of the senior liabilities.

The restructuring, which was proposed and implemented at the instruction of the senior lenders, consisted of the following key steps:

- A new holding company structure was created, comprising four newly incorporated holding companies: Newco Parent, Holdco, Midco and OpHoldco. Each holding company was a special purpose vehicle incorporated in Luxembourg.
- A new money term loan facility of €75 million was made available to certain operating companies. Only those senior lenders that consented to the senior coordinating committee's proposal and signed the lock-up agreement were invited to participate in this new money facility.

- One of the Dutch holding companies in the group (referred to as 'DH6') transferred its COMI for the purposes of the EU Insolvency Regulation from the Netherlands to England.
- Following the shift in COMI, administrators were appointed to DH6 following the acceleration of the senior liabilities against the company.
- The administrators of DH6 entered into pre-agreed arrangements to sell:
  - all of the shares held by DH6 in its direct subsidiary DH7, along with all of the liabilities of DH7 and its subsidiaries; and
  - an inter-company receivable, held by DH6, to OpHoldco for nominal consideration.
- Before the preceding step, various intercompany balances between what would form the 'rump' group (containing DH6 and its parent companies) and the post-restructuring group (containing DH7 and its subsidiaries) were tidied up through transfers and contributions of intercompany liabilities between the rump group and DH7 and its subsidiaries, so as to ensure that both debtor and creditor sides of such loans were transferred into the post-restructuring group.
- Following the purchase referred to above, OpHoldco purchased the total amount of the senior debt, the second-lien debt and the mezzanine debt in exchange for the issuance of new debt instruments by OpHoldco and Holdco to the senior lenders. This sale was consummated pursuant to the powers afforded to the security trustee under the intercreditor agreement to sell such liabilities.
- After the debt transfers set out above, the guarantees given by the company, as well as the security and guarantees given by DH7 and its subsidiaries in respect of the senior, second-lien and mezzanine debt, were released as part of the restructuring pursuant to the powers afforded to the security trustee (and as affirmed by the Court of Appeal) under the intercreditor agreement.
- The consideration given for the transfer of the senior liabilities to OpHoldco consisted of new facilities issued by Holdco and OpHoldco which, in combination, had a face value equal to the transferred 'old' senior liabilities. The issuance of part of the consideration by Holdco resulted in an intercompany balance between Holdco and OpHoldco equal to the face value of the Holdco facility.
- Pursuant to the steps above, and consistent with the valuation evidence obtained by both the company and the security trustee, both the second-lien and mezzanine liabilities were transferred to OpHoldco in the restructuring for no consideration. The PIK debt was structurally subordinated and was left outstanding in the rump group. (The PIK was unsecured and did not benefit from guarantee or security from subsidiaries).
- The hedging arrangements were novated down the group before the restructuring and remained in place thereafter.
- In order to undertake the steps referred to above, the security trustee required that the documentary conditions of the intercreditor agreement be met, and that a contingency fund be made available to fund the defence of any

challenge to its actions. In the event, the instructions of 100% of the senior lenders were obtained to undertake the transactions, and the contingency fund was returned to the company after a certain period.

- Only the senior lenders that consented to the terms of the restructuring agreement were entitled to receive ordinary shares in Newco Parent, the group's new ultimate parent company. Such entitlement was *pro rata* to their participation in the aggregate total of the senior liabilities. Each ordinary share carried one vote. Of the senior lenders, 93% consented to lock-up to the restructuring proposal and all consented to the restructuring agreement.
- By far the most numerous of the restructuring steps then related to the post-sale debt pushdown pursuant to which the new facilities borrowed by OpHoldco were pushed down the group to the obligors under the pre-restructuring facilities.
- Broadly speaking, the debt pushdown was achieved by novating the new facilities and offsetting the resultant intercompany balances against a mixture of the 'old' senior liabilities (which had been transferred to OpHoldco by the security trustee and were at that point intra-group balances) and existing intra-group balances.

9. Final closing structure

The final closing structure following these debt pushdown steps is shown in the simplified diagram on the right.

10. Comment

The successful completion of the European Directories restructuring has provided a template for a number of other restructurings in the European market in which the finance documents contain the same (or similar) widely used provisions in the intercreditor agreement relating to the release and forcible transfer of debt by a security agent upon enforcement. Its precedent has allowed other distressed companies to restructure successfully in a comparable manner.

It remains to be seen whether 'COMI shift' pre-packaged sales by administrators in the United Kingdom continue to be used to avoid the uncertainties surrounding insolvency regimes in other European jurisdictions as those regimes become better tested. In particular, one of the options that was considered (but rejected) by the senior lenders in European Directories was a private sale – as referred to in Section 3.251(1) of the Dutch Civil Code – by the security trustee of the shares in DH7 pursuant to the pledge granted to lenders over those shares. Given the complex tax consequences of COMI shifts and the prospect, at the time of writing, of other major European restructurings being implemented in this way in the Netherlands, the COMI shift pre-pack may become a less popular option.

Post-restructuring simplified group structure

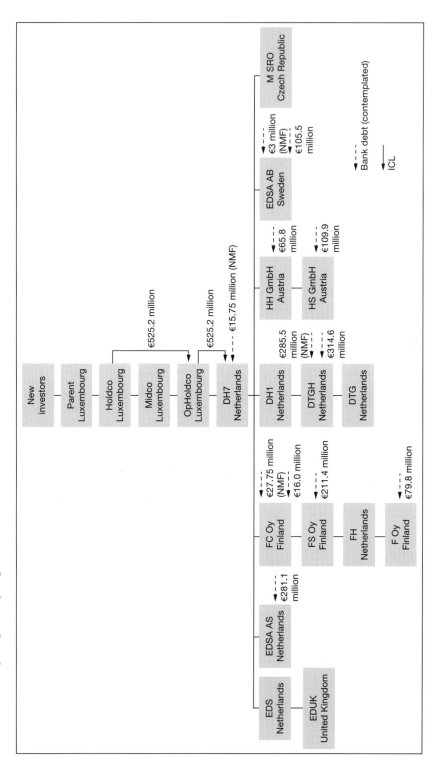

Rodenstock

Florian Bruder
Wolfgang Nardi
Leo Plank
Freddie Powles
Kirkland & Ellis International LLP

1.   Synopsis

Despite a lengthy and burdensome process with several setbacks, the Rodenstock group successfully avoided German insolvency proceedings and preserved its going concern by way of an English scheme of arrangement. The restructuring of its senior debt involved a €40 million new money facility and conditional subordination of certain debts (including senior debt). The existing senior lenders in turn received warrants representing 44% of the shares and a step-in right upon breach of certain covenants. The restructuring became possible only through a pioneering attempt to use the English scheme of arrangement to restructure the debt of Rodenstock GmbH. The company, which has its seat and centre of main interests in Germany, successfully argued that there was a sufficient connection to the English jurisdiction to apply the scheme merely on the basis that the senior lenders had chosen English law and jurisdiction to govern their lending relationship with the company. The restructuring has served as precedent for the use of the English schemes of arrangement in restructurings of other German companies, notably the restructuring of German PrimaCom AG.

2.   Background to group operations

At the time of its restructuring, the Rodenstock group, headquartered in Munich, Germany, was Europe's fourth largest manufacturer and distributor of spectacle lenses and frames. Its focus was on premium brands (including Rodenstock and Porsche Design) and progressive and high-end lenses, but it also had a value-for-money range. The group maintained around 40 sales offices across the globe and major production facilities in Europe and Thailand.

The main operating company in the group was Rodenstock GmbH, with a turnover of approximately €258.3 million. The group as a whole had an annual turnover of approximately €361.5 million.

3.   Pre-restructuring corporate and capital structure

Rodenstock GmbH was a corporate entity with limited liability, incorporated in accordance with the laws of Germany. The group included German and foreign subsidiaries and a German parent, but was ultimately owned by a private equity sponsor.

Rodenstock had outstanding senior debt of approximately €305.335,000 under its existing senior facilities agreement. The debt was secured by a market standard

collateral package, which included security over shares, interests, of accounts, movables, receivables (trade and insurance), shares, intellectual property and real estate. Certain security and guarantees that were provided by the existing guarantors may have been limited in scope, effect or validity, in particular due to German and Czech law limitations.

4. Financial situation of the group in the lead-up to restructuring, and restructuring triggers

During the global financial crisis of 2008 and 2009, Rodenstock suffered a deterioration in its business that led to a breach of certain financial covenants under the existing senior facilities agreement during the second quarter of 2009.

4.1 Trading performance and additional exposure

Rodenstock's financial situation deteriorated mainly due to a significant decrease in trading performance. In 2008 the group suffered a significant decrease in lense sales due to the economic downturn and a loss of market share to competitors. The deterioration continued in 2009 and the group attempted to address its causes by implementing certain operational restructuring initiatives. However, these initiatives had a temporary negative impact on profitability as a consequence of exceptional items of expenditure that were necessary for the restructuring initiatives.

Additionally, in 2010 the German Federal Cartel Office levied a significant fine on Rodenstock for alleged breaches of the German Act against Constraints on Competition.[1] Furthermore, the group had liabilities under its pension benefits of approximately €200 million.[2]

4.2 Covenant breaches, waivers, forbearances and restructuring agreement

The deterioration in the group's performance culminated in a breach of certain financial covenants under the existing senior facilities agreement during the second quarter of 2009, for which the company obtained waivers to present a restructuring proposal. Among other things, the waivers prohibited the senior lenders from accelerating the debt on the basis of any event of default that was the subject of the waivers.

At the time of the restructuring, Rodenstock had outstanding senior debt of approximately €305,335,000 under the existing senior facilities agreement. No unpaid due and payable amounts were outstanding under the existing senior facilities agreement. Rodenstock always continued to pay all its debts as they fell due, and was not insolvent as a matter of German law.[3]

However, the group was likely to face liquidity issues in April 2011 and, had the restructuring measures not been implemented, may have been unable to avoid insolvency.

---

1   See www.bundeskartellamt.de/wDeutsch/archiv/PressemeldArchiv/2010/2010_06_10.php.
2   See Handelsblatt, September 28 2010, Rodenstock-Verkauf gescheitert, www.handelsblatt.com/unternehmen/industrie/rodenstock-verkauf-gescheitert/3549638.html.
3   Cf Mayer-Löwy/Fritz, ZInsO 2011, 662 ff, for a discussion about the relation between the German over-indebtedness test and the English scheme of arrangement.

5.   Composition of lending syndicate and syndicate dynamic

The syndicate primarily consisted of major banks. Only very few CLOs and hedge funds were present in the lending group.

Following a meeting with Rodenstock in mid-2009, the senior lenders formed a senior coordinating committee comprising the agent as coordinator and four additional initial members. However, the lender group was fractioned and even after the formation of the coordinating committee, the senior lenders still did not appear to act as a homogenous group with aligned interests in the negotiations (even though it was held in the later scheme proceedings to be one class of creditors, ie, the rights of the senior lenders were all aligned and similarly affected by the restructuring). One of the reasons may well have been that the debt was widespread and many parties with diverse interests needed to come to the table.[4] A single voice in the press even questioned whether the syndicate would be able to come to any kind of settlement, as they had not even been able to agree on the straightforward transaction that had been offered by another private equity sponsor.[5]

Rodenstock, the sponsor and the senior coordinating committee all retained their own legal advisors.[6]

6.   Restructuring negotiation process

Overall, the restructuring process started slowly and seemed, at that time, primarily driven and controlled by the sponsor. Only later, following the withdrawal of another private equity sponsor's offer, did Rodenstock and the senior coordinating committee take charge of the process in light of the imminent threat of insolvency proceedings. Ultimately, the parties chose to pursue a restructuring by way of an English scheme of arrangement to preserve the going concern value of the group.

6.1   Restructuring proposal and new business plan

In the second quarter of 2009 Rodenstock notified its senior lenders that it had breached certain financial covenants. In the first waiver requests, Rodenstock indicated that the group's ultimate shareholder would present a restructuring proposal to the existing senior lenders. In order to address the current economic situation and to prepare for a restructuring, Rodenstock proposed a new business plan. The respective waivers allowed Rodenstock to formulate a restructuring proposal and to seek a restructuring opinion that was needed to protect creditors from:

- any liability that might arise under German law as a result of delaying the insolvency of a distressed company by lending new money, extending its credit or subordinating its claims; and
- potential equitable subordination risks.

---

4   See Handelsblatt, September 28 2010, Rodenstock-Verkauf gescheitert, www.handelsblatt.com/unternehmen/industrie/rodenstock-verkauf-gescheitert/3549638.html.
5   *Ibid.*
6   See www.juve.de/nachrichten/deals/2011/01/blick-nach-vorn-rodenstock-erhalt-mit-clifford-hilfe-finanzspritze-von-banken.

6.2 Offer by another private equity sponsor and other implementation mechanics

In 2010 another private equity sponsor made an offer, supported by the sponsor, to invest €42 million and acquire the majority in Rodenstock. In turn, the sponsor would contribute €28 million and remain a minority shareholder. Although the senior lenders were not prepared to take a haircut, as originally planned, the transaction had the potential to reduce Rodenstock's debt by €80 million, to approximately €220 million.[7]

However, an agreement could not be reached, and the private equity sponsor subsequently withdrew from negotiations. It was reported that this was due to the fact that some senior lenders could not agree on the conditions for the contemplated €80 million repayment and additionally claimed further conditions and fees.[8]

Subsequently, management announced a new round of talks with senior lenders. In light of these circumstances and the large group of senior lenders, single press reports seemed to suggest that the chances of restructuring outside insolvency were quite low.[9]

During the course of the restructuring discussions, the parties considered various other implementation mechanisms.

6.3 Restructuring agreement and scheme of arrangement

Following lengthy negotiations, Rodenstock, the members of the senior coordinating committee and certain other senior lenders entered into a binding term sheet. The term sheet provided the framework for the proposed restructuring with a view to principally implementing the restructuring by means of a scheme in case the restructuring could not be implemented consensually or by way of any other method. In case the restructuring could not be implemented, not even by way of the scheme, the only alternative available seemed to involve a share pledge enforcement. This was unpalatable from the lenders' perspective, as it would have caused uncertainty regarding whether Rodenstock would have filed for insolvency.

At that time, the restructuring proposed by Rodenstock did not gain unanimous support from the senior lenders. However, the company succeeded in attracting enough support from senior lenders (in both number and value) to effect the restructuring agreement in January 2011, committing the majority of senior lenders to support the restructuring and implementation through the scheme (except in case of any material adverse change). The support ran up to 88.6% in number and 93.36% by value at the time of the scheme meeting in April 2011.

6.4 Overview of benefits from senior lenders' perspective under the proposed restructuring

Existing senior creditors were incentivised to participate in the restructuring, in

---

7   See Handelsblatt, September 18 2010, *Rodenstocks Rettung rückt näher*, www.handelsblatt.com/
        unternehmen/mittelstand/rodenstocks-rettung-rueckt-naeher/3542010.html?p3542010=all.
8   See Handelsblatt, September 28 2010, *Rodenstock-Verkauf gescheitert*, www.handelsblatt.com/
        unternehmen/industrie/rodenstock-verkauf-gescheitert/3549638.html.
9   *Ibid.*

particular by a margin uplift to the existing senior facilities, the option to participate by way of equity and a step-in right in case their debt were jeopardised.

Upon the scheme becoming effective, senior lenders were entitled, among other things, to participate in the new money facility and to receive, in addition to the cash-pay interest, an additional margin uplift to the existing senior facilities of either 2% on a 'pay if you want' basis or 3% on a 'payment in kind' basis at the election of Rodenstock. In addition, the restructuring provided for warrants representing 44% of the company's ordinary share capital to be issued to senior lenders, and for a lender step-in right.

Aside from the warrants, the restructuring provided for a step-in right that allowed the interest in the group to be transferred to the senior lenders under certain circumstances. In essence, this step-in right allowed the senior lenders to take over the business entirely in case their debt were jeopardised.

Additional complexity was caused by a potential change in German law set to come into effect on January 1 2014. Under current law, German companies must file for insolvency within 21 days of becoming 'over-indebted'. However, the company is not 'over-indebted' – and hence there is no obligation to file – if the company can show that, despite apparent 'over-indebtedness' on its balance sheet, it is predominantly likely to preserve its going concern. The complexity in Rodenstock arose from the fact that this 'going concern' exception itself is set to expire and will no longer be available from January 1 2014, unless the German legislature extends it beyond that date (as it has done in the past).

To address this concern, the scheme implemented a mechanism for the conditional subordination of certain classes of debt (including senior debt) owed by Rodenstock with effect from January 1 2014 if and to the extent that such conditional subordination is required to avoid over-indebtedness of Rodenstock within the meaning of Section 19(2) of the Insolvency Code. This mechanism will ensure that subordinated claims will be satisfied only after all prior ranking claims, including all unsecured claims, have been satisfied in full.

6.5 Envisaged role of management

The restructuring envisaged that the existing management of the group would continue to manage the group following the restructuring and promote its success for the benefit of all stakeholders. In this regard, the restructuring foreshadowed implementation of a new management incentive plan, in order to encourage certain members of management to continue with the group.

6.6 Dissenting creditors

In January 2011, after the restructuring agreement became effective, a further alternative proposal was put forward by the later dissenting creditors. This alternative proposal was not favoured either by management or by a majority of the senior lenders. The dissenting creditors originally expressed their opposition to the scheme on grounds of jurisdiction, discretion and on the merits, but withdrew their opposition at a later date.

7. Implementation of the restructuring by English scheme of arrangement

7.1 Implementation method

The term sheet attached to the restructuring agreement provided the framework for the proposed restructuring and set out each party's rights and obligations.

Ultimately, implementation by way of a scheme was agreed to be the most suitable and promising option for the senior lenders to maintain a variation of their rights that was necessary to enable Rodenstock to implement a restructuring which its management believed would keep it from insolvency proceedings at the end of or after April 2011.

7.2 Mechanics of the scheme of arrangement

(a) Overview of timing

Event	Time and date
Court order to hold a single scheme meeting	March 23 2011
Voting/proxy form deadline	April 12 2011
Scheme meeting	April 14 2011
Sanction hearing	April 19 2011
Lodging of sanction order with the registrar of companies	April 20 2011
Execution of the restructuring documents	April 21 2011
Effective date of the scheme	April 21 2011

(b) Scheme meeting

For the scheme to become effective and binding on Rodenstock and the senior lenders, it had to be approved by a majority of at least 75% of the aggregate voting value of the scheme creditors (ie, the senior lenders affected by the scheme) that were present and voting either in person or by proxy at the scheme meeting. Subject to the discretion of the chairman, the voting value attributable to a scheme creditor was determined as the amount owing to a scheme creditor in its capacity as an existing senior lender on the date of the scheme meeting and by or from Rodenstock in its capacity as borrower under the existing senior finance documents.

Rodenstock had satisfied the court that there should be only one class of scheme creditor, as all creditors had rights arising under the senior facilities agreement and

all had those rights and obligations amended under the scheme in materially the same way. Therefore, the court directed a single scheme meeting of all scheme creditors to be convened.

The scheme meeting was held on April 14 2011. All but 11.4% in number and 6.64% by value voted in favour of the scheme. The dissenting scheme creditors consisted of funds managed by one manager.

(c)   ***Court sanction of the scheme***
In addition, a further court hearing was required to sanction the scheme for it to become effective and binding on Rodenstock and the senior lenders. On April 19 2011, after the requisite statutory majorities of the scheme creditors had approved the scheme at the scheme meeting, the case came before the High Court of Justice for the sanction hearing.

In the sanction hearing, the court was clearly satisfied that the formal and substantive requirements for an order sanctioning the scheme were met. However, the scheme application gave rise to serious questions of jurisdiction and discretion, which were extensively discussed in the sanction hearing (see transcript, *Re Rodenstock GmbH*, High Court of Justice (Ch) Case 2135/2011).

(d)   ***Execution of the scheme restructuring documents***
Pursuant to the scheme and following the day of the delivery of the sanction order to the registrar of companies (ie, lodgement date), Rodenstock and the authorised persons were irrevocably and unconditionally authorised to enter into, execute and (where applicable) deliver as a deed the scheme restructuring documents on behalf of each scheme creditor.

7.3   **Jurisdiction and discretion to sanction the Rodenstock scheme**
The creditors that voted against the scheme also objected to the sanction of the scheme, asserting mainly that the court had no jurisdiction to sanction the scheme or that it should not sanction the scheme as a matter of discretion. For a long time, until shortly before the sanction hearing, it looked as though the Rodenstock scheme would be one of the rare contested schemes. As such, it would have resulted in arguments being put forward on both sides in relation to the ability of the English court to sanction a scheme of a non-UK company incorporated in and having its centre of main interests in another EU member state. The situation was particularly challenging, as there was no clear guidance on jurisdiction to sanction a scheme of arrangement pursuant to the UK Companies Act 2006 in these circumstances.

Shortly before the sanction hearing, the dissenting creditors declared that they would no longer oppose the scheme. However, since they had not positively stated that they supported the scheme, the court concluded that it must satisfy itself that it had jurisdiction and in fact should sanction the scheme as a matter of discretion. Notwithstanding that the hearing was uncontested, the court thus considered the question of its jurisdiction in considerable detail.

Following a detailed discussion in the sanction hearing, the court held that the court had jurisdiction to sanction the scheme and would exercise its discretion to do

so. The court was satisfied that there was a sufficient connection to the United Kingdom based on the fact that the senior lenders had collectively chosen English law and, for their benefit, exclusively by virtue of a "single agreement" which "regulates ... the relationship between each of them *inter se*, and between them as a body and the company" (2011 EWHC 1104 (Ch), Paragraph 68). Furthermore, he was satisfied that the scheme would be effective in practice in binding the opposing creditors.

(a)   *Jurisdiction*

The court based its finding on the conclusion that the phrase "liable to be wound up under the Insolvency Act 1986" (cf Section 895(2)(b) of the Companies Act 2006), being the touchstone of the court's jurisdiction to sanction the scheme, is designed simply to identify the types of company which may be subject to the scheme jurisdiction. The Insolvency Act 1986 confers jurisdiction to wind up both insolvent and solvent unregistered companies with no express jurisdictional restriction to the company's place of incorporation, centre of main interest or establishment. To the extent that the scheme company is solvent, the same principle applies to scheme jurisdiction for non-UK companies, even if incorporated in and having its centre of main interests in another EU member state; nothing in either the EU Judgments Regulation or the EU Insolvency Regulation (both of which came into force far later than the provisions on the court's jurisdiction to sanction schemes) was intended to (or does) restrict the scope of the 'liable to be wound up' touchstone of jurisdiction – that is, a company's eligibility for the application of a scheme of arrangement.

However, the court left open the question of whether and to what extent the scheme creditors must satisfy jurisdiction pursuant to Chapter II of the Judgments Regulation. It concluded that it was unnecessary to resolve this issue because more than 50% (by value) of the scheme creditors (ie, Rodenstock's senior lenders) were domiciled in England.

(b)   *Discretion*

Furthermore, the court held that it also had the discretion to sanction the scheme, as it was satisfied that the matter had a sufficient connection to the English jurisdiction, as well as that the scheme would be effective in practice in binding opposing creditors to a variation of their rights.

Rodenstock raised the question of whether the choice of English law and jurisdiction constituted a sufficient connection with the scheme jurisdiction to justify the application of the scheme to the matters of a company that was not organised under the laws of, and did not have its centre of main interest in, the country where the scheme was approved. The court was not convinced that the senior lenders' choice of English jurisdiction could be interpreted as a deliberate decision to subject themselves to the court's scheme jurisdiction. It considered several other factors that could fortify the necessary connection, as would be the case in ordinary litigation (eg, that the restructuring and the scheme had been devised and negotiated in England; that all senior lenders had voted at the convening hearing and intended to participate in the sanction hearing). However, it found no real substance in these arguments, referring in particular to the explicit objection to

jurisdiction and sufficient connection. That said, it acknowledged that the choice of English law led to the result that their rights were liable to be altered by any scheme as far as English law would recognise the jurisdiction of the court that sanctioned such a scheme.

Ultimately, the court concluded – although "on a fairly narrow balance" – that the choice of English law and jurisdiction was on its own sufficient connection to permit the exercise of the court's scheme jurisdiction. In this finding, it clearly relied on the fact that the parties had collectively chosen English law and jurisdiction "by a single agreement governing what is in substance a single facility or set of facilities to which they have all contributed" and "not merely a series of individual creditor/debtor relationships". The single agreement "regulates ... the relationship between each of the senior lenders *inter se*, and between them as a body and the company" (2011 EWHC 1104 (Ch), paragraph 68).

Finally, the court was satisfied that the scheme would be effective in practice in binding the opposing senior lenders, in light of the fact that they would be entitled to enforce their rights by litigating in Germany after waiving the jurisdiction clause.

The court acknowledged that the German Higher Regional Court of Celle, still subject to appeal, had not recognised a scheme relating to Equitable Life on the basis that an English court's decision to sanction the scheme could not be characterised as a judgement within the meaning of Article 32 of the Judgments Regulation. In light of the fact that, on appeal, the Federal Court of Justice would have to refer the issue to the European Court of Justice, he did not see any prospect for recognition in Germany under the Judgments Regulation in the short to medium term and therefore refused effectiveness on this basis.

However, following the opinions by German law experts Hans-Peter Kirchhof and Professor Peter Mankowski, the court was convinced that in any litigation between dissenting senior lenders and Rodenstock in Germany, German courts would, pursuant to the Rome Convention, apply English law and, based on the application of English law, conclude that senior lenders' rights had been varied by the scheme. For this reason, it held that the decision to sanction the scheme would be legally effective in Germany and that it therefore had discretion to take such decision.

On the merits, the court ultimately held that the scheme should be sanctioned, being satisfied that it also met all substantive requirements.

8. Conclusion

Overall, the Rodenstock restructuring demonstrated how a silent restructuring, avoiding the stigma of insolvency, may be undertaken – even if the company, including its centre of main interests, is based in Germany and even if the terms of the restructuring may not find the support of all affected lenders.

That the Rodenstock restructuring could be successfully implemented was mainly due to the fact that – by way of an English scheme of arrangement – all lenders could be forced to come to the table and agree on a restructuring. Rodenstock was thereby able to avoid insolvency and preserve the going concern value. Among other things, the scheme introduced the concept of a conditional subordination of certain debts in order to address the imminent expiration of the going concern

exception to the 'over-indebtedness' test under German law (scheduled for December 31 2013).[10] Ultimately, the senior lenders did not formally take over Rodenstock, but only secured their interest through receipt of warrants representing 44% of the shares and by step-in rights upon certain covenant breaches providing essential influence.

More generally, Rodenstock has proven that the scheme is an effective tool, even for non-UK companies, including those based and with their centre of main interests in other EU member states. In the decision sanctioning the scheme (2011 EWHC 1104, Ch), the court elaborated in detail and confirmed explicitly that a scheme may be applied to matters of non-UK companies as long as there is a sufficient connection to the scheme jurisdiction. As such, the court accepted that the senior lenders had collectively chosen English law and, for their benefit, exclusive English jurisdiction for their relationship among themselves as well as with Rodenstock. This was explicitly confirmed by Mr Justice Hildyard in *Re PrimaCom* (2012 EWHC 164, Ch). Hildyard further clarified that EC Regulation 44/2001 provides jurisdiction to sanction a scheme concerning a company which has its centre of main interest outside England even if the majority of the affected creditors are not domiciled in England.

This makes the scheme an effective tool in particular for many LBO restructurings. If structured to reflect the option of a later scheme, it should be largely irrelevant where the respective company has its centre of main interests. For LBO restructurings with a straightforward class composition, there should no longer be a need to enter into ineffective court insolvency proceedings and thereby risk the going concern value. Whether this applies only to matters in which the parties have agreed on English law and jurisdiction has been left open by the court in the Rodenstock decision. It remains to be seen whether English schemes may also be applied to matters where the majority of the lenders amended the governing law and jurisdiction to suit the Rodenstock decision or to matters that are not governed by English law and jurisdiction at all.

For other countries, the scheme could well serve as a blueprint for an out-of-court restructuring (at least for solvent restructurings).[11] Rodenstock demonstrated that there is a need for such proceedings, in particular for syndicated loans, and commentators in Germany have also acknowledged such a need and have begun to advocate the introduction of an out-of-court restructuring proceeding.[12]

Although the authors advised Rodenstock in its restructuring, the chapter reflects only publicly available information.

---

10   According to the 'stricter over-indebtedness' test scheduled to come into force on January 1 2014, a company is solvent if the going concern prognosis for the business is positive and the assets valued at going concern values are larger than the face value of the liabilities. If the going concern prognosis is negative, the assets valued at liquidation values must be larger than the face value of the liabilities. A going concern of the business will no longer exclude over-indebtedness of the company.
11   Cf Laier, GWR 2011, 252; Mankowski, WM 2011, 1201 (1209).
12   Cf Mankowski, WM 2011, 1201; Eidenmüller/Frobenius, WM 2011, 1210 (1219); Laier, GWR 2011, 252.

Conclusion

Kon Asimacopoulos
Kirkland & Ellis International LLP
Justin Bickle
Oaktree

We hope that this publication demonstrates that the practice of European restructuring has increasingly become an exercise in devising creative and often groundbreaking solutions to legal constraints and practical obstacles. The case studies in this publication bring to life the talent to be found in European restructuring practice today, and the relatively few restructuring-related failures is a testament to the hard work and dedication of the principals and advisers involved.

About the authors

Adam Al-Attar
Barrister, South Square
adamal-attar@southsquare.com

Adam Al-Attar, BA (Oxon), BCL, is a barrister at South Square called to the bar of England and Wales (2007) and the British Virgin Islands (2011), and specialising in corporate insolvency and restructuring with a focus on banking and financial services-related insolvencies, including Lehman Brothers and MF Global. Recent UK restructurings in which he was involved include IMO Carwash, Cattles plc and Punch Taverns. Recent foreign restructurings and related proceedings include Fuji Food Holdings in the Cayman Islands and Hong Kong, and Pioneer Iron and Steel Co in the British Virgin Islands.

Kon Asimacopoulos
Partner, Kirkland & Ellis International LLP
kon.asimacopoulos@kirkland.com,

Kon Asimacopoulos is a partner in Kirkland's European restructuring group, based in London.

Mr Asimacopoulos is recognised in *Chambers & Partners*, *Legal 500*, *IFLR 1000* and the *Euromoney Guide to the World's Leading Insolvency and Restructuring Lawyers* as a leading corporate restructuring and insolvency lawyer, and is often engaged to act in the following scenarios: acting for debtors and insolvency practitioners of national and multinational corporations in cross-border insolvencies and reorganisation transactions; and acting for debt and equity investors – including a number of leading investment banks, private equity houses and hedge funds – in par, stressed and distressed transactions. These engagements extend to acting for committees of lenders and shareholders in distressed and restructuring scenarios. Mr Asimacopoulos also acts for a range of stakeholders in complex commercial disputes, including administrators in contentious insolvency scenarios, investors in rights enforcement actions, and corporations and individuals in a variety of disputes.

Justin Bickle
Managing director, Oaktree
jbickle@oaktreecapital.com

Justin Bickle is a managing director in the European control investing team at Oaktree in London and a member of the strategy's investment committee. Oaktree currently manages approximately $80 billion worldwide and is listed on the New York Stock Exchange.

Before joining Oaktree seven years ago, Mr Bickle was a partner in the financial restructuring department of US law firm Cadwalader, Wickersham & Taft LLP, where he specialised in European debt restructurings.

Mr Bickle is a board member of various Oaktree portfolio companies and is responsible for structuring and executing Oaktree's control investments across Europe. He serves as a member of the advisory board of the Private Equity Institute at Säid Business School, Oxford University, is a member of the Dean's Advisory Council at Plymouth Business School, and is chairman of the English National Ballet.

Mr Bickle is a UK solicitor and law graduate from the University of Exeter.

Florian Bruder
Lawyer, Kirkland & Ellis International LLP, Munich
fbruder@kirkland.com

Florian Bruder is an attorney in the restructuring and insolvency department of Kirkland & Ellis International LLP's Munich office. He advises in financial restructuring and insolvency cases, as well as related litigation and arbitration, with special focus on the areas of high-yield and distressed debt, as well as corporations undergoing transnational and multinational restructuring. Mr Bruder is licensed in Germany.

Melissa Coakley
Senior associate, Clifford Chance LLP
melissa.coakley@cliffordchance.com

Melissa Coakley is a senior associate in the Clifford Chance LLP London banking and finance practice, with six years of dedicated restructuring and insolvency experience. Since February 2010 Ms Coakley has been seconded to the Dubai office, advising on the Dubai World, Nakheel and Dubai International Capital restructurings, among others. Previous experience includes advising the senior lenders and the agent in respect of the Monier restructuring; advising the Bank of England in respect of Northern Rock; and advising the senior lenders in respect of the Eurotunnel restructuring.

Bruno Cova
Partner, Paul Hastings
brunocova@paulhastings.com

Bruno Cova is co-chair of the Milan office of Paul Hastings. He focuses his practice on mergers and acquisitions, restructurings and white-collar crime. Mr Cova started his career in Milan and London, before working as general counsel for Eni

E&P, chief compliance officer for the European Bank for Reconstruction and Development and group general counsel for Fiat. Immediately before joining Paul Hastings, he served as chief legal adviser to the commissioner appointed by the Italian government to restructure Parmalat. Mr Cova regularly advises distressed businesses, their shareholders and creditors in distressed situations, and has been involved in the majority of Italian restructurings over the last several years.

Mr Cova is recognised as one of Italy's leading restructuring lawyers by *Chambers*, *Legal 500* and other publications. He won the Client Choice Awards 2010 and 2011 for insolvency and restructuring in Italy, and the *Top Legal Award* 2010 for restructuring.

Ben Davies
Associate, White & Case LLP
bdavies@whitecase.com

Ben Davies is an associate in White & Case's financial restructuring and insolvency group in London. His experience includes advising banks, noteholders, funds, insolvency practitioners and companies in relation to a wide range of transactions, including financial restructurings, cross-border acquisition finance, general bank lending and high-yield and emerging-market debt offerings.

Mr Davies has completed a secondment to the loan syndications and trading team of the BNP Paribas London office, as well as spending time in White & Case's Hong Kong office.

Eduardo J Fernandez
Partner, Willkie Farr & Gallagher LLP
efernandez@willkie.com

Eduardo J Fernandez is a partner in the corporate and financial services department of Willkie Farr & Gallagher LLP in Paris. He holds an AB (government) from Dartmouth College and a JD from NYU School of Law. A native New Yorker, Mr Fernandez commenced his career as an

associate in Willkie's New York office and has, during more than 15 years based in Paris, specialised in M&A, private equity transactions and corporate finance transactions.

In particular, Mr Fernandez regularly represents private equity sponsors (eg, PAI Partners, IK Investment Partners and Apax MidMarket Partners) on leveraged buy-outs and distressed M&A transactions. He also led the Willkie team advising Oaktree Capital in Oaktree-led restructuring of the SGD Group.

In addition, Mr Fernandez advises a number of corporate clients on significant acquisitions, disposals, strategic alliances and corporate finance (notably debt private placement) transactions.

Carlos Gila
Senior adviser, Oaktree
carlosagila@yahoo.es

Carlos Gila is a frequent lecturer, widely recognised as one of the leading Spanish financial and operational crisis management professionals. He is a hands-on expert in turnarounds and workouts, with extensive experience in bankruptcy reorganisation, the restructuring of troubled businesses, and acquisitions and divestures.

Mr Gila began his professional career as a strategic management consultant at Andersen Consulting; he then established and led Gila & Co to become the groundbreaking turnaround firm in Spain for over a decade. Mr Gila is now senior adviser for and serves as non-executive director for company boards, chairing audit and governance committees.

Mr Gila graduated with a BA in finance from the University of San Francisco and an MA in law from *Universidad Europea*, and earned an OPM from Harvard Business School. He received the prestigious TMA International Turnaround of the Year Award in 2011.

Mark Glengarry
Managing director, Morgan Stanley
mark.glengarry@morganstanley.com

Mark Glengarry is managing director in Morgan Stanley's investment bank. He provides financial advice for corporate borrowers across the restructuring spectrum. Before joining Morgan Stanley, Mr Glengarry was a financial restructuring partner at White & Case LLP. He has worked on some of the biggest European restructurings in the market, including the €206 billion Greek private sector involvement, and the financial restructurings of SAS Airlines, Wind Hellas and Almatis.

Martin Graham
Vice president, Oaktree
mgraham@OakTreeCap.com

Martin Graham has been a vice president at Oaktree since 2007, having previously worked at Freshfields Bruckhaus Deringer, Cadwalader and Goldman Sachs. He specialises in cross-border debt restructuring, as well as distressed debt and special situations private equity investing. Mr Graham holds degrees in law from the universities of Glasgow and Oxford.

Mark Hyde
Partner, Clifford Chance LLP
mark.hyde@cliffordchance.com

Mark Hyde has been a partner at Clifford Chance LLP since 1993 and global head of its insolvency and restructuring practice since 1998. He is regularly listed in UK and global insolvency and restructuring publications as a leading practitioner. Mr Hyde is a member of R3, INSOL and a member and past president of the Insolvency Lawyers Association. He has worked on some of the highest-profile restructurings and insolvencies over a career spanning more than 25 years. Career highlights for insolvency work include acting for the liquidators of Banco Ambrosiano; advising the

government of Brunei in relation to the collapse of the National Bank of Brunei; and advising the insolvency officeholders of Barlow Clowes and the Peregrine insolvency officeholders in Hong Kong. Restructuring career highlights include advising Lyondell Basell and Dubai World on their restructurings and advising the lenders in the Metronet, NTL, Kirsch Group and Monier restructurings.

Partha Kar
Partner, Kirkland & Ellis International LLP
partha.kar@kirkland.com

Partha Kar is a restructuring partner in the London office of Kirkland & Ellis International LLP, with a wide range of cross-border restructuring and insolvency experience. He has acted for financial creditors (including non-bank funds), turnaround advisers, corporates (debtors and creditors) and insolvency practitioners/appointees in multi-jurisdictional restructurings and all classes of insolvency proceeding; directors, shareholders and creditors of companies that are financially impaired or subject to solvent reorganisation; and vendors and purchasers of distressed debt or equity. Mr Kar has worked on all stages of this work, including contingency planning and strategy, negotiations, documentation, post-restructuring/appointment and exit. He has been recognised as a leading restructuring lawyer in the *Legal 500* and *Chamber UK* and one of the "Hot 100" lawyers in Europe for 2011 by *The Lawyer.*

Nicolas Laurent
Partner, Bredin Prat
nl@bredinprat.com

Nicolas Laurent is a partner at Bredin Prat whose primary areas of practice include bankruptcy/restructuring and mergers and acquisitions. He has recently advised SNCF, the operator of the French railways, in its recovery proceedings for SeaFrance, its wholly owned subsidiary operating ferries across the Channel; the coordination committee

of senior banks in the restructuring of Consolis, a leading construction operator in Europe; TowerBrook on the buy-out of Autodistribution, a leading French automotive spare parts distributor, in the context of pre-packed safeguard proceedings; and DHL on the disposal of its French courier business to Caravelle, a leading French turnaround fund.

A member of the Paris Bar since 1998, Mr Laurent received his law degree from the University of Paris, Sorbonne and taught bankruptcy law there from 1996 to 1997. He is a member of the French Association for Turnaround.

Karen McMaster
Special counsel, Cadwalader, Wickersham & Taft LLP
Karen.McMaster@cwt.com

Karen McMaster is special counsel in the financial restructuring department of the London office of Cadwalader, Wickersham & Taft LLP. She focuses on debt restructuring and reorganisation, including contingency planning, insolvency and options analysis, and advising in relation to new financing. Ms McMaster has considerable experience devising and implementing creative restructuring solutions for a diverse range of clients including collateralised loan obligation funds and distressed investors, sponsors, corporates and creditor committees. She has represented the interests of stakeholders on a number of bank/bond structures and other complex European cross-border restructurings. Before joining Cadwalader, Ms McMaster was a managing associate at Linklaters LLP in its London restructuring practice.

Wolfgang Nardi
Partner, Kirkland & Ellis International LLP, Munich
wnardi@kirkland.com

Wolfgang Nardi is an attorney and partner in the finance department of Kirkland & Ellis International

LLP's Munich office. He advises on all aspects of financing in the areas of private equity transactions and corporate finance, with a particular focus on international acquisitions financing and restructuring. Mr Nardi has particular expertise in restructuring transactions involving an English scheme of arrangement. In addition to being a licensed attorney in Germany, Mr Nardi is licensed as a solicitor in England and Wales.

Holly Neavill
Partner, Latham & Watkins
holly.neavill@lw.com

Holly Neavill is a partner in the London office specialising in complex cross-border restructurings and insolvencies, encompassing debt and equity restructuring, distressed M&A activity, formal insolvency procedures and contingency planning, and debtor advisory work. She has substantial experience with legal systems and workout procedures across Europe and the United States, serving a diverse client base comprising creditors, steering committees, private placement noteholders, bondholders, banks and other financial investors, as well as debtors and sponsors/ equity investors.

Ms Neavill has represented the committee of junior bondholders in the €2.8 billion financial restructuring of SEAT Pagine Gialle SpA, the listed Italian directories business; acted as international counsel to AfriSam Group, a Southern Africa cement-producing business in connection with financial restructuring; represented Schoeller Arca in the first of its kind private court-sanctioned enforcement sale; and represented the Renova Group as majority shareholder in the Sfr3.1 billion financial restructuring of Oerlikon AG.

Yushan Ng
Partner, Cadwalader Wickersham & Taft LLP
yushan.ng@cwt.com

Yushan Ng is a partner in Cadwalader London's financial restructuring department. Before joining Cadwalader in 2012, he was a partner in the

restructuring and insolvency group at Linklaters LLP.

Mr Ng regularly acts on complex cross-border and domestic restructurings, insolvency proceedings and financings, with particular experience in representing institutions that invest in distressed situations or finance impaired credits. He has been heavily involved in engineering and executing market-leading loan-to-own strategies in a number of high-profile restructuring transactions.

Elaine Nolan
Partner, Kirkland & Ellis International LLP
enolan@kirkland.com

Elaine Nolan is a restructuring partner in the London office of Kirkland & Ellis International LLP. She advises strategic investors, sponsors, insolvency practitioners, turnaround managers, directors, debtors and creditors in all forms of national and international financial restructurings and insolvencies. Ms Nolan has been involved in a number of recent high-profile restructurings, including advising the European Directories group, the Fitness First group, certain bondholders of the Petroplus group, Sankaty Advisors LLC on the purchase of a portfolio of loans from the Lloyds banking group, the Civil Aviation Authority in relation to the Thomas Cook Group and Regency Entertainment Leisure & Tourism SA. She also advises leading investment banks, hedge funds and private equity houses in relation to their diligence and review of European investment opportunities in par, stressed and distressed transactions.

Samuel Pariente
Partner, Bredin Prat
samuelpariente@bredinprat.com

Samuel Pariente is a partner at Bredin Prat, specialising in financing work, including restructuring, banking, acquisition finance, real estate financing and project finance.

Before joining Bredin Prat in 2007, he worked

as an associate at an American firm in New York, London and Paris. A member of the New York Bar since 2000 and of the Paris Bar since 2007, Mr Pariente received his French law degree from the University of Paris, Sorbonne, an LLB from King's College London and an LLM from Harvard Law School.

Adam Paul
Partner, Kirkland & Ellis LLP
adam.paul@kirkland.com

Adam Paul is a restructuring partner in the international law firm of Kirkland & Ellis LLP. He represents both debtor and creditor clients in complex US Chapter 11 reorganisations; advises purchasers and sellers in myriad bankruptcy transactions and acquisitions; counsels boards of directors and senior officers regarding fiduciary duties and restructuring strategies; and advises financially troubled companies regarding the structure of various commercial transactions outside of bankruptcy.

Most recently, Mr Paul was recognised in the 2012 edition of the *Legal 500 US* and in March 2012 was selected by *Law360* as one of its annual "Rising Stars", a list of five restructuring lawyers in the United States under the age of 40 to watch.

Mr Paul regularly represents clients from the United States, Europe and Asia in cross-border restructurings, and is a frequent speaker and author on restructuring issues.

Leo Plank
Partner, Kirkland & Ellis International LLP,
Munich
Lplank@kirkland.com

Leo Plank is an attorney and partner in the restructuring and insolvency department of Kirkland & Ellis International LLP's Munich office. He advises in financial restructuring and insolvency cases, with special emphasis on representation of institutional investors in the areas of high-yield and distressed debt, as well as

corporations undergoing transnational and multinational restructuring. He has particular expertise in leveraged buy-out restructurings and complex transnational issues. Dr Plank is a licensed attorney in Germany, as well as an attorney at law in New York and a solicitor in England and Wales. He has authored various professional publications, in particular in the areas of restructuring, recapitalisation financing and insolvency law.

Freddie Powles
Associate, Kirkland & Ellis International LLP
frederick.powles@kirkland.com

Freddie Powles is an associate in the European restructuring group of Kirkland & Ellis International LLP in London. He specialises in advising sponsors, debtors, creditors and strategic investors on the restructuring of stressed and distressed businesses. Recent representative matters include acting for debtors and stakeholders in restructuring negotiations in relation to Klöckner Pentaplast, European Directories and Rodenstock. Mr Powles holds a degree in experimental psychology from the University of Oxford.

Teun Struycken
Partner, NautaDutilh
teun.struycken@nautadutilh.com

Teun Struycken is a partner in the loan finance group of NautaDutilh in Amsterdam, the Netherlands. He specialises in the law on restructuring and insolvency, secured transactions and asset finance.

Mr Struycken has substantial experience with the restructuring of multinational and domestic groups of companies, and advises both lenders and borrowers. Representative matters include the cross-border restructuring of European Directories, Schoeller Arca, Endemol, Vivacom and Pfleiderer, and the domestic restructuring of Kroymans, Thieme, Selexyz, Phanos and Koop.

Richard Tett
Partner, Freshfields Bruckhaus Deringer LLP
richard.tett@freshfields.com

Richard Tett is a partner in Freshfields' restructuring and insolvency group, with over 15 years of restructuring experience. He has worked on refinancings, in and out-of-court restructurings, distressed M&A, formal insolvency appointments, US Chapter 11s, pension deficits, insurance workouts, telecommunications, commercial mortgage-backed securities and bondholder restructurings, and insolvency aspects of structured finance.

Non-confidential matters on which Mr Tett has advised include Endemol, Deutsche Annington, Carl Zeiss Vision, La Seda de Barcelona, EMI, Primacom, McCarthy & Stone, Paroc, Bank of England (Bradford & Bingley, Landsbanki and Kaupthing), Honsel, TMD Friction, XL Airways, Amtel Vredestein, Schieder Möbel, Polestar, and the separate acquisitions of the London Eye and Budget Rent-A-Car Group's Europe, Middle East and Africa assets.

Mr Tett is a qualified solicitor-advocate (civil) and a member of the Insolvency Lawyers Association, the Association of Business Recovery Professionals and the Turnaround Management Association.

Alan Tilley
Principal, Bryan Mansell &Tilley LLP
atilley@bmandt.eu

Alan Tilley is an experienced turnaround manager and has significant expertise in international turnarounds, helping to preserve enterprise value for businesses operating in the zone of insolvency. He was the 2008 recipient of the Turnaround Management Association's (TMA) international chairman's award for outstanding service to the international turnaround profession, and Insolvency & Rescue UK Turnaround Manager of the Year 2010. Mr Tilley is the co-author of the Institute of Chartered Accountants in England and Wales' best practice guideline on turnarounds, 2011, and co-winner of TMA International Turnaround of the Year award for La Seda.

Mr Tilley qualified as a chartered accountant with Arthur Andersen in the United Kingdom and France, and between 1976 and 1994 held senior and chief executive positions with Grove Cranes, Lansing Bagnall and Simon Access. He began as a turnaround practitioner in 1994, undertaking the management buy-in of Lynton Group. Mr Tilley was European managing director of Glass & Associates between 1997 and 2007 and is past president of TMA UK and TMA International's vice president of international relations 2010-11.

Globe Law
and Business

Related titles

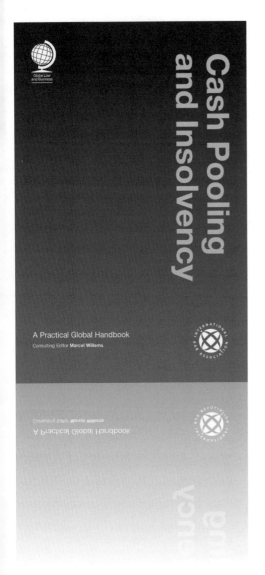

CW00969471